Killing Time

Praise for *Working Class Boy*

Working Class Boy is a stunning piece of work – relentless, earnest, shockingly vivid. Barnes … doesn't just have a scarifying story to tell. He has a grippingly effective way of telling it: one that does full justice to the grim facts without overcooking them … You can't fake such a tone. You have to earn it.
– *The Australian*

Nothing will prepare you for the power of Jimmy's memoir. A fierce, graphic, bawdy account of his working class childhood – truly harrowing, and yet often tender and funny. I couldn't put it down because, above all, it is also a story of resilience and bravery.
– Sam Neill

Visceral, brave, honest. A deep, guttural howl of a book, it speaks of the pain and hurt that haunt so many men. And it may just save lives.
– Magda Szubanski

Barnes writes with verve and style to present a fascinating story of flawed and compelling personalities, not least his own. The result is unexpectedly compelling.
– *Rolling Stone*

Barnes's way of addressing the reader directly, while largely ignoring his rock-star status, edges towards a unique voice.
– *The Listener*

Reading about [Barnes's] harrowing early life gives a greater understanding of both the belting lyrics and the softer, sometimes haunting, music he has produced … This moving account … shows in grim detail the enormous effort Jimmy had to put in to become the man he is.
– Booksellers New Zealand

Praise for *Working Class Man*

Rare is the man who has lived this hard, this fast
and this dangerously – only to survive and chronicle
it all so superbly.
– Lisa Wilkinson

All the mind-boggling excesses and the emotional
extremes are revealed here, with brutal honesty and
sparkling wit. Jimmy has found his real voice, and it's
imbued with a spirit of generosity that knows no bounds –
just like the man himself.
– Neil Finn

What a brave writer ... The legend who strides the stage
with so much power and charisma reveals the boy who hid
in a cupboard then found salvation in song, the rock star
who had it all and spent it all, and the man who loves his
family and his music.
– Lindy Morrison

Jimmy has always been a force of nature, living on the
edge, giving high-octane performances ... Yet, as this book
shows, his wrestle with his hidden demons was taking a
huge toll. Something had to give, and this searingly honest
account lays it out in spades.
– Peter Garrett

A story as dark as pitch but so compelling, so powerful and at times so close to unbelievable – how can this man still be alive? – it sets a new bar for rock 'n' roll survival stories ... What lifts this memoir is its searing honesty, and Jimmy's tender, sincere regret for what the circus he ringmastered did to his own wife and family. Also to himself.
– Jennifer Byrne, *Australian Women's Weekly*

This is a story of excess and success. This is a story of pain and gain. Most of all this is the story of an inspiring love affair like no other. *Working Class Boy* broke my heart. *Working Class Man* has put it back together.
– John Purcell

Only a fool would declare the circus animal's rage spent. But in these two books, he's broken it down and owned every part of it with the kind of honesty, clear-eyed insight and riveting storytelling that miraculously defies the damage done.
– *Sydney Morning Herald*

Jimmy Barnes

Killing Time

Short stories from
the long road home

HarperCollins*Publishers*

www.jimmybarnes.com
: @jimmybarnesofficial
: @jimmybarnes

We gratefully acknowledge the permission granted by copyright holders to reproduce the copyright material in this book. All reasonable attempts have been made to contact the copyright holders; the publisher would be interested to hear from anyone not acknowledged here, or acknowledged incorrectly.

HarperCollins*Publishers*
Australia • Brazil • Canada • France • Germany • Holland • Hungary
India • Italy • Japan • Mexico • New Zealand • Poland • Spain • Sweden
Switzerland • United Kingdom • United States of America

First published in Australia in 2020
by HarperCollins*Publishers* Australia Pty Limited
Level 13, 201 Elizabeth Street, Sydney NSW 2000
ABN 36 009 913 517
harpercollins.com.au

A catalogue record for this book is available from the National Library of Australia.

ISBN 978 1 4607 5948 6 (hardback)
ISBN 978 1 4607 1310 5 (ebook)
ISBN 978 1 4607 8605 5 (audiobook)

Cover design by Mark Campbell, HarperCollins Design Studio
Cover image © Jesse Lizotte/Trunk Archive
All photos from the collection of Jimmy and Jane Barnes unless otherwise noted
Typeset in Bembo Std by Kirby Jones
Printed and bound in Australia by McPherson's Printing Group
The papers used by HarperCollins in the manufacture of this book are a natural, recyclable product made from wood grown in sustainable plantation forests. The fibre source and manufacturing processes meet recognised international environmental standards, and carry certification.

*This book is dedicated to my beautiful wife, Jane,
and my darling children.
I love you so much.*

*I also dedicate this book to the memory of
my dear schnauzers, Oliver and Snoopy,
who passed away in 2019.
I miss you guys so much.
I cry for you every day.*

Contents

Introduction

When I was deciding on a title for this collection of stories, I had a number of ideas I tossed around in my head and shared with others. Again and again, though, I came back to the phrase 'killing time'.

Partly, it was down to the fact that I'd recently provided the lyrics for a Don Walker song with that title on the last Cold Chisel album, *Blood Moon* – lyrics that I was particularly happy with and meant a lot to me. But mainly it was because it's a phrase that has many meanings for me and conjures up particular periods and events in my life, many of which I've written about in these pages.

I spent most of my childhood killing time, waiting for something to happen. Something good. But it never seemed to come along. As I recounted in *Working Class Boy*, my first book, I was always hoping my mum and dad would get it together, but they never managed it and eventually our family fell apart. So I bided my time and escaped into my own world, as kids often do.

Then I started school and thought everything would be better: I'd get away from home and my life would change. Instead it just led me to another set of problems. Suddenly I had to fit in, which was hard for me to do, and that pressure made school just another scary place. To get through it, I kept my head down and tried to fly under the radar. Just killing time till school finished and I could escape elsewhere.

In the meantime I grew up physically, if not emotionally – I wouldn't really grow up for another fifty years or so. As a teenager I started hanging out in gangs. In those days it wasn't just time we wanted to kill but everything and anyone – especially anybody who got in our way – and at times even ourselves. Somehow I managed to survive and get older, though none the wiser, and it wasn't long until I joined a band and went on the road.

God knows, since then I've had a lot of time to kill. Like I said in my second book, *Working Class Man*, I've been on that road for over fifty years. But I'll let you in on a little secret here. Rock 'n' roll is not glamorous. You spend most of your time travelling from town to town, hoping to make it to the next venue in time for your show. That isn't always easy and you often start to think that the whole world has conspired to stop you getting there.

In the old days before we had money, we'd travel in cars that were real bombs, held together with gaffer tape and prayers. Blowing smoke and leaking oil across the country, we'd drive on dirt roads without a turn for hundreds of kilometres as we stared out the windows, bored, trying to kill time by thinking about where we'd rather be. We would run out of petrol in the middle of the night and get stuck in some one-horse town halfway across the Nullarbor Plain with no shop or petrol station and have to siphon petrol from a car parked in the shadows to get us to the next place. Then kill time again while waiting for the sun to come up and the servo to open so we could fill up and drive on for another two blisteringly hot days to reach our show.

As we got better at what we did, we could afford to fly occasionally. But the journeys could still seem impossible or interminable. Sometimes the wind would blow so hard or the rain would fall so heavily the runways would be closed. Then you could do one of two things. You could sit in the airport waiting for the storm to clear or you could fork out more money for a cheap hire car and drive, hoping the highway wasn't flooded too. That was always the better option, as you knew in your heart you had to do something to try to get to the next show on time, to do what it was you were born to do, what you loved.

Even when things work out and you get to where you are going in plenty of time, as happens more often these days, touring is still all about waiting – waiting for the venue to open, waiting to get into the hotel, waiting for the soundcheck to start, waiting for the hall to fill up – until you can finally get out there and play music to people. All in all, I've spent many, many more hours killing time than making music.

Musicians kill time in different ways. Some write songs, watch television or catch up on sleep (always a good thing to do). Others keep fit by heading to a local gym or going jogging. Or take in the local tourist attractions. In my early days, all of that seemed a bit dorky, not rock 'n' roll enough. And sleep was definitely overrated.

I preferred to go out drinking and looking for trouble. I was always the one asking 'What's happening? What's going on? Where's the action?' Anything to use up my excess energy. Anything to satisfy my cravings. Anything to stop myself from really looking at my life and the train wreck that was always just about to happen.

I kept this up for many years. But even I began to tire of it. How much trouble can one man start? You get to a point where you either grow up or your liver asks for a transfer to Joe Cocker for a rest. To channel my energies in a different direction, at one point I trained in karate. This knocked out two birds with one stone: I got fit and learned how to kill more than just time. It kept me alive, but it didn't keep me out of trouble. Plus, at heart I am a pacifist.

It took many more years for me to realise I was heading for disaster. I wasn't just killing time, I was killing myself and the people around me. So, eventually, I left that life behind.

Now I spend a lot of my spare time on the road reading and writing books. Don't tell me, I've finally grown up! After all those years I spent looking around, searching for excitement, it feels great to sit quietly, look inwards, reflect on the past and dream about the future. These days I have found a little peace. My world is still turning, but it doesn't entirely revolve around me anymore. Well, not as much.

And I don't have to be in the thick of the battle with my demons all the time. I can step back and let them fight among themselves. I've got better things to do with my time. Every now and then I have to go toe to toe with the ghosts of my past, but they don't possess me or overwhelm me. I look at them, see what I can learn from them, and then let them go. They don't own me anymore.

Don't get me wrong. I'm aware those demons are still around. Addiction doesn't just lie down and let you walk away. I know I need to keep my wits about me, but I am walking on my own two feet now. And after all those years on the road, all those years of drifting, with no sense of belonging anywhere, I finally feel that I have found my place in the world. I have a beautiful wife and family who all love me, and I love them with all my heart. I have friends I care about. I have stepped out of the shadows and I can feel the sun on my face and I like it. My head is held high and I am looking forward to what life has planned for me.

I still write songs about the bad old days, of course, trying to make sense of it all. Songs about how easy it is to lose faith and hope and fall into a downward spiral. Songs like 'Killing Time'. I can write about such things because I've been there. It's hard to look back too much, but I know it's healthy. While keeping an eye on where you're going, you need to remember where you've been.

Like many other things, writing is more of a pleasure these days. Putting together my memoirs was sometimes like pulling teeth. It was a harrowing exercise, and at times nearly killed me. But in these stories, although I was sometimes facing up to sad, frightening and occasionally embarrassing episodes, for the most part I have been able to take a lighter look back and, while reflecting on some dark times, relive some of the funniest and most absurd moments of my life, and recognise the joy, inspiration and kindness that others have brought me during my long journey. They include other musicians, roadies, producers, mentors, friends, sometimes total strangers. And, of course, my wonderful family — couldn't have done it without them.

Thanks to all these people, I'm no longer just killing time. Not anymore. Now, every moment is precious.

Enjoy.

Jimmy

'Killing Time'

I have no faith in you or me
There is no hope that I can see
We pray for help that never comes
Our fields are dry, no water runs
We curse the sun that burns the land
And slap the teeth that bite the hand
Of those who try but don't succeed
All left to die, alone they bleed

It's killing time
It's killing time

It's killing time
Too late to pray
Can't walk away
It's killing time
We made our choice
We have no voice
It's killing time
It's killing time

With lips pulled tight, the venom flies
You spit the words that make me cry
The clouds are black
There is no sky
No sun no moon
There are no stars at night

I'm lost at sea, caught in a storm
Can't navigate, I'm so alone
Back to the wall, nowhere to turn
I will lash out, or I will burn
It's killing time

It's killing time
It's killing time

It's killing time
The dam has cracked
No turning back
It's killing time
I see it all
I start to fall
It's killing time
It's you or me
So set me free
It's killing time
It's killing time

(Lyrics courtesy of Sony ATV Publishing)

There Are No *Stars at Night*

We were prepped and ready.
Houston, come in Houston, this
is the command module.
There were five of us setting
off on this momentous journey.

This was our day. Our moment. Our time in the sun.

Ignition.

Houston, we have lift-off.

We were trying to do something that had never been done before. At least that's what we thought. It had been a lifetime in preparation. Five lifetimes in fact. Every moment of every day. Through good, bad and pain beyond belief. Everything had brought us to this launch and now there was no going back.

Houston, we have detached from the booster and are heading into orbit.

We were off on a journey into uncharted territory, a journey we knew we might not survive. We might never come home. But we had nothing to come back to anyhow.

Maintain your course and God speed. Houston out.

We hadn't been chosen for this mission by anyone outside the fold. We'd chosen each other. We'd been drawn together, to this point in time and space, from disparate parts of the universe to undertake this journey. Of all the people I'd met in my short life, these were the guys I knew would stick by my side through thick and thin. Our lives would become so entwined that at times we wouldn't be able to tell each other's thoughts and dreams apart. Each of us holding a piece of a puzzle that when put together might lead us to greatness – or send us crashing out of control, never to be seen again.

Houston, we have a problem.

The first of many problems, and no one there to help us. We were alone and hurtling away from home, at light speed.

Houston? Do you read me? Houston, come in.

Nothing. The radio was silent now, except for white noise and old signals, sounds and voices that were years out of date and held no meaning for anyone anymore. From here on we'd hear nothing apart from the noise we made. And out here no one could hear us scream. Not yet, anyway.

There was a feeling of relief we got from leaving all those voices from the past behind. The voices that had told us we weren't good enough, that we'd never be worth anything. Now we were alone in a vacuum, held together by a single belief: we could do this, and it would be better to die trying than turn back. Besides, we didn't have enough in the tank to make it back. This was always going to be a one-way trip, and we all knew it.

In front of us were cold, starless skies, almost endless darkness. Only an occasional glimpse of the sun. Then it would shine so bright it would blind us. But it never lasted long.

We would journey on like this for years, every now and again touching down somewhere new, then leaving before we'd even acclimatised. We could never stay in one place too long. The motion was all that kept us alive.

If ever the light got too bright or the heat too intense, we'd simply load up and move on. To another realm, another world, another galaxy. There were always new horizons to chase. And we were never satisfied. Always in need of something else, yet never sure what it was. We'd find enough to keep us going, but never enough for us to stop, contemplate, stay put. We had to keep moving, pushing ourselves, digging deeper, looking for something we weren't even sure existed. Peace? A place to belong?

Houston, come in. Houston? Do you read me?

Occasionally, out of desperation, we'd seek the comfort of home, a voice from the past. But static – the cold, scratching sound of emptiness – was all we could hear. Home had given up on us. In fact home had given up on us long before we'd left. Maybe that was why we'd made this journey, why we'd taken this giant step.

Many times, over the years, we were battered and bashed so hard that we nearly broke apart and scattered like dust in the wind. But somehow we held on. Somehow we kept believing. Believing in ourselves. There was something worthwhile out there, waiting for us. So we journeyed on night after night, knowing we'd eventually run out of fuel and be left drifting, unable to change course. Just space junk spinning in the void.

Aeons passed. By then our ship, once sleek and menacing, had been patched back together so many times it no longer shone. It was covered in scratches and cracks. Eventually it would disintegrate completely and we, its occupants, would be cast into space, tethered together for a while by bonds we knew could snap at any moment. When that finally happened, we would drift apart once and for all. Each of us lost, on our own, forever.

Houston can you hear us? Houston, come in. Are you reading us? Houston?

Always, even in the darkest of times, we were searching. For a reason to keep on believing. For a spark or a sign, something to point the way. A light to lead us home. But all we found, for a long, long time, was darkness.

There are no stars at night.

Yes, Sir, *Whatever You* Want, Sir

It must have been back around 1980 when I made my first visit to Thailand. I had never been to Southeast Asia before and couldn't wait to see where Jane came from.

I'd heard stories about the food and how one false move in a restaurant could have your mouth set on fire so badly you might never regain your sense of taste. I didn't think that was going to be a problem for me because at that time I never touched hot food. But this particular trip would change all that, and by the time I left Thailand, I would be eating chillies with the best of them. Well, not quite, but I could finally eat *some* chillies.

I was so taken by the place from the minute I arrived. I loved it. The people were so warm and friendly – it was the Land of Smiles, as they say – the food so tasty. In my life, I'd never had it so good. This was like the opposite of where I'd grown up. Let's face it, Scottish food was never spicy at all. It was a whole new world for me.

We stayed at the house of one of Jane's favourite relatives, Uncle Chai. His home was like no home I had ever seen. There were gibbons living in the trees. Gibbons. I thought they were monkeys, but apparently gibbons are nicer. Who knew? The house wrapped around a lake, which was covered with the most beautiful lotus flowers and giant lily pads and was full of fish. Not like the fish we caught in the Port River in Adelaide, bream whose growth had been stunted by chemicals poured overboard from cargo boats waiting at the docks to be loaded with God knows what. No, these were big, colourful fish. Goldfish on steroids.

Everything looked exotic to me. I had never seen anything like this place before. It was breathtaking.

Uncle Chai owned the Charles Jourdan shoe factory. All those beautiful shoes were made right there in the compound where we were staying then sent to France to be exported around the world. Eventually, I had a mould of my feet made and was able to order handmade shoes and have them delivered to me anywhere in the world. I was very spoiled.

Now, Uncle Chai was a traditional kind of guy, living in a traditional house. He'd drink tea from delicate antique cups beneath huge, dark paintings from where stern-faced ancestors stared down at him. Both his mother and father were Chinese, and he'd been born in China and brought up in Thailand. His father, Jane's grandfather, had moved from China to Thailand before the Second World War.

I woke up on my first full day in Thailand to the sound of haunting, high-pitched Chinese music drifting across the lake. I had to go for a walk to find out where it was coming from. Uncle Chai was sitting in his study, playing an instrument I'd never seen before. He was hitting the strings with soft mallets and they had a magical sound to them, like they were being played for a princess in the Forbidden City. His room was full of his own beautiful paintings and they were at various stages of completion. It seemed he was a man of many talents.

I liked Uncle Chai from the day we met, and we became good friends. Later he would take me out to eat and see if he could find things that grossed me out – pigs' ears and tails, intestines, sugar-cured river fish, goose feet. Even if I didn't like the idea, I always ate whatever he put in front of me. It was a challenge. He would laugh as I chewed the offending item for way too long and then have a terrible time swallowing it. He knew where to find the best and most unusual food in Bangkok. And he always had somewhere new for us to try.

On my first night, Uncle Chai took us to Chinatown in Bangkok for fish-ball noodle soup. Now this place was not your typical upmarket noodle place. In fact, it wasn't even a restaurant. It was a street. A small back street. A small back street that led to a wharf. During the day, men fended off water rats there as they loaded goods onto small cargo ships that took produce to and from China and beyond. But come sundown, the narrow laneway was hosed down, tables were set up, the buildings festooned with lights, and the dingy alley became the best fish-ball noodle soup shop in Bangkok.

If you didn't have someone to guide you to it, you would never find it, and I got the feeling that if the people who worked there didn't like you, you wouldn't get served. I even started to think that if you stumbled into the alley at the wrong time, you might end up in the hold of one of the cargo ships, ready to be sold somewhere where they don't ask any questions.

I was with Jane and Uncle Chai, so I thought I could rest easy. We sat down and ordered bowl after bowl of the best-tasting fish-ball noodle soup I had ever eaten or have ever eaten since. Meanwhile the rest of the clientele kept a wary eye on me as they slurped their noodles. I started to feel I didn't belong there. And, sure enough, when I looked around, there were no other Westerners. In fact, I hadn't seen any anywhere near the place. Then I noticed that some of the mothers in the room were pointing our way and whispering to their children, who seemed to be mesmerised by me.

'What are they saying, Uncle?' I had to ask.

'They are telling the kids that if they don't behave, the *farang* will take them.'

Even I was worried. I looked up and down the alley to see what might have crawled in. 'What's a *farang* and why are they scared of it?' I asked. Whatever it was, it must have been frightening, as the kids seemed terrified out of their minds.

Uncle just laughed. 'It's you. You are the *farang*. You. Ha, ha, ha!' Then he explained that *farang* is the Thai name for Westerners.

Uncle Chai laughed again and waved the waiter over to order another round of whatever we were eating. It seemed like I was the first *farang* to eat at this establishment and the parents had jumped on the chance to use me to scare their children into behaving themselves.

*

On my second day in Thailand, I thought it would be good if I got a haircut. Nothing extreme, just a wash and a trim, to make a bit of an effort for the family. I looked like a wild man compared to everyone else in the house.

At that time I had long, curly hair. Dare I say it, almost a mullet. No, fuck it, it was a mullet. My hair was naturally curly and had become curlier still because I hadn't combed or brushed it for five or so years. Whenever it got too matted, I just cut bits off. I kept it clean, but it was messy. A year or so earlier, I'd been to a hairdresser in Sydney and she'd found a tick in my neck, dead as a doornail. I used to take a lot of drugs back in those days and I think the poor tick had probably bitten me and then died of a speed overdose. One bite followed by a massive heart attack. Either that or it had talked itself to death. But I'm getting off track here.

Uncle Chai lived on a little street, or *soi* as the Thais call it, right next to the Regent Hotel. The Regent had an old-fashioned barber. I could get a trim and a shave with a cut-throat razor in air-conditioned comfort directly across the road. So it didn't require a big effort.

Bangkok, 1980. 'This is a long, long way from Glasgow.'

Off I went, without Jane to translate for me. Surely in such a big hotel they would speak English, I thought. As it happened, they didn't, but I thought I'd manage to make myself understood.

'Can I get a little trim and a shave, please,' I asked, miming the process of shaving and cutting hair.

The barber smiled warmly at me. 'Yes, sir, whatever you want, sir.'

I sat down and was treated like a king. Hot towels were applied to my face and the seat was laid back and before long I was being shaved for the very first time with a cut-throat razor. Where I came from these razors were not much used for shaving, but for fighting. Glasgow had become famous in the 1960s for thugs carrying cut-throat razors, who were more than happy to slash anyone who crossed them in any way. They would slice people's faces open from ear to ear, leaving a scar like a permanent smile. In a way, Glasgow was also the land of smiles, whether you wanted one or not.

Despite my reservations, the shave went really well, though it took me a few minutes to get used to someone holding a blade to my throat and not demanding money – I had to fight the urge to give the guy my wallet. Once I got over that, it was perfect. My face hadn't been so smooth since I was a young fellow.

Next was the haircut. I could see in the mirror that two of the barbers were discussing how to approach my hair. They spoke to each other in hushed tones, only stopping to take a look at my head from many different angles. The shop was full, but all the other customers were Thai men with straight, black hair. My mop was a new animal for them: wild and out of control.

Finally, it appeared that they had come to some agreement about how to cut it, and the poor guy who must have drawn the short straw stepped up and prepared himself for the task. I nervously tried to make conversation, but I got no real answers.

'Have you, er, have you cut curly hair before?' I might have looked a little worried by this point.

The barber certainly did. 'Yes, sir, whatever you want, sir.'

I knew straightaway that he had no idea what I was saying, but I tried again. 'Don't cut it too short. Just a little trim, please.'

Now he looked even more concerned. He had to deal with my hair and the language barrier. 'Yes, sir. Whatever you want, sir.'

I realised I was in for an adventure and that all the talking in the world wasn't going to change anything. 'I'll just sit quietly now. Is that all right with you?' I said softly.

'Yes, sir, whatever you want, sir.'

He walked around the chair a few times in one direction. I was sure I could see beads of sweat forming on his brow. Then he slowly walked in the other direction. He was obviously wondering where to start. A look of resolve appeared on his face. Like a man who had just walked onto the gallows. He swallowed, then he sprayed water on the mop I called my hair, hoping that would make it easier to tackle.

After standing for about thirty seconds in silent meditation, he dived in. Not with the scissors, though, but with a round brush and a blow dryer. He spent the next twenty minutes straightening my hair, rolling long, tangled knots around the brush and then teasing them slowly but painlessly out. He was obviously a craftsman and this procedure would require all the skills he had gathered over his long career.

Then he stood back and studied me. Slowly, I lifted my eyes to the mirror, not knowing what to expect. It was still me, but I now looked like I did when I was seventeen years old and had just joined Cold Chisel, when I would regularly try to brush out my own hair.

My hair was fuzzy, straight and long. The curls and knots were gone. I looked half human and half tumbleweed. I wondered if that was it, if I should get up.

'Er, are you finished now?' I asked sheepishly.

He smiled at me. 'Yes, sir—'

I couldn't help myself. 'I know, I know. Whatever I want, sir.'

But he wasn't done. He grabbed a pair of scissors and a comb and went back to work.

Clip. Clip. Clip. His hands moved in an almost maniacal way. I couldn't believe what was happening to me. I tried to tell him to stop. 'I think that will do, thanks,' I said nervously.

He smiled reassuringly. 'Yes, sir, whatever you want, sir.' And then he went back to sculpting my hairdo, like a gardener trimming a hedge. I was half-expecting my hair to take the shape of an elephant or some other magical work of topiary. Every now and then, the other barber, who seemed to be the boss, walked over, looked as worried as his colleague, whispered something in Thai and walked away again.

Clip. Clip. Clip.

My hair was flying all over the shop and being blown around by the air conditioning, which seemed to be working overtime in an attempt to cool the situation.

Clip. Clip. Clip.

'Is it going to be all right?' I asked, craving reassurance.

'Yes, sir, whatever you want, sir.'

Swish. Swish. Swish.

My hair that was once tangled was being transformed, thinned, trimmed, teased, torn, tucked, tumbled, twisted, treated and tossed around my head like never before.

Clip. Clip. Clip.

The floor looked like the deck of a shearing shed. Curls lay in piles all around me. I sat dumbstruck, watching in disbelief. I no longer looked like the man who had walked in forty minutes earlier. And I certainly didn't look like any of the other customers. I closed my eyes and prayed silently to God, any god – I wasn't fussy by this point – to do something to help me and the poor man who had been given this thankless task get through the ordeal in one piece.

Dear God. I know I haven't been in touch a lot lately. But I've been busy. You know how it is. What with work and travel and all. But I did mean to call you. Honestly. If you are listening, please help me get through this haircut. It's not a big ask and I know how busy you are. Even just a little help would go a long way. And, oh, yes. Amen. Do people still have to say that these days?

Clip. Clip. Clip.

Then it was time for the blow dryer and the brush again. After ten more minutes the barber put down his tools, with the satisfied look of a painter who had just created a masterpiece. He stood there examining me. I slowly opened my eyes and looked at me too.

At least I thought it was me. But it was not my hair. The person in the mirror looked like an extra from *Planet of the Apes*. I had a sort of lioness cut. My hair had been preened and coiffed until it wrapped around my head and neck like a motorbike helmet. God hadn't been listening.

I was afraid to ask, but I managed to spit it out. 'Are you finished now?'

He must have heard the trembling in my voice. All my confidence was gone. I was a shadow of the man I'd been. I had a new hairdo and a bright red face.

He looked at me, smiled again and said, 'Yes, sir, whatever you want, sir.'

Next he applied so much hairspray that I got the feeling my hair might not move for weeks. Then he removed the cape, brushed the hair off my shoulders and smiled at me, before holding up a mirror so I could see the back. It didn't look any better from that direction.

He wrote the bill on a piece of paper and I paid as quickly as possible. I had to escape before he could do any more damage. I bowed uncomfortably, like every *farang* does on his first trip to Asia, pressed my palms together and raised them to my forehead the way I thought Thai people did, then turned away.

As I stepped out of the door of the hotel, Jane arrived. She took one look and nearly fell over laughing. I had to laugh as well. I mean, what else could I do?

But then I spotted a large ceramic pot of water by the door of the hotel. I ran to it, leaned over, stuck my head in the water, pulled it out and shook myself like a dog. My hair bounced back to something like it had looked before I went to the barber.

I took Jane by the hand and we walked away saying nothing. But eventually I had to speak. 'Don't let me do anything here on my own again, would you, baby?'

She smiled and said softly, 'I won't, my love. I won't.'

You've Given *Me Enough*

'I'm going for a walk.'
  They all know where I am
walking to. I'm going to get
something to drink before
we start recording.

I might even organise some cocaine too. I did the same thing yesterday and the day before that. I've been smashed every day since I arrived in Los Angeles and it's the same every time I come here. The place gets me down, and I'm down pretty low already. Much lower and I'll be gone. And the drugs are so cheap. For me, LA is a trap, a death trap.

It's the late 1990s and I'm here to record a new album with my mate and amazing producer Don Gehman. It's the follow-up to *Soul Deep*, an album we made for fun in my studio at home in the Southern Highlands, which has gone on to become the biggest-selling record I've ever had. In fact, it's one of the biggest-selling records in Australian music history. That first soul record has become so big that everyone thinks I was setting myself up for my old age, changing direction and choosing music that's easier to sing. But it was the opposite. I wanted to do something different before I charged ahead and played harder than ever before.

So now here I am, nearly ten years later. Because I learned so much about singing during the making of that first soul record, I've decided to do a second and see what happens. I'm under incredible pressure. Not so much from the critics but more from myself. I want it to be more soulful, more real. It's to be called *Soul Deeper* and I know I'll have to dig real deep if I'm going to make it work.

'Are you sure you don't want to sing for a while and then get a drink?'

Don does his best every day to keep me on the straight and narrow. He knows what I'm up to and he knows he's fighting a losing battle. He tries to be the voice of reason. It seems to be part of his job, dare I say a large part of his job: get the best out of me before I push myself too far and begin to fall apart.

I drove Don Gehman so crazy he started wearing my album tapes.

Don knows what I'm going through. You see, Don is a friend of Bill Wilson. That means, at some point, he was probably nearly as bad as I am now. But then Don changed, after he hit rock bottom and reached out to Alcoholics Anonymous for help. Bill Wilson started AA and if you were a friend of his it meant you were a member of the club. And it was a big club. You'd be surprised how many people have hit rock bottom. But rock bottom is not the same for everybody. What Don calls rock bottom and what I call rock bottom are two very different places.

'The horn section aren't here yet,' continues Don. 'Why don't we go to an AA meeting? There's one just down the road. It will only take an hour. I know what I'm talking about. This will help, Jimmy. Trust me,' he pleads.

We go through this every day. I never listen. I haven't even begun to think about how difficult I must be making Don's life.

'I would rather stick pins in my eyes, thanks Don.' And I laugh as I walk out the door in search of fuel. Rocket fuel.

It's way too early to start taking drugs. That won't happen until at least midday. Fucking drug dealers just don't wake up early enough for my liking. In the meantime, surely a little vodka isn't going to kill anybody?

I come out of the dark, air-conditioned recording studio into the burning sun. There is something about the concrete and the heat in LA that gets to me, and God it makes me thirsty. I don't want to be outside for too long. This is a different studio from the one we've been using for the last few weeks, so I'm not sure which way to go. I head out and turn left into a lane. There has to be somewhere to buy booze around here. It's a shitty neighbourhood and there are drunks everywhere. I'm keen to join them.

I start to plan my day. Stock up with vodka, enough to last me until the end of the session. While I'm out, get a big pile of money from the ATM, so that as soon as the drug dealer shows his face, I'm ready to get off mine. Then back to the air conditioning as quick as possible. Before I die.

I walk towards the main street I can see at the end of the lane. Small, scraggy trees line the way, only about three or four feet high, with not a lot of leaves on them, so there's little shade.

I pick up the pace and keep my eyes to the ground. I don't want to talk to anybody in a place like this. It feels a little dangerous.

'Excuse me, sir. Can you spare a little something for a hungry soul?'

I hear the voice but I'm too preoccupied with my mission to pay attention to it. I keep walking.

'Sir, hello. Can you hear me?'

I look up and there, sitting on the ground under one of the small trees, trying desperately to find some shade, is an old lady. Grey hair and skin, faded clothes that blend in with this dull shithole of a town. Nothing shines here anymore. I think the glamour died in the 1930s.

Our eyes meet. She looks as though she is ashamed to be in the position she is in. I look the same. I stop and open my wallet. It's empty.

'I would give you something, but I'm out of cash,' I say, fumbling as I open my wallet to show her.

'Never mind, dear,' she says quietly. 'I only wanted to sell you some of my art.'

That's when I notice the pieces of paper and cardboard laid out in front of her. I hadn't even noticed *her* until she spoke, never mind her art. I thought they were just crumpled papers that someone else must have thrown away.

'I'm sorry,' I say, continuing on down the street. I'm on a mission, and I need to get on with it.

But there's something about her that sticks with me. Maybe the loneliness in her eyes or just the disturbing thought that a woman her age has to live on these streets. I don't feel secure in this neighbourhood, so how could she possibly feel safe here?

I walk on, thinking about her. Soon enough, I locate an ATM, withdraw some cash and find a market where I can get vodka. Then I head for the safety of the recording studio.

As I walk back up the lane, the old lady smiles at me.

I have to stop. I don't think this person has anything I need, but I squat down so she doesn't have the sun in her eyes.

'I haven't always lived on the street,' she says. 'I used to have a home.'

I can tell she is settling into a story that I don't really have time to listen to. But I sit on the ground next to her and get comfortable. I feel like running back to the studio and pouring myself a big drink, but it will have to wait.

'I used to be an art teacher. I had a family and a husband. I had a life. I even had a dog. Now I live on the street like a dog that no one wants.'

I can see her eyes are starting to fill with tears and I try to make a joke. 'But at least you're free to do whatever you like, eh?'

She smiles at me and I catch a glimpse of something in her expression that makes me smile too.

'So, tell me, what are you selling here, and how much does it cost?' I ask.

She starts to lay out a selection of pencil and smudged crayon artworks on pieces of cardboard and papers that had clearly once been wrapped around tins of food.

'I can't afford to buy real paper, so I have to make do with what I can find,' she explains.

There in front of me are drawings of rainbows and trees and flowers. They are not masterpieces, but they look like they were drawn with care and love.

'I'll buy a few,' I quickly say, hoping to help her out and get away as fast as I can. As nice as she seems, she doesn't smell too good.

I pull out a wad of cash and peel off twenty bucks. 'Is that enough for one of these?' I ask her, picking up one of the artworks.

'That's way too much, young man. Give me a dollar. That will be plenty. You have already given me enough.'

I'm a bit confused. 'What do you mean? I haven't given you anything yet.' I can feel myself thinking less and less about getting drunk and destroying my life.

'Living on the street is hard. People treat you like an animal. They walk past and don't even see me. You've stopped and given me your time. The thing I miss most about my old life is just having someone to talk to. Out here I am alone. Out here no one cares at all. Actually, you can have that drawing for free. I don't want to take any money from you.'

By this point my troubles feel like nothing. We sit and talk for a while longer and she tells me about her life and how it all fell apart after her husband died. And how her kids were too caught up in their own lives to even care about her.

They didn't need her anymore, so she was just cast aside like a piece of rubbish.

But even though she has nothing, she can still smile at me. 'I don't blame them. They have their own children and their business to take care of,' she says softly.

'How many drawings do you have on you?' I ask her. She opens her shopping bag and pulls out another pile of shabby bits of paper, all with sketches on them. I realise these aren't just sketches. They are dreams and memories.

'I'll take the lot,' I say and try to put five hundred dollars in her hand.

'I can't take that, young man. It's way too much,' she says and looks down at the ground. 'I told you: you've given me enough already.'

I want to sit and talk to her for longer, but I know that the studio is calling.

'Please take it. I think your drawings are beautiful and you are the one who has given me so much. I was just going to spend most of that money on booze and coke. And then I'd probably waste the rest.' I laugh. 'Sorry, that was a bad joke. I was hoping I'd stop feeling anything. But now I think I want to feel, because of you. So, please, take it.'

I put the money back into her hand and get up.

'I hope you are going to be all right,' she says.

I smile at her and walk away.

There will be no cocaine for me today. I walk back to the studio and grab some tape and stick her drawings around the walls.

Later I go for another walk, hoping to say hello, but she's gone. I never see her again.

Hold My *Hand*

'Oh, Jimmy, I thought it was so nice the way you swam down and took your wife's hand in case she was scared of the manta rays,' said Hannah. 'You're such a gentleman.'

Hannah, a surf photographer, was accompanying us on a one-day diving tour in September 2019, cruising around the Maldives looking for large, dangerous sea animals to swim with. My chest started to pump a little faster and swell with pride as she spoke, but inside I felt embarrassed. You see, the real story is a little different from what that young lady had seen. And if she'd known Jane and me well, she would have realised that things aren't always as they seem with us.

I am the one full of bravado. Always jumping up to be the saviour. The protector. The man of the house. But, it's all an act. In fact, my actions are fuelled by pure, unadulterated fear. It's been that way all my life. Since I was a child, I've been afraid of the dark, afraid of the unknown, afraid of everything. Sometimes that can make me a little dangerous, but mostly it makes me a little pathetic.

Jane, on the other hand, is afraid of nothing. She is courageous and strong. On many a flight, as our plane has hit turbulence and I have started to panic, the only things that have calmed me down are the sound of Jane's voice and the touch of her hand as she gently caresses my face and tells me everything is going to be all right. So many nights I have woken in a pool of sweat, heart pounding and unable to breathe, only to be held in Jane's arms and whispered back to sleep. She is my angel. My light.

Mostly, I am afraid of the unknown, the dark, the unseeable. I would throw myself in front of a bullet for my Jane, but ask me to go round the back of the house and fix a broken fuse in a storm and my mind immediately spawns a worst-case scenario. Vicious killers lurking in the shadows, waiting for an opportunity to pounce. The ones you never see until it's too late. The same ones that terrified my mother all her life. So much so that we moved house constantly, trying to keep one step ahead of them.

Every second night, I would wake to the touch of Mum's hand on my shoulder and the sound of her voice. 'Jim, son. I can hear someone outside.' Half-asleep, I would be bundled out of bed and into my mum's room with the rest of the kids. Was she protecting us or were we supposed to protect her? I never worked it out.

'Mum, there's no one out there. It's just the wind,' I would say, before she'd cut me off.

'Listen, son. Did you hear that? Shhhh! Listen. There it is again.' Her eyes would be darting around the room as she tried to remember: had she locked every window, bolted every door? There was always somewhere someone could get in.

'Mum, it's the wind, I'm telling you.'

By then I could see the fear in her eyes. She would be in a state of pure panic. How could anyone be this scared of nothing? I'd think. Yet what if she was right? Maybe something was out there, watching, waiting for a chance to get us.

Thump. Thump. A banging on the wall outside the bedroom. Mum's eyes would fill with tears.

What had happened to her? Where had all this started? Who had hurt her so badly that she felt the need to pass this sense of dread on to her children? You see, I am not the only one in my family who is like her. Mum successfully handed down her terrors to each and every one of us.

She passed on a different fear to my dad. He was terrified too. But he was terrified of her and what she would do if she was cornered. Or if she found out what he was up to. Either way, she might have killed him in his sleep.

I've often found myself in deep water. Thank God for Jane. *(Hannah Anderson)*

My mum, though, was afraid every day of her life. And every night as darkness fell the world closed in on her. Out there in the shadows, something waited. And if it got the chance, it might take her.

Did she ever search elsewhere for the source of her fear? Maybe what was scaring her was closer than she knew. Maybe it was inside the door. Inside the house. Inside her own heart. I know, because I'm like her, and the thing that scares me most is what's inside me. That coldness I feel when I shut down. The darkness that lies not far beneath the surface. Scratch a little and it starts to reveal itself, black and lonely. The sense that I care about no one really but me. I hide it from everyone and try to push it further down inside me in the hope that it will disappear.

That's where I come from. That's my demon. It took me years to be able to sleep with the lights out, and I still haven't quite got to the point of being comfortable alone, anywhere. But if my Jane is there, I am braver. At least I try to be. I want to be the one who protects her. Who looks out for her. I want to be someone better. Someone she can love. I want to be the one who would save her, if she ever needed saving. But, like I said, it's normally the other way round.

And now I have to own up to it.

'Er, Hannah. You know that photo you took?' I reply sheepishly.

'Yes, Jimmy.'

I can't lift my eyes from the ground. I can't look her in the eye.

'Jane swam down and held my hand. She knew I was terrified. She swam down and saved me. She always does.'

Big Jim

Just before the demise of Cold Chisel in the early 1980s, I bought a farm in the Southern Highlands of New South Wales. It was about six acres and had a little shack on it.

It was rustic, which means it was nearly falling down, but I loved it. I'd always wanted to live in the country, breathe fresh country air, and have space for my family and maybe a dog.

As much as I dreamed about country life, though, I was at heart a city slicker. I'd never really had a green thumb, and I still can't grow a thing. I wasn't particularly good with animals unless they were in my audience, and I wasn't much of a handyman – in fact, the only thing handy about me on the farm was that I lived there. But Jane wanted a vegetable garden and chickens, the whole thing, and I was happy to be her farmhand.

We settled in and life was good. Then one day my brother John turned up at our place towing a horse float. As he pulled into the driveway, I could hear thumping and kicking coming from inside it. It sounded dangerous.

John went to the back of the float, dropped the door and brought out what looked to me like a really big horse. A really big, angry, red horse. I thought I saw steam coming out of its nose, but I might have been wrong. John told me he was an ex-racehorse, just over sixteen hands, which is quite large as horses go, I now know. He had a flaming red, or chestnut, coat with a white chest and white feet, and a white blaze on his forehead and apparently he liked to run. He was magnificent.

John said, 'You can't live on a farm without a horse. It wouldn't be right.'

I stood open-mouthed for a short time then said, 'That's great. I know what you're saying, John, but I can't really ride.'

That was the least of my worries according to John. 'It's not hard, son. Just jump on and hang on. Cowboys do it all the time. And they're throwing ropes, catching cows and cracking whips while they do it. How hard can it be?'

So that was it. I was the proud owner of a racehorse.

'Does he have a name?' I asked John as he jumped back into his car.

He got back out. He couldn't wipe the grin off his face.

'Big Jim. That's his name. Big Jim. That's why I bought him. He was meant to be with you.'

I looked at Big Jim. He was nice enough. In fact, he was very handsome. But he was bloody big and he scared the hell out of me. He had a wild look in his eyes that made me think he had plans for me. Later I'd come to understand that he'd been scared too.

I decided it would be best to take some lessons before I started riding him by myself. There was a guy named Angus who had a riding school not far from us, at Fitzroy Falls, and he said it would be fine if I brought my own horse. So we put Big Jim into his horse float and drove out to his farm. The area was beautiful. Green and lush. But there was a good reason it was so lush, and that was because it rained a lot there. And, as it happened, the day I took my first lesson was a very rainy day. Clouds hung over the paddocks, covering the whole place in mist. It was really pretty, but it didn't look like good horse-riding weather to me.

'Shall we call it off and try again tomorrow?' I asked Angus.

'Jimmy, I thought you were Scottish,' he replied. 'You guys love the rain. And this is perfect riding weather. Put on your Driza-Bone and let's get started.'

Before I could think or protest further, we were in Angus's lunging yard. This was a space about the size of two tennis courts with a high-railed wooden fence around the outside. As I saddled up, the rain started to come down heavier. By the time I was ready to get on Big Jim, it was bucketing down.

'Don't worry, Jimmy,' Angus said, smiling at me, 'at least it's not windy. Horses hate the wind.'

As if on cue, the wind started to gust around the yard.

Angus shrugged his shoulders and laughed. 'Oops, spoke too soon. Get on, mate.'

Just before I climbed up on Big Jim, I found myself looking straight into his eyes. They looked particularly wild that day. Dark and glassy, with a fire burning in them. I could see it.

'Are you sure he's all right?' I asked Angus.

'He'll be fine. It's not like he's been eating oats or anything like that,' he said in a matter-of-fact tone.

'I fed him oats this morning,' I cried out.

'Why did you feed him that?' Angus asked anxiously, pulling me away from the horse.

'John, my brother, told me that's what racehorses eat.'

Even Angus looked really worried now. 'I think you'll find that is only when they are racing, Jimmy. It makes them a bit loopy. But anyway, you're in the yard, I'm here with you, and he can't go far, so hop on.'

Against my own better judgement, I climbed on. I was sure the beast could smell the fear in me. He moved from side to side beneath me as if waiting to get into the starting gate.

'Now, just gently squeeze his flanks with your heels and he will start to walk,' Angus instructed. 'Not too hard. You don't want to spook him.'

I was the one who was spooked. 'Like this?' I asked and ever so gently began to squeeze.

'Yes, that's right.'

Big Jim didn't move.

'Try squeezing a tiny bit harder,' Angus said.

So I did and Big Jim went from standing still to galloping at high speed, straight towards the fence at the other end of the yard. My arms flew wildly around as I lost even the small amount of control I initially thought I'd had. When he got to the fence, he stopped dead. I wasn't quite so lucky and continued to travel forward at the speed of sound. Over Big Jim's head and over the fence and into a large puddle of mud.

I was furious. I got up and walked back through the gate and into the yard, went straight up to my big red equine friend and gave him a severe talking-to. Not too hard. Just enough to let him know I thought his behaviour wasn't cool. 'Don't you ever do that to me again, all right, or else,' I screamed at him, before climbing straight back onto the saddle.

Big Jim never threw me again. From that day on we were the best of friends. Inseparable. No one else could ride him but me. I was the only one he trusted and he was the only horse I trusted. When he was hopped up on racing feed, he didn't like to walk or trot: he went from standing still to galloping in one stride. Just like me.

We reached an understanding, and running wild around the countryside of the Southern Highlands was how we related to each other. I rode Big Jim every day I was home for about ten years, come rain, hail or shine. He calmed me down when I was angry and cheered me up when I was sad.

He even starred in one of my film clips, the video for 'No Second Prize'. That was the first big single from my first solo album. It was a time when I thought my world was about to fall apart, but it became the most successful phase of my

For most of my life I was out of control, but not with Big Jim.

career. I truly believe that part of the reason for that success was the film clip with Big Jim.

Originally, the director wanted me to ride a movie horse and race alongside a moving train. 'Let's get you riding a beautiful big black stallion,' he said.

I preferred to be on Big Jim. 'I can ride these days,' I said to him, 'but I've only really ever stayed on the back of Big Jim. Any other horse might throw me off. And if you want me racing a train, Big Jim is your horse. He's a fucking racehorse.'

The director agreed but wanted to dye Big Jim black.

'I think he looks magnificent as he is,' I said to him. 'I'm not painting him for anyone. Get someone else to ride a black horse.'

The director relented. Like I said, Big Jim and I had an understanding. He became the star of the clip and he stayed a beautiful chestnut colour. I was merely an extra and managed to stay on the horse.

Big Jim came to know me as well as anyone did. He had to listen to all of my darkest secrets as we ran flat out around the countryside or stopped at mountain lookouts, peered out to the horizon, smoked big joints and contemplated life. Well, he never smoked – he preferred uppers – it was only me.

Some days I would ride him down the mountain into the town of Bowral, tie him up outside the pub and go in and have a beer. Then I'd get back in the saddle and off we'd go, galloping away up the hill. The locals thought we were crazy. If only they'd known the half of it.

The Yakuza *Driver*

In 2013, my very good friend
Don Walker began doing
things I'd never thought I'd see
him do. For a start, he became
excited about outdoor sports.

Now, I don't mean just watching people play sports, because he had always been keen on watching rugby league. Suddenly, he seemed to be actually participating himself – and he wanted to share his activities with his friends.

'Jim, I tell you. This is the best skiing you will ever see. It's in northern Japan, Niseko to be exact. I've been going for a few years now and it is an amazing place,' Don said in his slow North Queensland drawl. This was a guy who, as far as I knew, never did anything fast. Even his speech was restricted to the kind of language that could really only be spoken when you were in deep thought and sitting down on solid ground. Preferably flat ground. Flat and mostly dry. And, if possible, not only dry but also cleared as far as the eye could see. And ideally somewhere in Queensland – it always sounded better if there was sugar cane growing within spitting distance.

But now he was talking crazy. In one sentence he calmly mentioned snow, mountains and moguls as if they were things he had dealt with all his life.

'Yes, these mountains, Jim, just keep getting higher and higher. These mountains are higher than Dave, our old tour manager from Byron Bay.' He laughed to himself. 'And to get off them you have to negotiate blizzards and moguls. Moguls are really big speed bumps in the snow that are put there with the sole purpose of killing skiers. Oh, yeah, and there are black runs too. You know what a black run is, don't you, Jim? It's like a cliff with skid marks on it. Skid marks that were carved into it by an unsuspecting skier who didn't know what he was doing, and foolishly thought he could make it down in one piece, and nearly killed himself in the process. Believe me, I know.'

Don rubbed his leg as if remembering some painful old injury. 'And the snow is thick. Really thick. Thicker than that Macedonian promoter we used to work for in Wagga Wagga back in the early eighties. So thick you might not make it off the mountain in one piece unless you know what you are doing.'

This was all a bit of a shock and I had to pause for a minute to take it in. Jane had got me into skiing in the early 1980s, but I never thought I'd see Don on the slopes. In fact, I'd never really seen him bend his legs before, let alone slide down a mountain.

'Are you telling me that you have taken up skiing, or am I hearing you wrong?'

He wasn't really listening to me and continued with his speech. 'I tell you Jim, it is just breathtaking up there in the cold, crisp mountain air. A cold, howling wind blows straight down from Siberia, and we all know how cold it gets in Siberia. It's so cold that it cuts right through you. Quicker than a speed dealer in the Cross with a flick knife. Cuts right to the bone too. You really know you are alive up there, I'm telling you.'

The most I'd seen Don do outdoors was drink coffee on the street outside Café Hernandez in Kings Cross. And even then he was always waiting for a table indoors to become available. But now I realised I could see the effects of this new outdoor activity on his face. I hadn't noticed previously, but he was slightly more weather-beaten than I remembered. And, if I wasn't wrong, he had white circles around his eyes from wearing goggles. This was fucking nuts. It had to be a prank.

'And the food, Jim, there is nothing like it. Sushi, you know, raw fish, Jim? Yep, they don't even bother to cook it because it's that fresh. You know how much I love it. And yakitori. Bloody chicken and onions on sticks. What a great idea! And tempura. That's like fish and chips but there's no chips. All sorts of fried vegetables – what a great way to get the kids to eat their veggies. And you don't have to hunt for this food, it's all right there at the bottom of the slopes waiting for you to ski in and get it. It is phenomenal. The culture, the food and, of course, the whisky. Do you still drink? You must have tried Japanese whisky in your day, Jim. It's smooth as silk. Smoother than a Los Angeles record company A&R man. There is nothing better after a hard day's skiing than sipping a large whisky in my favourite bar while the snow is falling outside.'

I could see his eyes glazing over and sense he was longing for distant shores and foreign mountain ranges.

'You should see this bar, Jim. The entrance is a little fridge door and it opens up into a beautiful room overlooking silver birch tree–covered hills.'

He stopped to draw a breath and I jumped in. 'Are you fucking serious? You can't be.' I looked him straight in the eyes. 'You are, aren't you?'

I laughed as it slowly sank in. My friend of over forty years, a man I thought I knew and was comfortable with, had taken up a hobby. One that did not involve smoking Cohibas, drinking coffee and reading newspapers or being a lounge lizard in one of the many clubs and bars around Darlinghurst. He had taken up what was clearly a sport. And a very physical one to boot. I was flabbergasted. 'You think you know someone and, *boom*, this happens. Fuck me!' I exclaimed.

'You and Jane should come skiing with us,' said Don. 'We go every year in February. If you book now you'll still be able to find some good accommodation.'

This was an offer I could not refuse. The chance to see Don Walker wearing something else besides a country-style dress shirt, straight-leg jeans and R.M. Williams riding boots was too much for me to resist. I'd seen him wear a balaclava for a photo shoot, but never outside a studio before.

'Yeah, all right then, I'll talk to Jane and see what I can do.'

And so the wheels were set in motion. Jane and me, our children and assorted grandchildren would all travel to Niseko on the island of Hokkaido, in Japan, to ski with Don Walker and his family. Was this a dream? And, if so, would it end well? I would have to wait and see.

*

The following February, we caught a plane to Tokyo, one of our favourite places. When Jane and I were young, we used to go there quite often. In fact Jane had lived there while trying to escape me, but that's another story and you'll have to read one of my earlier books to catch up on that.

Jackie, my younger son, speaks fluent Japanese, so he was chosen as our interpreter.

'We need to book a few restaurants,' I said to him.

Jackie knew that we loved to eat and was keen to book for us, partly so he could tag along too.

'Yeah, Dad, just give me a list and I'll organise it all.'

Top of the list was a restaurant called Inakaya, in the Roppongi district, one of my favourite places in the world to eat. The food is Japanese country-barbecue style. The freshest produce is grilled over flames right in front of you by highly trained chefs kneeling behind the grills, wearing traditional dress, including headbands around their foreheads. They are keen-eyed, hold razor-sharp knives at the ready, and look like samurai waiting to pounce on unsuspecting enemies.

As you enter the room, the chefs yell out at the top of their voices, 'Irasshaimase!' Then the rest of the staff answer, equally loudly, 'Hai. Irasshaimase!' This is repeated every single time anyone enters the room. At first, I couldn't understand what they were saying, but I soon found out it is a traditional welcome.

Inakaya is so good that one time many years ago, Jane and I ate there three times in one night. On that particular trip I had arrived in Japan for a working holiday with one thing on my mind: to take Jane straight to Inakaya for dinner. This was our restaurant. This was our place to go on dates in Japan. We were so excited about the evening to come, but no sooner had we checked into our hotel than the phone rang.

'Eh. Hello. Is Jimmy Barnes, please?' a Japanese voice asked.

'Yes, it's Jimmy speaking,' I answered politely.

'Ah, Jimmy-san. I am representing your record company in Japan and we would like you to join us for dinner.'

I started to panic. All I wanted to do was eat at my favourite restaurant in the world and now it looked like I was going to have to go somewhere else. I squirmed in my seat, trying to think of a way out of it.

'It would be a great honour if you could join us, Jimmy-san.'

There was no way out of it.

'Yes, of course. When and where would you like us to meet you?' I bit my lip and tried not to sound disappointed. In case you don't know it, I am a creature of habit, dare I say compulsive, even obsessive. And every time I go to Japan,

Inakaya in Tokyo, my favourite restaurant in the world

the first thing I want to do is head to my favourite place to eat. So this guy had thrown me a curve ball and I wasn't happy.

'We would like to take you somewhere a little bit different. We have booked a Korean barbecue restaurant for you. It is very nice. We will send a car to pick you up at eight o'clock from your hotel and we will see you there.'

I hung up the phone.

'Arrrrgh!' I didn't want to eat Korean food in Japan, I wanted to eat at our restaurant. But I was going to have to go, so I needed a plan.

A few minutes later I said to Jane, 'We can go to Inakaya early for an entrée and then get back here in time for the car.'

Jane looked bemused, but she knew me and knew I was getting crazy about this upset to my plans. 'That will be fine, darling, but we just can't eat too much too soon. We will have to pace ourselves.' She smiled at me. Jane knows that pacing myself is not my strong suit.

'Of course, of course,' I said, starting to mentally run through what I would eat even before I'd finished speaking.

So, at six o'clock we arrived at Inakaya to be greeted by the raised voices of the samurai staff.

'Irasshaimase!'

'Hai. Irasshaimase!'

We ordered everything we could eat in one hour then dragged ourselves back to the hotel. The car arrived and took us to the Korean barbecue place. It was fine, but not where I wanted to be. We sat squirming in our chairs and pretended to be very jet-lagged and then after an hour or so excused ourselves and were driven to our hotel by someone from the record company.

'So sorry you are tired, Jimmy-san. The main course was just coming when you had to leave. Please take my card and call if I can do anything for you while you are in my country.' The record company man bowed and handed me his card, then got back in his car and drove away. I think I awkwardly bowed to the car as it left. Then we stood in the driveway and continued to wave. As soon as the car was out of sight, I turned to Jane. 'Great, now we can go back to Inakaya and eat some more.'

Jane looked at me in disbelief but smiled. She knows me too well. Off we went to our restaurant for the second time that evening. Again we were greeted by the staff.

'Irasshaimase!'

'Hai. Irasshaimase!'

The maître d' had a puzzled look on his face, but he politely ushered us in and we sat down in the exact spot we had sat in three hours earlier.

We proceeded to eat everything that was put in front of us for an hour or two. Then, when we could not possibly eat another bite, we paid the bill, bowed and headed home.

Later that night, after a short sleep, Jane woke up and said, 'You won't believe this, but I'm hungry again.'

Jane can eat more than most men I know. Big men.

'Yeah, so am I,' I replied.

Jane knew what was coming next.

'Why don't we go back to Inakaya? It's open until 2 am.'

Jane laughed. 'I'm in. Let's go.'

We got dressed, went downstairs, jumped in a cab and headed back to our restaurant for the third time that night. As we walked in, the staff began shouting.

'Irasshaimase!'

'Hai. Irasshaimase ...'

They tailed off quickly when they realised it was us again. The maître d' took us back to the same seats and started bringing food even before we'd ordered it. We've been to this place many times since, and every time we walk in I'm sure they remember us.

*

Anyway back to the skiing trip. On the second day, after a night at Inakaya, we all caught the bullet train to Hokkaido. Then, after a bus ride up to the snowfields, we arrived in Niseko.

There was a message waiting at reception from Don, welcoming us to Japan and enquiring about our plans for dinner. Jane had learned from an Anthony Bourdain show about an amazing place called Torimatsu and was very excited about going there. It was in a little town just half an hour from Niseko called Kutchan. So we made a booking for nine people and quickly changed so we could head straight there. After travelling all day we were starving. We sent a message to Don, asking him and his family to meet us at the restaurant. We had the hotel book us a car with a driver because we didn't know where Kutchan was and we didn't want to drive in the snow.

When we headed down to the car, snow was gently falling and the whole town looked like it was covered in a fresh white blanket. It was just like a postcard, the perfect start to our stay. We jumped into the car and the first thing I noticed was that our driver didn't look like your usual chauffeur. He was young, slick and wearing a beautifully cut suit, and I was sure I caught a glimpse of tattoos under his jacket sleeves. He turned and greeted us and we could immediately tell he wasn't from these mountains – he looked more like he should have been driving a Yakuza boss. But although he didn't say much, he was polite and seemed to know what he was doing and exactly where to go.

It was a cold, cold night and the drive was exciting. Within about thirty minutes or so, we pulled up outside the tiny little restaurant in a tiny little town in the middle of nowhere. The driver jumped out and opened Jane's door.

'Please just call when you are nearly finished and I will be right here waiting for you,' he said in hesitant English. He handed me a card, bowed and jumped back into the car, then *swooshed* away into the soft white night.

We entered the restaurant and there were Don, Firoozeh, his beautiful wife, and Leili, his daughter, waiting quietly by the desk for us. Although the restaurant wasn't very big, we were shown into a little private room off to one side, which had a low table and a tatami floor. It would be a true Japanese experience, like travelling back to feudal times. I was sure the restaurant must have looked the same for over a hundred years.

There appeared to be only two people working in the kitchen, a very old man and an old woman I assumed to be his wife. He stood fanning a grill full of hot charcoal with a paper fan, waiting for the first orders to be placed. We struggled to take off our fancy shoes with too many buckles and laces – should have worn slip-ons, I immediately thought – and then went to sit down. The kids and the girls slid into position in seconds, just like they belonged there. But Don and I were shuffling our feet around, trying to work out where and how to sit down.

Meanwhile the chef's wife slowly organised drinks. It was lucky that Jackie was with us, as neither of the proprietors seemed to speak any English. Jackie translated and the woman laughed at us and we nervously laughed with her as we pointed at pictures on the menu and wondered what we were ordering.

Don and I were still struggling to get seated. Low tables and tatami floors are obviously something you have to be brought up with to be able to get into any sort of comfortable seated position. And Don and I clearly hadn't been brought up with them.

'Are you all right sitting on the floor, Don?' Firoozeh asked.

'Yeah, yeah. No worries. I just have to see if my legs are going to bend that way. Yep, that's it. I've got it. There you go. There you go. No, that's not right …' Don was trying to sit with his legs tucked under his backside, but it was never going to work for him. 'Let's have another go. Oh. Oh. No, that's not much better. Ah, oh, there you go, perfect.'

Don was now sitting in a position that he clearly hadn't been in since first grade: legs crossed, slightly red in the face, not comfortable.

'Are you sure you're all right, Don?' Firoozeh asked again.

'Yeah. This is just perfect. Couldn't be more comfortable,' he lied.

In the meantime I was trying to get my legs to bend into positions that weren't natural for any Scotsman to be in. Where I come from, you don't see legs bent like that unless they've been broken. I couldn't even remember sitting like this at school.

'Fuck. Oops, sorry. Ahhh, shit, this hurts …' Finally I said, 'This is not going to work, unless I can sit over there against the wall. Then there might be a chance.'

So Jane swapped places with me and I settled in with my back against the wall. All at once I felt surprisingly comfortable. It occurred to me then that I always like to have my back against the wall. Well, maybe that's an exaggeration. But at least now I'd be able to sit still for a while.

The chef sprang into action and it wasn't long before the first course arrived. It looked good too. No one was sure what it was, but we were starving. As the hostess placed plates in front of each of us, Jackie leaned over and spoke to me. 'Dad, this is the house speciality. I saw it on the TV show. It's grilled fish sperm sac.'

I pushed the plate away immediately.

'Geez, I've never eaten this before and I don't know what it is, but it's good. Just slips down real easy,' Don said, trying to sound adventurous.

Jane picked up her chopsticks and grabbed a piece. She had just got it to her mouth when I piped up, 'You know that's fish sperm, don't you?'

Jane immediately threw it back onto her plate. Don turned a slight shade of green and pushed his portion away. It was then that Jackie was made to explain the whole menu. Fortunately, there were no other surprises to be had and we settled into what was an amazing meal. Countless servings of fresh fish, beef, pork and vegetables, all tasting like they were harvested in the backyard, were placed in front of us, beautifully grilled and plated up, with each dish tasting better than the last. It was incredible.

Finally, after a meal that had gone on for hours, we were nearing the end, just waiting for our green-tea ice cream. At this point I thought I would sneak up and pay the bill. Don had invited us to Japan, so I wanted to buy our first dinner.

Don at the top of his game. There's only one way to go from here.
(courtesy of Don Walker)

I excused myself from the table. 'I've just got to go to the bathroom. I'll be right back.'

Don looked me in the eye and I had the feeling he knew what I was up to. But I got away before he could straighten up and get the blood flowing again in his by-now almost crippled legs.

'I want to pay the bill, please,' I said in feeble Japanese while miming signing a cheque to the chef's wife. She laughed, but I realised she had understood. I wasn't far from the table and I could still hear Don moaning as he tried to get up. I quickly pulled out my credit card to hand to her before he got there, but again she just laughed. Then she pointed to a sign: 'Cash only. No credit cards, please.'

I fumbled again for my wallet. I wasn't worried, as I had about one thousand dollars on me in Japanese yen. But then I picked up the bill and read it. I nearly choked when I saw the price. Seven hundred and forty-eight thousand yen. I quickly converted it in my head. No, that can't be right, I thought, and started to re-do the conversion. My maths wasn't that bad. If I was right, I didn't have nearly enough cash.

Just then Don walked up. 'No. NO. No, you don't. This is my shout. I invited you. Give that bill to me,' he insisted.

'I'm not sure you want this one, Don,' I joked.

'Nah, mate, I got it.' He dug deep for his wallet then tried to hand his credit card to the woman. She started speaking Japanese to him and Don looked at me.

'They don't take credit cards here,' I explained.

'That's fine, I've got cash,' Don announced.

'I hope you have a lot.' I looked him in the eye and handed him the bill.

'Fuck,' he said quietly as he examined the bill. I could see him doing the numbers in his head just as I had done. It was clear he hadn't got any better results than I had.

'That's about ten thousand dollars, I think.' He swallowed hard. 'I don't have that much.'

We both stood looking at each other and then at the bill and then back at each other.

'I've got a car with a driver. I could go and get cash from an ATM,' I said to him.

'I'll come too and we can split it,' he insisted.

We excused ourselves from the table. 'Ah, sorry folks, we are going to go out and get some cash. They don't take cards here,' we explained. 'We'll be right back.'

We stepped out into the cold and now not quite as magical night in search of cash. We found an ATM. It would only allow me to take a few hundred dollars out.

Don pushed me out of the way. 'Here, let me have a go,' he said anxiously and proceeded to try every card in his wallet. It seemed that I had already emptied the machine. Obviously ATMs in these small towns didn't carry a lot of cash. We jumped back into the car and asked the driver to find another bank.

We must have visited every ATM within fifty kilometres, but we still had nowhere near enough to pay the bill. Then I remembered that I had plenty of Australian money in my room. But it was a half-hour at least each way and we'd already been away for an hour and a half.

At this point, the driver, who obviously understood English better than he spoke it, turned to us and said, 'Excuse me, are you having trouble here? Can I help you?'

I explained how the restaurant didn't take cards and the bill was much bigger than we had anticipated and so we needed a lot of cash.

'Let me pay your bill and you can pay me later,' he said.

Of course we both thought then that any hire-car driver who is carrying ten thousand dollars with him had to be more than just a regular chauffeur. He was definitely a yakuza man.

'How much is your bill?' he asked politely.

'Seven hundred and forty-eight thousand yen,' I said sheepishly.

'No, it can't be,' he said, looking alarmed and slightly angry. After a minute of what I think was cursing in Japanese, he got on his phone and spoke to his boss. His tone was short and gruff, but polite. I reckoned he must have been talking to the head yakuza driver. I hoped Torimatsu would not be burned down by the time we got back.

As we drove there, the driver made it clear that the restaurant must be robbing us and said he would speak to them. 'It is not honourable to steal from tourists,' he barked under his breath, his voice taking on a menacing tone.

I rang Jane. 'Where are you?' she asked. 'The kids have all gone and Firoozeh and I are sitting here at the bar. The place is empty except for us. Do we need to start doing the dishes? I've called Jackie and asked him to come back and help translate.'

I explained our predicament and told her we would be there soon. And not to wash up. We arrived just as Jackie walked in.

'What's the problem, Dad? Mum tells me the bill was a bit big. Let me have a look at it, please.'

I handed Jackie the bill, whispering as I did, 'It's bloody ten thousand dollars.'

Jackie looked at me. 'No, it's not.'

'Yes, it is, son,' I said and went through the conversion with him. 'Seven hundred and forty-eight thousand yen is about ten thousand dollars.'

Jackie laughed. 'It's only forty-eight thousand yen, Dad. That first symbol that looks like a seven is the yen sign. I've got enough to pay it.' He pulled out his wallet as Don and I stood there looking like idiots.

Next day we hit the slopes with Don and, true to form, he skied like he spoke. He skied like a Queenslander. Slow and measured. And I swear he's the only person I've ever seen skiing without bending his legs.

After a while, I told him we would catch up at the end of the day for a green tea and skied off at high speed. We met at the fridge door and never mentioned the dinner again.

Life is a *Butterfly's* Dream

It was one of those hot,
steamy Sydney nights when
the humidity is just high enough
to make it uncomfortable
but not oppressive.

Summer seemed to be well on the way, even though it was another month before it officially started. Lightning was flashing over the Blue Mountains, and low, distant rumbles of thunder could be heard off the coast, quiet and menacing.

Jane and I were staying at Jane's parents' seventh-floor apartment in Neutral Bay. It was small but comfortable, and from the balcony we had a striking view of the Sydney skyline. There was no air conditioning, so we had the balcony doors wide open and a soft cool breeze was coming off the harbour.

Jane was pregnant with our second child, Eliza-Jane, and our baby, Mahalia, was asleep in the other room. We had just spent an hour or so watching a mini-series called *Shōgun*. The show was set in feudal Japan and was about the samurai who fought and died for their lords, the shoguns. It constantly made references to ways to die with honour: to die as a warrior or to take your own life when the alternative was to die a shameful death. On this particular night, the theme seemed to be that life is a butterfly's dream, and that death is not an end but a transformation and, for many, a release from the darkness of life.

I went out on the balcony and smoked a rather large joint and contemplated the meaning of life and death, then reached the conclusion that I was not ready to think about such deep matters. Not at that moment anyway. Back in those days, the idea of death, especially suicide, stirred something deep inside me that was not comfortable. In fact, it was terrifying. Not just because I was afraid of death but also because, I realise today, I had come so close to death so many times as a young man and even as a child. At this time, I hadn't really looked far enough into myself to understand it, but subconsciously I knew that suicide was something that had at one time, when I was very young, seemed preferable to living. For now, though, I was still running from that idea.

I went back inside and sat with my Jane and hoped that she would make me think of happier things. We turned the television off and listened to the now distant rumbling of the storm. It was followed by silence, peaceful and calming. I sat holding Jane in my arms. I closed my eyes and breathed deeply. It seemed like there were no troubles in the world. Then ...

Thud. A loud, strange, dull noise. I looked at Jane. We both knew something was wrong.

'What was that?' she asked softly.

'Sounded like someone in the car park,' I replied. From the apartment, you could look straight down to the entrance to the car park below, where car bonnets jutted out from under the building, all in a row like a cheap car yard. So I stood up and walked to the balcony. The area was dimly lit. After my eyes adjusted, I could make out the figure of a man lying on the ground.

'Don't worry,' I said to Jane. 'It was just some bloke bouncing off one of the cars down there. He's probably drunk and on his way home.'

But I couldn't look away. There was something not right about it. The sound had been like something I'd never heard before. And I'd heard plenty of drunks as they bumped and moaned their way through parked cars. In fact I'd done that many times myself.

I continued to watch, waiting for him to pick himself up and carry on staggering until he hit the next parked car that jumped out in front of him. But he didn't get up.

'Hey Jane, there's something wrong here, baby. I don't like it.'

Jane joined me on the balcony and we both stared down. The longer we looked, the further away the ground seemed.

'Oh my God, Jimmy, look!'

The man on the ground hadn't moved, but slowly a circle was spreading out around his head. It took me a second to realise it was blood. His blood. Oozing out from his skull.

'Maybe he hit his head on a car or something,' I whispered. But I already knew it was much worse than that.

'Oh, Jimmy, I think he jumped from one of the apartments. You'd better go and help him.'

I quickly put my shoes on and raced to the lift. I was filled with fear. I knew what I would find and I didn't want to see it. That lift was one of the slowest in the world, but on this night it seemed to reach the ground in seconds. I warily stepped out of the door into the semi-darkness of the car park. The fluorescent light above the cars flickered on and off.

He was alone on the ground in front of one of the cars. No one else from the building had come down. I tried to see if he was breathing. There was no movement.

'Oh, mate. Why? Why did you do this?' I reached out and touched his hand. I didn't want him to be alone. Not now.

My heart was pounding and I screamed as loud as I could: 'Help! Somebody help me!'

I heard a window open and a faceless voice yelled back, 'There's nothing you can do. Leave him. He was always gonna jump.'

'Come down and help me with him,' I pleaded.

But I got no answer and I heard the window shut. I was standing alone in the dark sometime after midnight with this poor lost soul, just as his spirit was leaving his twisted, broken body, and no one cared.

Now these were the days when mobile phones weren't attached to everybody's ear. I could have run to the apartment to call an ambulance, but I didn't want to leave him there in the dark alone. So I sat, with my head in my hands, wondering what to do next.

Then the lift door opened and bright neon light splashed across the car park, like the lightning I'd been watching a few minutes earlier. It was Jane.

'Is he all right?'

Her voice told me she already knew the answer to that question but was hoping she was wrong.

'Get help quick, baby. I think he's dead.'

Jane ran back to the lift and headed for our apartment. Along the way she banged on doors, but no one would answer. Finally one door opened, but with the safety chain on, and a voice from behind the door spoke to her. 'This was always going to happen. He's tried before, but never like this. He checked himself out of the hospital earlier today. He knew it was too soon and tried to go back, but those places don't work that way. He told them he was going to jump, but they wouldn't take him back in. It's the law. Poor bastard.'

Bang. The door shut.

Alone again, Jane ran as fast as she could to our apartment to ring an ambulance and the police. She called out to me from the balcony that she had to stay with Mahalia. Someone else would have to wait with the poor lonely shell of a man lying on the floor of our dark car park, and clearly it was me.

It took a long time for help to arrive. Meanwhile I sat on the ground next to the body. I cried and I sang and I told him my darkest secrets. I felt for him. I was just like him, but I hadn't quite sunk as low as he had. I would, of course – I just didn't know it then. But not until much, much later.

Life is a butterfly's dream. And I still had to go through my own metamorphosis.

Rockin' *Rod*

Rod Stewart was one of the singers I looked up to when I was a young fellow. Like me, he was from a working-class background.

And like me he'd obviously grown up listening to soul and blues music. In fact, I don't think anyone in the world had listened to or been influenced more by Sam Cooke. But Rod hadn't stolen from Sam. He had listened and learned and then he had taken what he'd learned and applied it to what he was doing himself. In doing so, he became one of the best and most recognisable rock singers of a generation. In fact, if you look at his career as a whole, he in turn influenced singers all over the world. Including me.

In 1979, Cold Chisel toured with Rod. Now, Cold Chisel opened up for a lot of big acts around that time, and we gained a bit of a reputation for making it difficult for bands to follow us. We were never malicious about it, we were just competitive, and we wanted to make it as hard as we possibly could for any band that came on after us to go about their work. But when you're dealing with the cream of the crop – people like Rod, for instance – there is only so much you can do. No matter how well we played, or how outrageous we tried to be, Rod walked on stage afterwards and was still bigger than life. His band were great, his sound was great, his lights were great – he was just fucking great at everything he was doing.

I did get the feeling, though, that he missed being the underdog every night, the one who had to rise to the challenge and try to outshine the headliner. Now he was established, with a huge career, he had it all to lose, and was under incredible pressure from his record company to hold on to his success. We, on the other hand, had nothing to lose and just wanted to rock. Rod had been the wild one, the one who did whatever he wanted, whenever he wanted. The bad boy. But now, every night, he had to play it safe, while bands like us opened for him. Bands that were still wild. Bands that were still bad.

We chatted a few times and I could tell he was the real deal. He loved music and touring and all that came with it. So we got on well. And he spoke positively about us if the press asked his opinion, although I don't think he was asked often. It wasn't long until we all started drinking down at the bar of whichever hotel we happened to be staying at. At first, it was just us and Rod's band, but gradually Rod turned up more and more. It was like he was going to show us young upstarts how a real rock band misbehaved.

One night he had his piano player accompany him in the mezzanine bar at a hotel in Christchurch. A scattering of tables and customers flanked a baby grand piano positioned close to the low rail around the mezzanine. After each song, Rod complained about the acoustics and suggested that his band move the piano over a little, or he would get on top of the piano to see if the music sounded any better up there. Song by song, the piano was shifted closer and closer to the rail.

You see, Rod could do this. He had enough money to throw the piano off the balcony. What did a baby grand cost? Thirty or forty thousand dollars? Nothing if you are one of the biggest rock stars in the world. And he knew that this was something we could never do.

So he kept singing and the band kept moving the piano a little nearer to the edge. When they got there, they lifted the end of it onto the rail. That's when the hotel security started panicking, obviously alarmed about the potential damage to their establishment. But they had no effect on Rod. He just kept singing.

Then the police arrived. Rod was tipped off by someone and immediately rushed away to his suite. The rest of us had no idea what was happening until the police entered the foyer. By the time they reached the bar, the piano was balanced precariously on the mezzanine rail. As the police and hotel security wrestled it back from the brink, we all made our escape. It seemed that Rod was still one of the lads.

We reunited at another bar in the hotel, not far from the scene of the crime. Rod didn't appear for a while, but once the police had well and truly gone he sauntered in and sat next to me. We had a good laugh about what had just happened while enjoying a quiet drink. Just as Rod started telling me some stories about the good old days, up came a rather big, drunken guy who wanted to give Rod a hard time. It appeared he preferred Rod singing 'Maggie May' rather than 'Do Ya Think I'm Sexy?', his recent hit.

Rod was polite. He obviously had to cope with people like this all the time. I, on the other hand, usually dealt with such intruders a little differently and was already positioning myself to smash the guy. Then, out of the blue, the guy grabbed Rod's shoulder and really started getting in his face. So Rod leaned forward and headbutted the bloke, sending him flying to the floor and ending their meeting abruptly. He then turned back to me and continued with what he'd been saying, as if nothing had happened.

'Er, do you think you ought to get out of here?' I asked.

Rod just laughed and said, 'Why? This guy won't start any more trouble.'

'I'm not bothered about him,' I stressed. 'I'm more worried about the police coming back.'

'Yeah. Yeah. You're probably right,' he replied casually. 'I'd better go. It's been good talking with you guys, though. Always good to slum it with the riff-raff.' And up he got and went to his suite.

I felt like I should have been taking notes. Rock Star Behaviour 101. Luckily I have a photographic memory. Shame it's not developed.

Sunset *Cruise*

Jane and I celebrate our wedding anniversary on 22 May. At least we try to celebrate it then. But, if the truth be known, we often completely forget about it.

Canoeing with me. What could possibly go wrong?

Not because we don't care or because we don't love each other, but because, I like to think, we celebrate our marriage every day. That sounds corny, yet it's true. I know that every day I wake up and think how lucky I am to share this life with Jane. (I'm not totally sure she does the same; you're going to have to wait for her book to find that out.)

It's just that our lives are so busy that sometimes we don't get a minute to stop and think, and then some things slip by us. I remember once, in late May one year, we were both exhausted and sitting in front of the television set, trying to get a rest. We had a night off from relentless touring somewhere and we'd decided to do nothing but lie around watching TV. It was good. Then one of the actors on the screen said, 'Happy anniversary, darling. I love you so much.'

We both looked up at each other and said, 'Oh no! We've missed it again, haven't we?'

'Can we celebrate tomorrow?' I asked.

Jane smiled at me. 'Absolutely, baby.'

Then we leaned over, gave each other a kiss and went back to resting. No big deal.

This sort of thing happens often. But we don't stress. We celebrate our love enough.

I tend to be a bit more over the top than Jane and try to make a big deal out of any anniversaries I do remember. I've done things like booked out a whole cinema and had a private screening of *Romeo and Juliet* played for us while a waiter served champagne and caviar. One year I rented a boat. I arranged for it to be parked in Sydney Harbour and filled with beautiful flowers, champagne, candles ready to be lit and flower petals ready to be thrown on the bed. All we needed to do was to get out there and we could spend the night alone. We don't get a lot of time alone, as we are constantly surrounded by people, so this was going to be special. I didn't tell Jane, as I wanted it to be a big surprise. But Jane had forgotten our anniversary and had decided to rent a boat herself that day for a party with a group of gay friends. I went along too and tried to get us back on land early enough to get to the other boat, but everyone was having too good a time. And then it was too late and we were too tired to be bothered.

You see what I mean? These things don't always go as planned.

Another time a few years back, we were at home in the Southern Highlands and we both remembered our anniversary. We thought we'd have a quiet romantic dinner together. Normally, we'd still be joined at some point by six or eight other people, but on this night, for once, it was just us.

It was cold that night, but I had the idea that if Jane rugged up I could get the canoe out and take her for a sunset paddle along the river and sing to her as the sun was going down. Romantic, right?

'Come on, darling,' I said. 'It'll be beautiful with the sun setting, and I'll sing to you and all the birds will sing to you too. There will be kangaroos and all sorts of other animals out. You'll love it.'

She wasn't convinced. 'It's too cold. Let's just sit by the fire and, if you really have to, you can sing.'

You can tell how much she loved me singing to her. I must admit, though, I don't really sing *to* her, more like *at* her, but that again is another story.

'It will be so nice and relaxing,' I said. 'All you'll have to do is sit and enjoy it.'

Soon we were out the door and I was pushing the canoe into the river. It's a Canadian, so it normally takes at least two people to carry it. In fact, it's so big I should have been smashing champagne over the bow as it hit the water: 'I hereby name this boat the ...' You get the picture. But I was determined and launched the beast myself.

There were a few wobbles as we boarded, but besides that it was all going to plan.

'Arrivederci Roma!' I sang at the top of my voice, wearing my best Italian hat. I looked and felt just like a real gondolier.

Jane sat nervously in the front, dodging the water that I occasionally splashed over her, mostly by accident but occasionally on purpose to check she was awake.

'I think this is far enough, baby,' she said just as I was hitting the chorus of the second song.

'No worries, my love.'

We couldn't go that much further anyway, as there was a little waterfall ahead. So I stopped pretending to be Italian and turned the boat around. Lost in the scenery and the moment, I wasn't really concentrating as much as I should have been. A big mistake.

I don't know quite what happened or exactly what went wrong, but halfway through the turn, I tipped the boat over.

Shit.

'Waaaaaaaa!' Jane screamed.

The outside temperature was by now about five degrees. We were lucky the water hadn't yet frozen.

I surfaced just in time to hear Jane scream again. That was when I realised that the boat was in only four or five feet of water. So we could stand up.

But Jane was still not happy. Standing or drowning, it made no difference.

'Oh. My. God!' she shouted at me. 'How could you do that?'

I couldn't help but laugh. Another big mistake.

'What are you laughing about?'

I could see Jane was now crying. This was not going well. I struggled to stop myself laughing. It was nervous laughter. I wasn't laughing at her, more at the situation.

'My love, you will have to stop crying and help me turn the boat over, or we will freeze to death.'

The canoe lay half-submerged. Miraculously, we managed to set it upright, empty it and drag ourselves back in. Then we sat in deathly silence as I paddled us carefully home.

Jane sat looking straight ahead, saying nothing. I didn't dare sing again. When we arrived at the dock, she got up, jumped quickly out of the canoe and marched towards the house.

'Even getting wet and all, it was still really nice wasn't it, baby?' I yelled after her.

She didn't answer.

Oops. Spoke too soon. Sorry, darling!

Sneaky
Pete

Young Peter McFee joined my
band in the mid-1980s as a
technician for my lead guitarist,
Mal Eastick. Now, Mal was a fussy
guitar player and I was fussy too.

We only wanted to work with the best people. Mal and I couldn't stand the sound of out-of-tune guitars, particularly if we were on the same stage as them. Then there was a chance that blood would be spilled, and I couldn't stand the sight of blood either. Especially my own.

Peter came highly recommended by the last tech, who was leaving us. When I say 'leaving us', I mean we'd sacked him. So the recommendation didn't mean that much really. But after the first few shows Peter had proved himself and got the job. I never heard anything go wrong, and Mal seemed to like him. He was going to work out fine. He was very nervous around me, but I knew he would settle down with time.

Soon after, I invited Peter up to my room with a few friends to celebrate his new job and he quickly accepted. I heard the doorbell as I was getting changed. Then he knocked on the door. *Bang. Bang. Bang.*

'I'm coming. Hold your fucking horses. Who the fuck is that?' I opened the door, scowling. It was Peter. He looked sheepish. He had obviously had a few drinks already.

'Come in, mate. Take a seat. Relax. I'll order up some room service. A couple of my mates are on their way over, so it'll be fun.'

It was long after midnight and I'd already had a lot to drink too. In fact I had been drinking solidly since about 1973, but that's another story. I was flying and thought I'd have a bit of fun with him.

'Now listen, Peter. You're new to the tour, so I'll tell you what we're going to do. You know that Mal, your boss, is the tightest man in the world, right? He still has the first dollar he ever earned and I doubt he will be spending it anytime soon.

Not on this tour anyway.' I looked Peter in the eye and kept a straight face the whole time.

'Ah, er, no, I, ah, never knew that,' he mumbled. 'It's not my job to know that, eh, is it?'

He was nervous. I could tell. I moved closer. He got more nervous.

'It's your job to know everything about your boss. To anticipate his every need and move.'

Peter just sat nodding. I backed away. He knew I was right. Of course I was right. It was my band.

'So, here's what we're going to do. We are going to order a pile of drinks and we will sign them all to Mal's room. You okay with that?' I smiled warmly at him.

'Er, yeah, I guess so.' He laughed uncomfortably.

I knew he was worried, but I pressed on. 'Come on, mate. It's all good fun. We're not going to kill anybody here.'

Peter regained a bit of his colour and agreed to my plan.

'Now, since you are his tech, it will be so much funnier if you sign his name on the room service bill and pretend to be him. Okay? Anyway, the staff all know me, so you'll have to do it.'

The colour drained from his face again. 'I don't know how he signs his name,' he piped up.

'That's why we're going to practise it before the drinks arrive,' I said. I handed him a sheet of paper and told him to sign Mal's name until he felt comfortable.

'They won't know what he writes like, so just get it so you don't panic. Make it look like you are signing your name. No hesitating or any shit like that.'

Peter sat there, signing away. 'Does this look right?' he asked shyly.

'Just keep doing it until room service gets here. They won't suspect a thing.'

Peter kept signing 'Mal Eastick' over and over until the doorbell rang. In came the room service guy with a bottle of vodka, a bottle of whisky and a bucket of ice. I don't remember how much the bill was, but it wasn't cheap. They had charged by the nip, so it was probably ridiculously expensive.

'Are you buying this lot, Mal?' I said, nodding to Peter.

'Er, em, what? Are you talking to me?'

I stared harder at him and lifted my eyebrows towards the waiter. 'Ahem,' I coughed. 'Are you buying the drinks, young Mr Eastick? You can sign it to your room.'

Peter looked blank.

I grabbed him by the shoulder and whispered, 'Sign the fucking bill, would you?'

He finally caught on. 'Yes, let me put that on my room. You're always buying the drinks, Jimmy. I've got this one.'

He was overacting, but he seemed to get away with it.

'Leave a really big tip for this guy for being so quick,' I said in an offhand way and then walked into the next room so I could laugh. I returned as the room service guy was leaving. Then I grabbed my list of all the rooms the band were staying in and found Mal's number.

Peter was watching me, a little confused.

I went to the phone and picked it up.

'Er, what are you doing, Jimmy?'

I looked up. 'Just hang on a second, Peter, would you, please?'

I dialled a number as Peter watched anxiously. He looked like he had developed a slight twitch.

'Better look busy, here comes the boss. Jimmy's there too.'
(courtesy of Peter McFee)

'Yeah, hello, Mal. Sorry to wake you like this. I know it's late. But we were just having a few drinks.'

Peter tried to interrupt me. 'Er, Jimmy, what are you doing?'

I waved him away. 'Hang on, mate, I'm on the phone.'

I went back to my call. 'Like I was saying, Mal, we ordered up a pile of drinks and you'll never guess what happened.'

Peter was turning as white as the high-thread-count linen sheets on the hotel bed.

'I went to the toilet and when I came out, I caught that sneaky little bastard who works for you – that's right, Peter – signing the bill to your room.'

Peter was by this time diving for the phone, trying to cut me off, but I was way too quick. I spun around and kept talking. 'You're right, he is a sneaky little bastard and we will have to sort this out in the morning. I've thrown him out of my room. Sleep well, mate. Sneaky little fucker, eh?'

I hung up. Peter was dumbstruck. He couldn't believe what I had just done. I was laughing so hard I nearly cried. Though he was visibly upset for hours afterwards, it didn't stop him drinking. I guess he thought it was his last night, so he might as well make the most of it.

Of course, the next morning I spoke to Mal, confessed and paid the bill and the whole thing was put to bed. I was glad someone made it to bed, because we never did.

Anyway, the reason I'm telling this story is because Peter, ever since that day, has been known as Sneaky Pete. That was over thirty years ago, and these days Sneaky Pete is in demand everywhere. He runs some of the biggest festivals in the world, and tours constantly with Elton John. He even works with Cold Chisel. But everyone in the business still calls him Sneaky Pete. Even his mum.

You Can *Leave Your* Hat On

There was a long period in my life when every day seemed to melt into the next. I'd be awake for nights on end, not knowing which way was up.

It might sound like fun to some of you, and if you'd asked me when I was a teenager if I would like that kind of life, I would have said yes. But when you are forty or fifty years old, it starts to wear a little thin.

Some people think that's how I should have stayed forever, though. 'Geez, mate. I liked the bloody band when you were fucked up and falling all over the stage, mindless, drinking vodka and jumping off things,' some of them say. 'Why aren't you like that anymore?'

And I have to reply, 'Because I don't want to be. You go and do that. I've had enough. I was lucky to get away with it then, never mind now.'

If I was still doing these days what I did when I was eighteen, I would think I was an idiot. You've got to grow up some time. In fact you have to grow, full stop. And change is what keeps us growing. So I'm glad I changed and I'm not that crazy anymore. But being in that state got me into some very funny situations. Let me tell you about one.

It was getting close to the turn of the millennium, a time of turmoil and change, and things for me were particularly blurry. I wouldn't always hear things clearly and I would agree to almost anything. One day I was in my studio, cleaning up after a party that had lasted for days and finished minutes earlier. My studio at the time was called The Jolly Roger. I had a pirate flag hanging over the door and anyone who entered ended up walking the plank one way or another. We used to get very messed up in that room, and not a lot of writing was done in there.

Anyway, I was in an altered state, completely fucked up, when the phone rang. A rather posh, English-sounding lady's voice on the other end said, 'Hello, Jimmy. It's Rachel Ward here. You know, Bryan Brown's wife?'

I knew who Rachel was. But I was having trouble clearing my throat, never mind my head.

'Yes, Rachel, how can I help you?'

There was a bit of an awkward silence for a second then she said, 'So, Jimmy, I was wondering if you, my dear, would do the Full Monty for me?'

Like I said, I answered a lot of things without understanding what was required in those days. Plus, I was a smartarse and Rachel was a very beautiful woman. So I didn't think twice and just said, 'What? For you, Rachel? Of course I will. Anytime.'

Then there were some pleasantries exchanged and a little chit chat before we hung up.

'Who was that, Jimmy?' Jane asked.

'Oh, it was Bryan's wife, Rachel, asking if I would do the Full Monty for her.'

Jane's ears pricked up. 'Really. Rather strange request, don't you think? Did she say when or where?'

I shrugged. 'I'm not sure what she wanted really. I guess we'll find out next time we see them.'

As you probably know, doing the Full Monty – stripping off in public – became a big thing after a popular 1997 English film of that name told the story of six unemployed steel workers and their attempt to make a bit of money and get their lives back on track by emulating the Chippendales male strip revue. After the film's success, blokes started taking their gear off everywhere. It didn't have that effect on me, though. If anything, it made me want to start wearing more clothes.

Anyway, I never thought about my conversation with

Rachel again for months and months. Then one day I was talking to Bryan on the phone, just having a laugh, when he said, 'Oh, yeah. Fuck, mate, I nearly forgot. I really wanted to thank you. It's good of you to do that thing for Rachel. She's so happy. You're a fucking top bloke.'

I didn't know what he was talking about. 'What's that, mate? Not sure what you mean.'

He laughed and said, 'You know, doing the Full Monty thing in public for her charity. Because you said you'd do it for her, a whole mob has agreed to do it too. The fundraiser is only going ahead because of you.'

I was speechless and hung up the phone. I sat contemplating the dilemma I was now faced with: letting down my mate and his wife who were trying to raise money for a charity, or making a fool of myself, completely fucking naked, in front of a room full of people I'd never met. It was a tough decision but I made it in seconds.

'Jane, I think Rachel Ward thinks I'm going to strip naked on stage for her charity. She has to be fucking kidding, hasn't she?'

Of all the people in the world, I would probably be the last person to want to strip off in public. You couldn't offer me enough money to do it. I'm a prude. I'm shy. So I just wasn't doing it.

'You'd better ring her and tell her before it's too late,' Jane said. 'I think you must have told her you would do it.'

Somewhere in the back of my head I did have some vague, uncomfortable memory of such a conversation. I thought for a second and fragments of the discussion came back to me. Had I said yes? Maybe, but I hadn't known she was serious. And she couldn't have thought *I* was serious, surely?

I rang Bryan back. 'Er, Bryan, what was it you were saying about the Full Monty, mate?'

Bryan chuckled on the other end of the phone. 'You don't remember, do you? You bastard.'

I back-pedalled. 'Yeah, yeah. Of course I do. I was just checking it was the thing I thought it was.'

Bryan didn't believe me. 'What did you fucking think it was?'

I pretended to be cool. 'Rachel wants me to do the Full Monty for a charity somewhere.'

He laughed again. 'Not only that. As I told you, when you said yes, she sold it to all these other dumb bastards. She pressured them into it, using you as bait. You, my friend, got eleven other fucking grown men, and not particularly pretty or fit-looking men – besides myself of course – to say yes to taking their clothes off in a room full of fucking strangers. And because I'm one of them there is no fucking way you're backing out of it now, mate.'

There was a brief silence on the phone, then I said, 'Nah. Nah. I'm not backing out. I was just checking that's what it was about. Of course I'm in. I'll get my gear off in public. Love to. Yeah. Pffft. No worries, mate. I do it all the time. Shit, yeah. I'm naked now in fact, and I'm in a public phone booth.'

I hung up. I was in big trouble.

But then I thought, there's no way she'll get this together. And I decided to pretend to myself that it wasn't happening and that it would just go away.

It didn't. The next thing I knew I was getting calls from friends telling me the event had been announced. Then Rachel rang again.

'Oh, hello, Jimmy darling. How are you? Just ringing to

let you know the good news. Paul Mercurio is coming on board to help with the choreography. It will be fabulous!'

Paul had shot to fame when he'd played Scott Hastings, a battler who wanted to do things his way in the leotard-filled world of ballroom dancing, in the movie *Strictly Ballroom*. Now, I could appreciate the challenge his character had faced in the film and I could appreciate how great a dancer Paul was, but Rachel could have hired Fred Astaire and it wouldn't have helped me learn to dance. In my career on stage and television, I'd done as much for ballroom dancing as Gene Kelly had done for cage fighting.

I tried to explain. 'You know, Rachel, I can't really dance. Left feet and all that.'

She quickly responded, 'You can't "really" dance. So that means you can dance a bit then, does it?'

Time to be blunt. 'No, I can't dance at all. And I certainly can't do steps. Choreography and all that is way beyond me.'

'Oh, Jimmy, you're a singer. When the music plays, you will just move with it. It's second nature to you, surely.'

I stopped her. 'Rachel, you've seen my show. And you've seen me move. Do you call that dancing?'

She suddenly sounded worried. 'Oh, yes, that's true. I have seen you and you are not very good, are you? But trust me, darling, you will not be the worst dancer in the ensemble. There will be a few chaps who will have trouble just walking, believe me, Jimmy. Maybe you should get some extra lessons with Paul. Then, who knows, you could end up being the best of the lot!'

I squirmed then pleaded with her. 'You don't really need me to do this, do you, Rachel? You've got Bryan there, and the others have said yes. You won't miss me.'

But Rachel was adamant. 'They all agreed only because of you. Even Bryan. He won't be happy if you pull out. So we need you, Jimmy. You're such a good sport. Come on. Tickets are on sale now. In fact, the event is nearly sold out. You'll be wonderful!'

I couldn't say no. Rachel is very persuasive and the event was certainly for a good cause. The proceeds from Aussies Without Cossies, as our show had been dubbed, would go to the Hope for the Children Foundation, which supports people struggling to look after their kids, particularly single mothers.

There was, it appeared to me, no way out of it. I thought about planning a move overseas for the whole family. But I was sure Rachel would buy me a plane ticket back for the show. I wondered if I could accidentally break a leg just before the event, but I wasn't good with pain either.

'Okay. Just let me know when the rehearsals are on and I'll do my best.'

*

Twelve poor sods were booked and lined up to reveal all in public. Bryan Brown, as mentioned. He had to do it. After all, it was for his wife. I was sure I'd seen Bryan bust a few moves at parties or in a movie or two, so he wouldn't be afraid.

Ernie Dingo. As the sole representative of our First Nations peoples, he had a lot to live up to.

Angry Anderson. He'd always been a bad boy and I'd seen him get his gear off at the drop of a hat at rock shows after too many drinks. It was going to be easy for him.

Graeme Blundell. Fuck me, I thought, he was Alvin Purple, wasn't he? He'd taken his clothes off for every sex-starved woman in that movie. He was naked more than he was clothed. This would be a walk in the park for him. Breezy, but still a walk.

John Jarrett. He always seemed crazy, even in *Play School*. It would be no different here.

Peter Phelps. I knew he was an actor and that actors were used to getting their gear off anytime, especially if their career wasn't going well.

Mike Carlton. Mike had a great head for radio. That's all I'm going to say. But even he couldn't wait to get it all off. What was wrong with him?

George Negus. All I could think of was years of credibility built up by *Sixty Minutes* gone in sixty seconds.

Jack Thompson. I knew Jack and didn't think this would be too much of a stretch for him. In the seventies, Jack had been the first male centrefold for the Australian edition of *Cleo*, and his bare body was pinned up in women's offices all over the country. It was a particularly low point for Australian female workplaces, I thought. Since then he'd taken his clothes off every chance he got. *GQ* functions, gear off. *Rolling Stone* function, yeah, get the gear off. So I wasn't surprised to see his name there.

Hugo Weaving was happy to be a part of the show too. Being a professional actor, he just saw it as a good laugh and a chance to hang out – and I use that term loosely – with a few of his mates. Hugo was making *The Matrix* in Sydney at the time and I heard a couple of bigwigs from *The Matrix* production team were planning to come along, astonished by the fact that someone could get such high-profile people to do something like this. It would never happen in America, they said.

The author and journalist Bob Ellis was in as well. Now Bob was a wild choice. He was from the Swinging Sixties, but would he swing on the night? I didn't fucking know and I didn't really care.

And then there was me. The only person in Australia to wear army boots, full army fatigues and a headband during blistering fifty-degree pub shows at the height of the Australian summer. I wouldn't even wear a singlet or take my shirt off. I was the least likely of all this mob to drop my gear on stage.

I was beginning to panic.

The first rehearsal with Paul Mercurio was arranged for a Saturday morning and I turned up at the studio to find Jack Thompson had got there long before Paul or anyone else. He was sitting alone, waiting to start, and he was already stark naked.

'Hi, Jack. How are you, mate?'

Jack was as he always is. 'James, my young lad. Yes, indeed. So great to be here smelling the grease paint again. Bring down the lights. Turn up the sound. I am ready for my role.'

I'd only said hi. 'Bit cold in here, Jack, don't you think?' I mumbled, trying not to look below his waist.

'Love the cold weather. I spent months in the snow filming *The Man from Snowy River*. I used to ride naked and bareback through the mountains while the snow was falling, Jimmy. Loved it. That's when you know you're alive. I tell you. Can't get cold enough for my liking.'

'But it is cold,' I said again, nodding my head down towards Jack's manhood. Which should not have been subjected to such cold weather. Jack didn't take any notice. He didn't give a shit.

That day only five of us turned up. Bryan, of course, he's a pro. Mike Carlton, who was more worried about learning the steps than being naked. Angry, because he was a pro too and wanted it to work. And Jack and myself. It was hard, I was told, to get all the cast together in one place at one time. I was glad about that, as I was having enough trouble dealing with Jack and his nakedness, never mind another seven of them.

Like me, Angry, Mike and Bryan opted to keep their clothes on for the rehearsal. Although I could see it in Angry's eyes: he wanted to join Jack.

We were ready to start work. Paul arrived and immediately asked Jack to get dressed.

'No, I think I'll stay in character, thank you, kind sir. I am an actor and I need to feel the part.' Then Jack lifted his face into the light, placed his hands on his hips and thrust them forward as though he was standing at the front of a boat in some sort of gay porn movie. If I hadn't known better, I'd have said Jack was completely pissed, and it was only ten o'clock in the morning. I thought I might try that at the next rehearsal.

For an hour, we stumbled and tripped around the area marked out to represent the stage. I could see that Paul was a little concerned.

'Er, Jimmy, don't panic. There will be lots of other rehearsals before the big night.'

After we finished, I looked at the rehearsal schedule and realised that I was working every single day they had booked. So this one rehearsal had been my only chance to learn the whole routine.

I begged Paul to cut me out of the cast. 'I'm just not going to be able to do it, Paul,' I said to him, almost in tears by this point.

'Jimmy, you're a showman. Don't stress, mate. You'll get it right in time. I'll come to your house and give you a few private lessons.'

I didn't think that would be enough, but I needed all the help I could get. Paul found a day when we were both free and we locked it in. I would be having private dancing lessons with Paul Mercurio, one of the best dancers in the country. I was a lucky guy, but would it get me through this?

*

A month later Paul turned up at the house, ready to teach me to dance. I felt bad for him. He really didn't know what he had taken on.

'Okay, Jimmy, find a place where we won't get disturbed and with enough room for us to walk through the steps.'

I'd made a point of making sure my teenage children would all be out of the house so I wouldn't embarrass myself. We went to the lounge room and started going through the steps.

'That's good, Jimmy. One, two, three, turn and step. Two, three, four, turn again and kick, and hold it there ...'

Paul was very encouraging. We'd been at it for about an hour when he said, 'You're doing well, mate. No worries, you'll be fine. You've got all the moves. Let's just do it once or twice more and you'll have it.'

He turned the music up loud. I started with my back to him and the music took off. I stepped confidently – two, three, four – and turned with my hands in the air and kicked. That's when I noticed my daughter and her five sixteen-year-old girlfriends laughing uncontrollably in the corner. I stopped, marched out of the lounge and said, 'Fuck it. I'm not doing this.'

Paul followed me, but I walked into my bedroom and slammed the door shut.

He knocked and said, 'Come on, Jimmy, you need to do it in front of people. It's good practice.'

I wasn't listening. 'Fuck off. I'm not doing it.'

Paul went away, but after about an hour he came back to the door. He must have realised I really wasn't coming out. 'Listen, Jimmy. Just don't think about it too much. It will all come back to you on the night.' Then he left.

I wouldn't get another run-through until the day of the show. Even then, we'd still be fully clothed. The only time I would get my gear off was on the night. What could go wrong?

The original idea that Rachel had was for us all to wear animal covers on our … well, you know what I'm talking about. Little animal covers that would look funny and cute. But the last thing I wanted was to be standing stark naked except for an animal tied around my dick in front of a crowd of strangers laughing uncontrollably. That would be a nightmare. So one day I surprised everyone with a suggestion. 'Guys, I think we should strip completely. No fucking animals. What do you all say?'

Bryan replied, 'Are you fucking serious, mate? I'll do it if you do. But are you sure?'

In a moment of madness, all the other guys agreed that we would go all the way – no furry animal covers. All except

Ernie, that is. He would not show the world whatever it was he had to hide and he insisted on wearing an elephant cover with small ears. It looked even worse than anything we were going to be showing.

As the big night drew closer, I became more and more nervous, and by the day of the show I was absolutely furious.

'How the fuck did I get into this? This is fucking stupid!' And I banged and shouted as I stomped around the house.

'It was you, Jimmy,' said Jane. 'You agreed to do it. Now you have to see it through.

'Why did I do it?' I cried. 'I would rather fight a tiger than take off my clothes on stage.' Now that was an idea. 'What if I tell Rachel I'll fight a tiger on stage instead?'

'Won't work, Jimmy. The show is happening with you, tonight. Get used to it.'

I had the feeling that Jane was enjoying my misery.

The 'undress rehearsal' went well and even though we got to keep our clothes on, I was so stressed I was unbearable. I needed to drink and I needed to drink a lot if I was going to do this. But I didn't want to fall over, so it would require precision drinking. This was a technique I'd developed over the years that nearly always worked. Drink until you can't feel anything but you can still move your legs.

My recollection of the event is still hazy. I remember arriving at the venue, the Sydney Cove Passenger Terminal, and looking out from behind the stage curtain. There were so many cameras, so many TV crews, and so many celebrities in attendance, from James Packer, Collette Dinnigan and Noni Hazlehurst to Andrew Denton, Jennifer Byrne and Thomas Keneally. And, oh my God, Nicole Kidman was in the front row. So embarrassing! To make matters even worse, my wife,

I managed to stay hidden even when I was on stage. *(Cameron Bloom)*

Jane, and my son David Campbell were in attendance too. The rest of the audience looked like they were after blood. We were the gladiators, only we would be completely nude. Fuck!

Backstage, all the guys were in various stages of nakedness and full of bravado. Laughing and joking with each other. I sat with my eyes to the ground and spoke to no one. I felt like I was about to explode. Then it was time and I could hear the MC introducing us. There was no turning back.

A mist seemed to settle over the stage. I could not see clearly and everything was shrouded and sounded slightly muffled. My senses were shutting down. I felt an ice-cold wind blowing under the stage door. Fuck me. There is no God.

Then the opening lines of 'You Can Leave Your Hat On' started playing and I switched to autopilot. The show started with a *bang*. Bright lights flashed, just as we would very soon. Astonishingly, I remembered almost every move. The movie and TV guys who never did a lot in front of a live audience all fell apart, all except for Bryan, who is a natural show-off and was a highlight of the night. But somehow Angry and I were okay. Maybe because we were used to playing to hostile audiences who wanted to kill us. In fact we liked the pressure.

I was half-naked in front of a bunch of screaming women and, I might add, a few screaming men. What the fuck? Another change of the lighting and more of my clothes, as if by magic, seemed to disappear. Very soon, the room was ready for the big finish. Did it just get colder in here?

We'd decided that we'd end up with only our hats covering us, and then on cue, we would throw the hats in the air. And the lights would go out. That short time between holding the hat in place and the stage going dark seemed like a lifetime. In that fleeting second, I saw my career fall apart, never to be repaired. I saw my wife leaving me because she was so embarrassed by my bad dancing. And I saw my children and all of their friends laughing hysterically. I even saw my dog take off his leash and run out the back door. I would be alone, forever.

Of course the lights didn't go out straightaway, so everyone got a good look. Damn that lighting guy.

As soon as they did, I was off the stage, dressed and out the front door before the rest of the cast had even made it to the dressing room. But then I was dragged back in and told to take my clothes off again for a photo with the two brave women who had paid more than thirty thousand dollars each to have their photograph taken with this motley crew – Betty Klimenko, who, among other things, had started and run the Mercedes-Benz Racing Team, and Nicole Kidman. Of course the ladies kept their clothes on.

As soon as that was done, I dressed and started making my way out again, only to be reminded that I had agreed to sing after the show. Rumour has it I sang with David, but I've blocked out so much of the evening I have no idea. I can't even remember what the song was. I asked David if he knew, but he confessed he was so traumatised by the sight of me stripping off that everything that followed remains a blur for him too. All I know is that I performed the whole song with my eyes shut, trying desperately not to look anyone in the audience in the eye. Especially Betty or Nicole.

I heard that Jack and Angry and a few others sat naked for hours afterwards enjoying the male bonding. And Mike Carlton was so excited he wanted us all to do it again soon.

No fucking chance, mate. I went home and washed. I felt I would never be able to wash away the shame. In fact it was a while before I could even speak to anyone, and I spent most of my time in my room. But eventually I drank and snorted enough not to care anymore and one day I re-emerged.

Jane was in the lounge room with a bunch of her gay friends. They all told me how much they'd loved the show. I went back to my room.

A few days later, Rachel and Bryan came over to the house to get me to autograph some photos that were to be sold at an auction. After telling me how the event had already raised more than half a million dollars, Rachel said, 'You are so funny, Jimmy. There were so many photos taken on the night, with so many cameras and from so many angles. But somehow you managed to hide behind someone or something in every shot. There is not one photo in existence that captures you in your entirety, if you know what I mean.'

It was little comfort. I smiled and signed as quickly as possible, without looking at the pictures.

I got over it eventually, but it will never happen again. These days, if I'm drunk, I don't answer the phone at all. Sometimes even if I'm sober I don't answer it, just in case. And the next time someone asks me to do something like that, I'll keep my hat, pants, shirt and shoes all on and run away, as far as my covered legs will take me.

The Claw
Hammer

My father, Jim Swan, came to a
Cold Chisel show in Melbourne
one summer night in the late
1970s. This was not that long
after we had first reconnected.

Me and Dad, ready for anything. 'What are you lookin' at, stupit?'

He wasn't really comfortable with the whole rock thing, and he certainly wasn't that comfortable with the whole family thing either. But he turned up at a little pub show in the city, near the university.

He'd always liked to dress well, and on this particular night he arrived in a suit and tie. He'd probably started the night out looking sharp, but by the time he got to the show he'd had a few drinks and the suit had lost a little of its edge, the pants now slightly wrinkled around the knees and their creases disappearing. In fact, he appeared a little shabbier with each drink he had, though he was still better dressed than most of the crowd. Luckily for him, he seemed to care less with each drink he had too.

The pub, like I said, was close to the university, so the clientele, were hippy, uni-student types. Lots of beads, flares and essential oils. The polar opposite of my father – the only oil anybody wore where I came from was residue from the car they were trying to hot-wire earlier in the night. I knew he was more than a little uncomfortable, and although he was trying his best to be calm and fit in, I could see he didn't.

Between sets I went to the back of the room to see how he was holding up. When I went to check on him before starting the last set, he pulled me in close and spoke to me. His accent seemed stronger than at the previous break – I think he became more Scottish the more he drank too.

'Jim, there's a fucking bloke. Least I think he's a bloke. He's got long hair like a lassie and a lotta beads on. And he keeps staring at me. It's geein' me the shits. If he comes back, ah'm going tae have tae belt him.'

I could see he was getting more agitated with every word.

'Dad, just ignore him. He probably doesn't mean any harm.' I tried to settle him down but it wasn't working.

'Ah, fuck. Here he comes again. Ah'm sick of him.'

A young student walked up and stood next to us at the back of the crowd. He was tall, wearing eye makeup and dressed in flares, a shabby top hat and op-shop tails. I watched as his eyes moved across my dad, alighting on him only for a few seconds. He was definitely having a good look.

Then I caught his eye and he quickly looked away.

Dad turned to me again. 'Did ye see that?'

I kept watching the student. 'Aye, ah did, Dad. Ah did.'

I was getting more Scottish as I talked to him.

Sure enough, before long, the guy was staring at Dad again.

Dad had been waiting for him, and this time he snapped. 'What are you fuckin' looking at, stupit?'

The young guy shifted his feet uncomfortably, and nervously but politely replied, 'You seem a little overdressed for this kind of show, don't you think?'

My father's posture had already changed by then. His shoulders were back and his feet were wide apart, as if he was ready to take a blow. He put his drink down and glared at the hippy then pushed his glasses up his nose. This was something I had seen my dad do many times when I was much younger. And it was normally followed closely by someone getting belted on the chin. But surely he wasn't going to hit the poor hippy, was he?

'What are you talking about? You look like a fucking claw hammer.'

I burst out laughing. 'That's funny, Dad.'

But Dad was beyond laughing. He had moved closer to his unsuspecting target, and his eyes were by this point burning a hole in the young hippy. I had to act quickly to avoid a bloodbath.

I put my hand gently onto my dad's shoulder and whispered, 'Maybe it would be better if you came down the front and watched the band, Dad. It would be nice to have you close to me.'

The sound of my voice seemed to calm him, so I smiled at him as I kept talking. His demeanour changed and he smiled back at me. His eyes softened, he unclenched his fists, and his glasses slowly slid back down his nose to where they'd been before the altercation.

'Aye, that would be nice, son.'

He smiled lovingly at me then turned and followed me calmly towards the stage, nodding proudly at strangers as we pushed our way through the crowd.

Dad had changed in his old age. And so the young student lived to parade about in fancy dress once more and interpretive-dance around another club.

He didn't know how lucky he was.

Warp Speed
Wayne

Superfast motorbikes and rock 'n' roll music go together well. In fact, they are made for each other. Most of the time.

On 15 September 1990, I was booked to play a show at the Australian Motorcycle Grand Prix on Phillip Island, near Melbourne. The show was on the Saturday night and the race the next day, but I was asked to get to the island early for a photo opportunity with motorcycle racer Wayne Gardner. In 1987 Wayne had won the 500 cc World Championship and he is one of the greatest racers Australia has ever produced.

I'd followed his career closely and jumped at the chance to meet him. We had a lot in common. We both loved crowds and speed, plus we both liked to get a lot of attention, though we went about it in very different ways. People used to think I was crazy, but Wayne made me look like an altar boy. He was afraid of nothing.

I arrived at the track late in the afternoon and was escorted over to the pits.

'Hey, Jimmy, great to meet you,' Wayne said. 'I love your music, mate, and can't wait to see the show tonight.'

I could tell he wasn't kidding. It was clear he was a down-to-earth Aussie bloke. 'Well, mate, I'm a big fan of yours too,' I replied, with a smile. Like many Aussies, I'd watched Wayne conquer every track in the world and bring motorbike racing to the masses. And this was his home. He was the King of Phillip Island.

The plan was for the press to simply take photos of us together. But then Wayne had another idea.

'Listen, Jimmy,' he said, 'why don't I take you for a lap of the track? You'll love it.'

I felt a knot form in my stomach. The kind of speed I enjoyed was quite different from the type he liked. 'I thought that your racing bike only had room for one person,' I replied meekly, trying to weasel my way out of it.

'No, don't worry, mate, I have a street bike right here.'

I could feel the blood drain from my face just thinking about it. 'Nah, it wouldn't be as fast as your racing bike and it'd be no fun for you … really, it's fine.'

Meanwhile the press were watching and listening, snapping photos and zooming in on me, trying to catch the fear in my eyes. I was confident I had them fooled with my relaxed demeanour, though inside I was panicking.

'Don't worry, mate,' Wayne insisted, 'it will go as quick as we need it to go. Hop on.'

Before I knew it, someone had handed me a set of leather gloves and a helmet. I was already wearing a leather jacket and biker boots, so now I had the whole outfit. There was no way to get out of this and save face.

I leaned towards him and whispered, 'Just don't kill me. Okay?'

Wayne looked at me and smiled. 'You'll be right, mate, I'll take it nice and slow.'

I had the terrible feeling he was lying to me, but I'd run out of excuses. I kitted up and jumped on the back of his bike as he started it up.

'Is the seat supposed to be this high?' I shouted over the screaming of the engine.

Wayne just laughed, said 'Hold on', and waved to the press gallery. Then he opened the throttle till the bike sounded like a jet engine, yanked the front of the machine up and did a wheel stand all the way out of the pits and down the first straight. I buried my knees under his bum and clung on for dear life. I was sure I could hear him still laughing as we went.

As soon as we left the press behind, I closed my eyes and tried to calm myself down. My heart was jumping out of

'Calm down, Jimmy, we're not moving yet.'

my chest. When we hit the next straight, I opened my eyes again, figuring I might as well see what we were about to smash into.

Bad idea. It felt like we'd just shifted into warp speed. Everything was gone before I could even focus on it, the crowd and the guard rails blurring until they were just streaks of light.

'Are you good?' Wayne hollered as we approached the first corner.

'Yeah, mate, no worries,' I lied, hoping the approaching corner would force us to slow down a little.

It didn't. After briefly dropping down a few gears, Wayne hammered it again and I nearly went flying off the back of the bike. As we approached another corner, I looked over his shoulder at the dials. We were travelling at 240 kilometres an hour.

The handlebars and the foot pegs scraped the ground as we leaned into the bends, creating a trail of sparks that made it look like the bike was on fire. I was convinced that at some point a peg or handle would dig into the track and we'd be flipped off at high speed. Already I could see the headline: 'Rock Singer Killed as World Champion Rider Shows Off to Press'. But we didn't die. Wayne was really good at this – the best. We just kept moving, faster and faster.

It was, though, utterly terrifying. Eventually, the world was passing by so quickly that nothing registered in my brain. I became completely numb.

Then, as suddenly as it had started, it was over – or so I hoped. Wayne slowed down a little as we completed one complete lap in what seemed like a millisecond. The world came back into focus and I almost regained my composure.

'You want to go around again, mate?' Wayne shouted. We were only doing about 120 kilometres an hour by this point, so Wayne had twisted himself round to look at me.

'No thanks, mate, I'm good,' I replied, gesturing frantically at the track ahead in the hope that he would look where we were going before we died.

Wayne whipped the bike into the pit lane and slowed down in front of the television crews and newspaper photographers, all eager to capture my reaction to the ride. I was so desperate to get my feet back on the ground that I jumped off before the bike had even stopped.

I fumbled with my helmet, my hands shaking so badly that I couldn't get it off. Wayne made matters worse by helping me remove it. 'There you go, mate. Geez, your hands are shaking a bit there. You okay?' he asked, grinning at the press.

Normally in those days, when something scared me that much, I either ran from it or smashed it, but fortunately I held myself back and did neither. I simply muttered, 'Thanks, Wayne …'

And then I turned to the press and said, 'Wayne just told me on the way round the track that he's going to get up with me tonight and sing a song. Won't that be great?'

Wayne turned as pale as I was. For once he was at a loss for words. 'Yeah, well, er, thanks, Jimmy … I, er …'

I waved to the crowd and we went our separate ways – him to tinker with his bike, me to drink vodka.

Wayne didn't make it to the show that night. I was told he was resting up for the race the next day, but I think he just didn't want to go around the stage with me driving. He wasn't the only one who could go at warp speed.

Child's
Play

'Look at the colour of the sea,'
exclaimed Jane. 'It's so beautiful!'
She always gets excited when
she takes me to new places.

This time it was Hyams Beach on the South Coast, about two and a half hours out of Sydney.

'I love it down here,' she went on. 'We used to spend summer holidays on the South Coast when we were little and lived in Canberra.'

I looked out to the sea. I had never seen a beach with such white sand or water that was such a beautiful shade of blue. So clear you could see right to the bottom. It was spectacular.

'It is very nice, my darling. Are there any sharks here?'

Jane ignored me, not wanting to put me off. But I knew. Of course there were sharks here. Hyams Beach is in Jervis Bay, a marine park. And that's where sharks like to live, in the fucking sea. I never brought it up again.

Jane, myself and the kids had rented a small house right on the beach for a few days and we couldn't wait to get out onto the sand and go for a swim. But I soon found out why I hadn't spent a lot of time on the South Coast. The water was freezing cold. Still, I wasn't going to let a little thing like the subantarctic water temperature stop me from swimming.

'Come on everyone, let's get in!' I ran and dived head-first into the water. Suddenly I could feel the breath rushing from my body and within seconds hypothermia was setting in. I looked at the children and they, just like the water, had turned a lovely shade of blue.

'Oh my God, it's cold,' I gasped. We were all in and out in a matter of seconds.

'Hey kids, let's play in the sand,' I suggested. We set up a blanket and tried to thaw ourselves out while gazing out to sea for a while, saying nothing, just taking it all in and waiting for the feeling to return to our extremities.

'Just look at the view!' Jane waved her hand to direct my gaze towards the idyllic scene before us – and her wedding ring went flying off her hand. The water was so cold her fingers had shrunk. I tried to follow the ring through the air, but the sun hit my eyes and I lost track of it.

'Nobody move! It's over there somewhere,' I shouted.

This was serious. I didn't want to lose Jane's wedding ring. So I got up and started looking in the area where I thought it had landed. The sand was white and fine and I realised that anything heavy, like gold, would sink straight in and might never be found again.

'I'll find it, Dadda.' My ten-year-old daughter, Eliza-Jane, or EJ as she's usually known, was up and running to where she thought it might be.

'Stop!' I shrieked. 'If we stand on it, we'll never find it again.'

The children froze. It was the second time they had done that in as many minutes.

'Okay, kids. You guys go over there and Dadda will hunt for the ring.'

Jane didn't seem that fussed, but I was determined to find it. I started scanning the surface of the beach to see if it reflected the sun. Nothing. It was gone.

'Oh well. You'll just have to buy me another one,' Jane said calmly.

I was not going to let this go. But what was I going to do? I sat and scratched my head.

'Jane, you keep the kids over there and stay off this section of the beach,' I said. 'I'll be right back.'

I got up and left the beach, grabbed the car keys and hightailed it to Nowra, the nearest big town. I had a plan.

I was going to rent or buy a metal detector. Surprisingly enough, it didn't take me long to find one. I guessed it wasn't the first time this had happened.

Soon I was running back to the beach, metal detector in hand. I looked like I was sweeping for explosive devices.

'Right, kids. You guys stay over there and I will perform the search,' I said, acting like I knew what I was doing.

I proceeded to map out a grid on the beach. I would search it section by section until I located the ring.

Two hours later, I had found nothing. It was an incredibly clean beach. Not even a bottle top had shown up. In the meantime Jane and the kids had made sand sculptures of mermaids. Not small ones; they were full size. But the sun was starting to go down and now the kids were bored to death.

I was still searching frantically. Jane stared at me in disbelief.

'Can I have a go with the machine, Dadda?' EJ was keen to help.

'Sorry, baby, this is serious stuff here. I have to do it. I need to find your mum's ring. So, best if you just stay out of the way.'

Back to work the grid I went for a second time. Still nothing. The sun was just about to set and I was exhausted. I dropped the metal detector and lay flat out on the beach, covered in sweat.

EJ rushed in and grabbed the device. 'Let me have a go.'

I wanted to stop her but was too tired. I stayed on the sand, resigned to the fact that I would never find the ring. I reached out and held Jane's hand. 'Sorry, baby. I tried.'

Suddenly I heard a beeping noise. I looked over and EJ was standing there with the metal detector, smiling at me. And holding her mum's wedding ring.

'I told you I would find it, Dadda.'

I had searched the beach methodically for three hours in the searing heat and found nothing. EJ had found the ring in less than one minute in near darkness.

'Right, I'd better take the metal detector back to the shop, eh?'

I headed for the car. My work was done.

EJ at Hyams Beach after finding her mum's wedding ring

Finishing
Touch

Down in the Southern Highlands
of New South Wales where we
live, there is a big, beautiful
property next door to us,
owned by a charming couple.

Michael and Eleonora Triguboff are both environmentalists and they both love the arts, so we get on really well with them. When they first bought the place, long before they started spending time down there, I asked if it would be all right if I could walk through their property with my dogs, Snoop Dog and Oliver. Those boys loved running wild through there, chasing anything that moved. They never caught a thing, but they liked pretending they were hunters.

The Triguboffs' property encompasses a fabulous garden with beautiful trees and a large area of natural bushland, so at any time of the day you could see kangaroos and wallabies hopping around. It was a great place to walk, especially when we had guests from overseas staying with us. My American friends in particular thought it was amazing that we lived in a place where you could see those animals all day. Being the nice people they are, our neighbours never seemed to mind our visits. In fact Eleonora said to me one day, 'It's nice that you walk on our land so that the place feels lived in.'

So I did for many years. And we talked whenever they came down, and got to know each other better. Eleonora had been the publisher of *Art + Australia* magazine and was highly respected in the art world and we had mutual friends, including Ben Quilty, a fantastic artist who had painted me for the Archibald Prize. Eleonora had been one of the judges of the prize.

After a while, the Triguboffs invited us to dinner at their home in Sydney with a bunch of their good friends from the art world. I was, as usual, mid-tour and was very busy and tired, but we liked them so much we agreed to join them.

We were made to feel at home as soon as we walked in. I couldn't help but notice that the house was full of beautiful paintings and sculptures. It was like a gallery.

Dinner was served and we were taken into the dining room to sit down. On the walls around the large, oval table, intriguing artworks were tastefully lit, and a light in the centre of the room hung low, creating a warm, intimate feel. Eleonora had evidently planned the seating to prompt some interesting conversations. I was placed between a man who I think was one of the main art buyers for Sotheby's in London and Gretel Packer, daughter of Kerry Packer, and a successful businesswoman and patron of the arts in her own right. Both were charming and friendly.

Everyone in the room clearly knew a lot about art – except me of course. So I sat there trying not to say too much, as I knew that would just reveal my ignorance. But the gentleman next to me kept trying to include me in the conversation. I think he knew I was uncomfortable.

'So, Jimmy, tell me,' he said, 'what do you look for in art and have you purchased very much at all? If you are in the market, I could help you. I would love to be of assistance.'

I wasn't sure what to say. In the end I decided to speak from the heart and not the head. 'I really don't know a lot about art as such, but I do own a few pieces. I only buy what I really like. If something moves me, then I think it's good and might try to buy it. It doesn't matter if it's by a master or a beginner.'

To my surprise the man from Sotheby's replied, 'I totally agree with you, and it sounds to me like you know a lot more than you realise.'

Now, I had really only formed my opinions on art by listening to my Jane. She always told me if you like it, appreciate it; if you don't, move on.

The conversations from that point on were friendly and entertaining, and the dinner was a lot of fun. But after the dessert was served I gave a little nod to Jane to signal that I needed to go home.

Jane announced, 'We would like to thank you, Michael and Eleonora, for inviting us here to dine with your lovely friends, but I'm afraid Jimmy has been touring incredibly hard and I need to take him home to rest.' And with that she stood up.

I did the same and reached for my jacket on the back of my chair. But as I put my arm into the sleeve, I heard a smashing sound and something that looked like glass shattered and fell all over Gretel Packer's head and shoulders. It was only then that I noticed the exquisite sculpture hovering above the table like a ghost. The low light and my bad eyesight had stopped me from seeing it – up to the moment when I put my arm right through the middle of it.

The table fell silent. Then the sound of art critics gasping for breath filled the air. No one said a thing. They just sat, mouths wide open, looking straight at me.

I dusted the broken pieces off Gretel's shoulders and tried to get them off her head without ruining her hairdo as well.

Then I did the only thing I could do. I excused myself. 'Well, goodnight everybody. That was a great meal, and what fabulous company. I hope we all meet again.'

And I walked out the door. Not a word about the sculpture.

In the hallway, though, I immediately apologised to Michael and Eleonora, who had followed us out. 'I am so sorry. I didn't see it. Was it made of fine glass or something? It was so hard to see.' I was almost hysterical.

Michael tried to calm me down. 'Don't worry, Jimmy. It will all be fine and, no, it's not glass; it's made of salt. I will get it fixed in no time.'

With that, I said sorry a few more times and we left. Jane and I hardly said a word the whole way back to the Southern Highlands.

When I got home, I had a stiff drink to calm my nerves while I worked on a long, apologetic email to Michael and Eleonora. This is what I ended up with:

Hi Michael and Eleonora,

Jimmy here. I have only now worked up the courage to contact you and apologise for not only trashing one of your pieces of art, but also for trying to talk seriously to your friends about art, life and the whole universe. I am a singer, and my life is singing, and trying to get to people's souls as basically and as honestly as possible. Art is way too deep for me. Unless you can wear it and change it and let it evolve in front of me. Which brings me to my goodbye the other evening. So sorry about that, I should have warned you that I am the clumsiest man in the world. I quite like the new piece, though, and I sincerely hope you guys and the artist do too. If not, I expect to be killed by a falling statue or a wayward paintbrush that has been thrown from a car moving at high speed by an artist (not anyone in particular) rushing to an exhibition of the newest art form in years – DEVOLUTION – which I started at dinner and perfected when I went home. I worked on a painting for hours and by the time I finished there was nothing on the canvas. So pure.

Fancy lunch, this time at my gig, and you can all sing?

I loved your friends and was honoured to be at your beautiful house. If you need any more work done on any of your pieces, please call.

Love and pleading for forgiveness,

Jimmy xx

PS Has anyone painted a scream yet? If they have, I'd be the last to know, as I am deaf in one ear and am seriously thinking of cutting off the other. I hate symmetry.

Saints that they are, the Triguboffs replied:

Dear Jimmy,

Please don't worry about your artistic involvement. Like you, we think the piece has improved.

We very much enjoyed having you and Jane over for dinner and look forward to seeing you both more often.

Warm regards,

Eleonora and Michael

The Golden
Buddha

Jane's family and my family
are completely different.
When we met, it was literally
two worlds colliding.

Jane's family history is exotic and wonderful, full of colour and magic, and can be traced back for a thousand years. My family history is grim and grey and the only miraculous thing about it is that I somehow ended up married to Jane. My forefathers were paupers who struggled to make lives with the cards they were dealt. Our history includes a short line of prize fighters and standover men. There are no long lines to be found anywhere. A few years ago the television show *Who Do You Think You Are?* tried to make a show about my family tree. They traced it back a few generations to Ireland, but at that point the trail disappeared. There were no records to be found. The only ancestors they could identify seemed to have perished in poor houses, been worked to death or died early of consumption. It was sad, because I'd been hoping to find out more about where I came from.

So you can see why, when Jane announced we were getting married, her family was shocked. They'd had much better things planned for her. Then I came along and ruined everything. It took a long time for me to get myself together enough for them to see some hope in me, but eventually it happened. Now they love me and have taken me into their beautiful family. Let me tell you a little more about them.

Jane's maternal grandfather, Khun Kong, left China before the Second World War. He was a wealthy Chinese businessman and he was smart enough to get his money out of the country before communism took hold. He moved to Thailand and started a new life. Eventually, that life included six wives and twenty-seven children. Jane's maternal grandmother, Khun Yai, was Khun Kong's fourth wife and his first Thai wife. Every wife had to be kept in the same fashion as the others, so it was a sign of wealth and power to

Jane's grandmother Khun Yai in Bangkok in the 1980s

have so many wives and children. Most men I talk to today say that if they told their wives there was a new wife coming, they'd be found dead soon after with an ice pick in their back. But Khun Kong was from another world and another time. He was a remarkable man in other ways too. He had eleven fingers and stood six feet four inches tall – a giant by Thai standards.

Khun Kong started a trading company in Thailand and worked hard and it wasn't long before he started buying up a lot of land in the area known as Chinatown in Bangkok. On one part of this land, sheltered by a tin shed, there was an old stucco statue of the seated Buddha that had previously been left out in the open, exposed to the elements, for many years. The paint that covered it had faded and only a few of the many cheap glass beads that had been attached to it originally remained. It didn't look like anything special. Khun Kong found out later that the Buddha had been moved from place to place for a couple of hundred years. No one wanted it because there were so many stone Buddhas in Southeast Asia and there was nothing particularly outstanding or attractive about this one, though it was large. Somehow it had travelled from the old Siamese capital, Ayutthaya, to Bangkok, before ending up in a rundown temple near Chinatown. Eventually that temple had closed and the Buddha had at some point been moved to Khun Kong's property. It had been forgotten, lost in time.

One day, some of Khun Kong's workers tried to move the Buddha, using a pulley and rope system to lift it. But the ropes snapped and the statue dropped to the ground, breaking off part of the plaster. Underneath it, the astonished workers saw gold. And when they removed the rest of the plaster they found they had a five-and-a-half-tonne solid-gold statue – at nearly three metres tall, the largest solid-gold Buddha in the world.

Later, historians traced its origins back to the thirteenth century in Sukhothai, the first capital of the Siamese Kingdom. When Ayutthaya replaced Sukhothai as the capital, the statue was moved there. In 1767, when Ayutthaya was besieged at the climax of the Burmese–Siamese war, the Buddha was covered in stucco to hide the priceless gold from the marauding Burmese soldiers. Eventually everyone who knew about the cover-up died. The seemingly worthless Buddha passed from place to place and finally ended up sitting outdoors on Khun Kong's land.

Obviously, when you find a national treasure, you can't keep it. So Khun Kong donated the statue to a local temple, and that's where it sits to this day. Known as Wat Traimit, the temple has become a major tourist attraction in Bangkok, mainly because of this incredible statue.

Jane's grandfather is buried in the temple. But over the years his part in the discovery of the Buddha has been slowly forgotten as other wealthy families have donated money to the temple and, in return, gained a more prominent place in its history. If you dig deep enough, though, you will find the truth.

We visit Khun Kong's grave and the Golden Buddha whenever we go to Bangkok. It is a huge part of Jane's family history. And because I married Jane I feel it's now part of my history too and I'm happy to help get the real story out there.

Sadly, I never got to know Khun Kong, as he died before I met Jane. But I wear a small gold Buddha from Wat Traimit around my neck. Partly it's to honour him and my connection to Jane's family. But there's also another reason.

Khun Kong and a young Uncle Chai in the late 1940s

The Buddhists say that you don't look at the images of Buddha because he was a god. He was just a man who looked so deeply into himself that he attained enlightenment. You look at the Buddha to remind yourself of the god in you. I'm still searching for the god in me, but I know it's in there somewhere. And sometimes I think of the story of the plaster being chipped away to reveal the Golden Buddha underneath as being a little like the story of my own life. I've begun the process of hammering away at the hard outer shell that has locked me in and kept me hidden from the light.

Who knows what I'll find? After all, everyone has a history. Everyone has a story to tell. Every life shines like gold sometimes.

Frankfurt
Cowboys

In 1984, Jane and I went to
Germany, where I planned to
write songs to take to America to
make my second solo album and
first album for Geffen Records.

This was a very important point in my career. The album would be called *For the Working Class Man* in Australia, but in America it would be released as *Jimmy Barnes*. It would be the first time I'd put out anything in the States since Cold Chisel's *East*.

I know what you're thinking here: 'Funny place to go to write songs for America.' But Geffen had some connection with a studio in Frankfurt called Hotline and they wanted me to write with a guy who part owned it. His name was Tony Carey and he was a keyboard player and singer who had left America to work the European market. At one time he'd played for Rainbow, the band started by Ritchie Blackmore, then he'd left the band and decided to pursue his own solo career. He was doing pretty well and he'd had a few hits in Germany.

But although he was talented and could write a good tune, Tony was going through a pretty dark spell and he spent most of his time drinking brandy and hiding in the studio. His problems were getting on top of him. I was much the same, so we were a match made in hell, and in the end I didn't really get anything I could use for the record. But I did learn a few tricks from him that would come in handy later on when I started writing more myself, and I got to hang out with some great musicians and even sing on a few records that were cut at the studio.

I spent one night singing, drinking and laughing with Jack Bruce, the legendary bass player from Cream. Well, I was drinking and I'm pretty sure Tony was too. I can't really remember if Jack was, but we did have a laugh. I think I even did some backing vocals on an album he was making there.

Jack and I hit it off straightaway. He was from Scotland too and we talked about the old country.

'I live in the northernmost part of Scotland, Jimmy. It's absolutely beautiful up there. Another world. I can see the northern lights from the front door of my house.'

It sounded magical. He invited me to come and stay and write some songs with him if I ever got up that way. It was a real shame it never happened. Jack was a great player and I was a big fan and I'd have loved to have had the chance to work with him again. Sadly, he died a while back. I have Tony to thank for introducing me to one of the greats.

Another night I sang with John Bonham's sister, Deborah, a talented lady who was there to make a country-sounding record. John, of course, was the legendary drummer from Led Zeppelin, one of the hardest-hitting timekeepers the world has ever seen. He'd died a few years earlier and I could tell Deborah missed him terribly. I told her how much of a fan of her brother I was, then I sat and watched, quietly demolishing a bottle of vodka, as she worked with Tony.

Tony had the newest drum machine on the market and he was programming the drums for her album on it. I don't know if he'd planned it, but he'd made the drum machine play something that was almost like John. Well, it was only a machine, but it had a similar sound: a massive kick drum and a machine-gun snare that took the top of your head off.

Soon Deborah had tears in her eyes.

Tony looked at her. 'Are you all right, darling?' He knew she was struggling and wanted to help. She wiped her eyes, looked at him and said with a wry smile, 'That machine sounds like John in a box.'

The session came to an end soon after that.

I had a lot of time on my hands while I was in Frankfurt, so I started listening to country music, which Jane had always liked. It took me a while to get it, but once I did I came to the realisation that good country music was really white man's soul music. It could tear your heart out if you let it, just like soul music did. I was particularly inspired by an album of duets that Ray Charles made, called *Friendship*. If you haven't heard that record, give it a listen. I still love it to this day. Ray sings songs with Johnny Cash and Willie Nelson and a whole lot of other great singers. This led me to seek out other country artists I'd never really listened to before. People like George Jones, Waylon Jennings, Patsy Cline and, of course, Tammy Wynette.

We also started to look out for some live shows in the hope of seeing some real cowboys perform. To my surprise, I discovered that Germany had a big country music scene, maybe because the country is home to several large US Army bases filled with thousands of homesick GIs. Then I found out that Johnny Cash was playing in Frankfurt with his wife, June Carter, the very next week at a big German country festival, and opening for them was Freddy Fender, a Mexican American singer. I'd heard Freddy on the radio and his big hit 'Before the Next Teardrop Falls' was one of my favourite songs of all time. So I grabbed a couple of tickets and a few days later Jane and I headed out to the festival.

As we walked into the venue, I quickly realised that the Germans like a good dress-up. There were guys and girls done up to the nines everywhere. The guys were wearing boots and hats with feathers and braided bands, and belt buckles so big you could probably see them from space. I immediately felt underdressed – I wasn't even wearing a cowboy hat.

The girls had so many layers of makeup caked on their faces they must have put it on with a trowel, and way too

Wasted days ... Freddy Fender looking sharp, 1984 *(Getty Images)*

much mascara. In fact they could hardly lift their eyelids, so they all looked slightly drugged. Or maybe they were, I don't know. Lots of them had really big hair to boot, teased up high and proud. I hadn't seen hair that big since I'd accidentally walked into a Les Girls show in Sydney.

Soon Freddy came out, dressed all in white, and I was happy because he sang his hits. We didn't have the best seats in the house because I'd bought the tickets so late, and we were quite a way from the front. He looked a bit like a mariachi from where we were – a small mariachi. But he still sounded good.

The crowd, as usual, were waiting expectantly for the main act. Opening acts always have a tough time – I knew, as I'd opened for many a show in my younger days. I couldn't help thinking that Freddy hadn't been as well received as he would have liked, and he didn't seem very happy as he left the stage.

Then Johnny came on and the crowd went wild. He was obviously having a great time, singing all his hits with June, including 'Jackson'. The German crowd knew every word and sang along. I'm not sure they knew what every word meant, but they certainly knew the songs. The show brought the house down.

Afterwards, the lights came up and the audience filed out of the place. Everyone was very polite and orderly, walking in single file down the aisles and out the gates. I had never really seen this much country music at one time before, and the first thing I thought as we stood up to leave was that I needed a drink. Maybe country wasn't really my thing yet.

We headed across the park outside, following the rest of the crowd. I figured the Germans liked to drink and they'd know where to go. I was right, and we ended up in a hotel bar that was packed to the rafters. There were hats and hair as far as you could see, so I knew we were in the right place.

At one point, I pushed my way past a group of men who were all dancing. I wasn't sure if they were dancing together or just happened to be dancing in the same area. They looked like a cross between German gunslingers and hillbillies, and I couldn't really tell if they were square dancing or slap dancing. It might have been a bit of both. I felt like an extra in a Village People film clip. Now I really needed a drink.

As I moved on towards the bar, I noticed a guy staggering around and bumping into everyone who tried to pass him. He was dressed in a bright red cowboy suit that was covered in dazzling rhinestones. He looked like a fucking mirror ball on legs. His hat seemed to be bigger than anyone else's in the bar too. It took up a lot of space.

I stood behind him for a while, waiting my turn. But the barman just ignored him and on either side of us people were pushing the red cowboy out of the way to get to the bar. So I stepped around him and went to order. As I did, he fell onto me and spilled his drink on my jeans. I looked at him as he stood up straight again. He was a mess. I offered a hand but he pushed me away.

I felt bad for him. I'd been in that state myself many times. And somewhere in my heart I had the feeling that I would get a lot worse before I got better.

I took another look at the guy and couldn't help thinking he was very dark for a German. Not only that, but his big moustache made him look like a Mexican bandit. He was obviously a huge Freddy Fender fan, but he wasn't happy. Neither was I really as I wiped his drink from my jeans.

'Thanks, pal,' I said to him. 'Just be careful, would you.' I was trying to be patient, as this guy was clearly having a bad night.

Then he leaned my way and fell again.

Now I was getting pissed off. I snapped. 'Hey, stupid?' I said, half shaping up to him. 'Who the fuck do you think you are? Fucking Freddy Fender?'

He stopped but said nothing. Just stared at me with a look of confusion on his face.

That was when I realised that he *was* Freddy Fender.

Recovering quickly, I smiled and said, 'Hey, Freddy, I loved the show. Let me buy you a drink. What will you have?'

Evidently I was the only Freddy Fender fan in the bar. No one else seemed to recognise him or, if they did, they didn't pay him any attention.

Freddy was so drunk he couldn't answer me. So I leaned towards the barman and ordered. 'One large whisky for me, a vodka and soda for my wife, and a large of whatever my new friend Freddy here is drinking.'

The barman scowled at me. 'He's had enough. No more for him.'

I looked at Freddy. He didn't even seem to know he was in a bar. I think he thought everyone was in his dressing room and he was wondering who we all were.

'Well, just the other two then. Don't worry about my new mate.' I winked at the barman and he went and got my drinks.

Jane and I stood and watched with dismay for a while as Freddy spilled booze over half of the crowd. If he doesn't get out of here soon, I thought, one of these huge German cowboys will kill him.

So I walked over to help him. 'Freddy, I think it would probably be safer if you went back to your hotel. Can I get you a cab or something?' I was trying to save his life.

He looked at me. I could see he was miserable – he had the same look on his face as he'd worn during his show. Then he stumbled, leaned close to me and grabbed my shirt. He breathed heavily on me just for a second – his breath could have killed an armadillo at fifty paces – clearly trying to get his eyes to focus. Then he said, 'Fuck you, man.'

At that point I thought that the next teardrop that fell would probably be Freddy's. But I would have to take a number if I wanted to belt him because it seemed that the rest of the bar were all waiting on their chance to bid him *Auf Wiedersehen* once and for all. I also got the feeling that because I was the only other foreigner in the bar, they all thought I was with him. I had to walk away. Freddy was on his own.

'Adios amigo,' I whispered as we left the bar.

A Song
for Rosa

'Let's go to La Jolla and visit
Deepak,' Jane whispered to me
as we lay in bed one night.
     'Sure,' I said. 'Where's La Jolla?'

'Just near San Diego.'

'Great. Where's San Diego?'

She knew I was kidding. I was trying to be funny. I do that a lot. It works sometimes and other times it just drives her crazy.

We were on one of the many trips we made to Los Angeles when I was trying to break into the American market. LA, the City of Angels, was where it all happened in the 1990s. If you wanted to make it big in the music business, you had to go there. The truth be known, I don't think that, deep down, I ever really wanted to make it there. I thought I did. But if I did, I disguised it well. Because I did everything I possibly could do to fuck it up. I fought with the record company. I fought with the agents. I fought with the punters at shows. I fought with everyone. I took a drink too often. I took too many drugs. I took too much of everything, except advice. I would not take advice from anyone. I was a self-wrecking machine.

Plus, I hated LA. I never felt safe there for a minute. Something about America made me feel afraid. More than just the thought of earthquakes and the ground shaking beneath my feet, or even the thought of California itself sinking into the sea, there was something about the whole country that felt like it was always about to explode. I just didn't like it. Still don't.

But we did have some dear friends in America, and it was always good to catch up with them. So we kept going back. On this trip we were accompanied by Elly-May, our youngest. She was only about five years old and she loved going away with us.

Deepak Chopra was one of those friends we liked to visit. He is a caring, loving man who is a great thinker. Deepak loves music and has long been fascinated by the effect it has on people, an interest that dates back to the time when he studied with the Maharishi Mahesh Yogi, guru of the Transcendental Meditation movement. In the 1970s, the Maharishi had noticed that when The Beatles played the *Ed Sullivan Show* during their first visit to the States, for the hour they were on television the crime rate in America dropped substantially. Music seemed to calm people down. The Maharishi was so taken by this observation that he surrounded himself with Western musicians. And Western musicians were drawn to him. They included, among others, The Beatles and Brian Jones from the Rolling Stones and, of course, their girlfriends and wives. The musicians studied with the Maharishi, meditating for days on end in search of inner peace and truth, and he changed the way they thought and even influenced their music. At least until he got caught chasing a few of the girls around the compound. Then a few of the musicians wanted to punch holes in his aura, and not long after they all went back to sex, drugs and rock 'n' roll – with just a little touch of sitar and tablas because they sounded good.

Deepak had maintained his interest in music and, after publishing a couple of books on mind/body medicine, had become something of a guru himself. Jane had been drawn to his writings and attended several of his workshops. I started to feel jealous and asked to meet him and we all got on so well we started spending a lot of time together. Part of what drew him to us, I think, was his interest in music and in my experiences as a singer.

I was always a little suspicious of the whole guru idea, and one day I jokingly asked, 'Hey, Deepak, are you a guru like the Maharishi?'

My mate Deepak. Yeah, I've read all of his books too.
(courtesy of Carolyn Rangel)

He laughed and said, 'Let's look at that word "guru". G-U-R-U: gee-you-are-you. You see what I'm saying?'

I never really knew exactly what he meant, but I pretended I did. 'Yeah, right, I get it.' I think he was saying no. Either that or 'We are all gurus.' Who knows?

Jane rang Deepak to see if he was at home or somewhere touring the world helping people. He was at home, and he wanted us to come to dinner the following Saturday.

'Oh, Jane. Dearie me,' Deepak said in his smooth Indian accent with just a touch of Californian thrown in for luck, 'it will be a fabulous dinner party. All sorts of very special, very talented people will be there and I want you to meet them. Jimmy will love it.'

So we booked a driver and a room at the Valencia Hotel, by the sea in beautiful La Jolla, and the next Saturday afternoon we set off. Then we hit the Southern Californian freeway system and came to a standstill for the next few hours. Before long, the heat and the traffic had completely ruined our holiday mood and by the time we arrived in La Jolla we were only just still talking to one another.

Our hotel room had a strange layout. We had to climb a steep flight of stairs from the front door to get to the lounge room, with its beautiful sea view, and then the bedroom. From the balcony off the lounge room, I could hear the sound of barking seals coming from just up the coast. Either that or our neighbour was a heavy smoker and had a terrible cough.

We decided it had to be the former, and we headed out to see La Jolla's famous seal and sea lion colony. The beach was covered in seaweed, and basking on the rocks nearby were hundreds of the very noisy creatures, all catching the afternoon sun. We stood and watched for five minutes or so. Elly loved the animals, but I got bored quickly and shouted, 'Well, we better get back and get dressed. We don't want to be late.'

Jane looked at me. 'Pardon, darling,' she said with a blank look on her face.

'We'd better get back and get dressed for dinner,' I shouted, trying desperately to make myself heard over the barking.

'What are you saying, dear?' Jane asked. She couldn't hear me for the noise.

'Let's go, my love!' I shouted, even louder. And then, growing increasingly annoyed: 'Do these fucking seals ever fucking shut up?'

'Pardon?'

I looked at her and smiled. 'Never mind,' I mouthed as I headed away from the din.

We walked back towards the hotel. Jane decided to take Elly-May with her and go to the shops to get a small gift for Deepak and his family. Unlike me, Jane was always very considerate of others. I headed to the room without her to shower. It had been a long, hot day and I was tired and wanted to cool down and relax a little before we went to dinner. We Scots don't deal with the heat too well.

I climbed the stairs, took off my clothes and jumped into the shower. I was still suffering from a bit of jet lag and the water falling over me felt so good. I could have stayed in there for an hour. But after just a few minutes, I heard knocking at the front door.

Bang. Bang. Bang.

If it's Jane, she'll have her key in her handbag and let herself in, I told myself, and went back to enjoying the cool, clean water.

Bang. Bang. Bang.

It was getting louder. And because it was getting louder I decided to ignore it. Fucking turn-down service. 'Go away!' I shouted from the shower.

Bang. Bang. Bang.

This time the door nearly came off its hinges.

I grabbed a towel from the rack and stormed, soaking wet, down the stairs to the door, almost slipping on the tiles, and leaving a trail of water right through the room. As I yanked the door open, I shouted, 'What the fuck do you want?'

Standing there were two well-built and extremely well-dressed African-American men. Both were in sharp, light-coloured, dare I say loud, suits. One suit was green and the other blue. Both men had razor-cut short hair and black-rimmed glasses. To me they looked like members of the famously dapper entourage of Nation of Islam leader Louis Farrakhan.

Just at that moment, my towel almost fell off. I quickly caught it around my knees and pulled it up. Then, in a slightly less agitated voice, I said again, 'What the fuck do you want?'

Both men were looking at the ground, a little embarrassed. Then the man in green spoke. 'Good evening, sir. We are here to pick up Rosa.'

I stared blankly at them.

'Is she here?' one of the men asked politely.

Standing there, as wet as a drowned rat, I sighed and replied, 'I don't know who you are talking about. Does it look like a Rosa is here?' And before they could speak again I said, 'Wrong room, gents. Have a nice day,' and slammed the door shut.

I dragged myself back to the shower, slipping and sliding along the way. I realised I'd been a little short with them, but they had nearly broken my door down.

Before long, Jane was home and we were getting dressed for dinner. A car picked us up and we arrived at Deepak's house in the foothills of La Jolla as the sun was setting over the sea. We were greeted by Deepak's lovely wife, Rita, and shown in.

'Ah, Jimmy and Jane, come in and meet my friends,' Deepak said and he proceeded to walk us around the room and introduce us to the extraordinary group of people he had assembled for dinner. There were millionaires and billionaires from all different parts of the world. There were doctors, scientists, freedom fighters, activists and even world-famous clothes designers.

'Jimmy, Jane, this is Donna Karan. Donna, these are my fabulous friends from Australia. Jimmy is the biggest singer in Australia. He's like Australia's Bruce Springsteen.'

I coughed uncomfortably. 'Ah, yes, well, I sing, but I don't know about that,' I said as I shook Donna's hand. It seemed that everyone in the room was the best in their field, and I immediately felt a little out of place. Jane, on the other hand, was completely at home.

Next, Deepak took us over to an elderly black woman who was sitting on the couch. She too looked like she felt a little out of place.

'Jimmy, Jane, this is Rosa Parks. Rosa is—'

I cut Deepak off. Of course I knew who Rosa Parks was. She was the famously courageous woman who, way back in 1955, in Montgomery, Alabama, had refused to give up her seat in the 'coloured' section of a segregated bus to a white person after all the whites-only seats had been filled. She'd had enough. It was a moment in time that started a protest that led to the largest demonstration against segregation of

Two beautiful souls: Deepak and Rosa at the party
(courtesy of Deepak Chopra)

the time, the Montgomery bus boycott. She was known as 'the mother of the civil rights movement'.

'It's so great to meet you,' I said. I almost got down on my knees. This quiet old lady had done what no one else would do at that time and, as a result, things had begun to change.

'Rosa is going to make a speech for us all tonight,' Deepak said.

This was amazing, and I was just starting to get my head around the idea of Rosa Parks speaking at a dinner I was at when Deepak continued, 'And Jimmy is going to sing for us too. How lucky are we?'

I turned to him so quickly I nearly got whiplash. 'I'm what? ... Er, well, yeah, yeah, okay.'

It was only then that I noticed the two large gentlemen standing directly behind Rosa. It was the two Louis Farrakhan guys who had nearly broken my door down. I smiled at them. But clearly they were thinking back to their earlier encounter with me – first impressions and all that. They didn't smile back.

'Gentlemen,' I said and held out my hand. They didn't move. I coughed nervously and walked away.

Drinks and dinner were served. Non-alcoholic and vegetarian, obviously. We loved it all, though, because we had spent a lot of time with Deepak and got used to that.

The speeches were about to start. I quickly pulled Deepak aside and asked, 'Do you have someone who will accompany me on the piano?' I looked around the room. I couldn't see a piano.

Deepak smiled, 'I don't have a piano or an accompanist.'

I started to sweat. 'Do you have a guitar player here?'

Deepak shook his head. 'No, Jimmy. No guitarist either. There is a concert violinist here from Austria ...'

That wouldn't work. I was panicking now. 'Do you have a guitar that I could use?'

Deepak smiled again. 'Relax, Jimmy. These are our friends. You can just sing alone. It will be great.'

A wave of sheer panic washed over me and sweat started to run down my back. I wasn't worried about the wealthy, powerful audience I had to entertain. Much more daunting was that I had to sing for Rosa Parks. Rosa had stood arm in arm with Sam Cooke as he sang 'A Change is Gonna Come', an anthem of the American civil rights movement, while the police in Alabama set dogs on them. Otis Redding had sung 'Try a Little Tenderness' right next to her while rubber bullets were fired over their heads as they protested on the streets of Montgomery. Well, actually I'm not sure any of that really happened, and I might have made it up, but those were the scenes that played in my head. And whether they'd happened or not didn't matter. I was just not worthy.

In shock, I stood there trying to think of something I could sing a cappella to this group. But then Rosa started to talk and I immediately forgot about everything else. Her story was heartfelt and heartbreaking. At the end of her speech Elly-May ran across the room, cuddled her and said, 'Oh, you poor thing. Why did they treat you like that?'

Rosa held Elly-May beside her, laughed out loud and asked, 'Does anyone have any questions about that time in my life?'

There were so many questions running through my head, but in an instant I raised my hand and said, 'Why do you think your voice had that impact? Why didn't the world hear the other voices? The ones that came before you.'

As I finished asking my question I sensed someone behind me. It was the man in the green suit from my hotel door. He grabbed my shoulder in what I can only describe as a Vulcan death grip and squeezed it so tight that I nearly passed out. Then he leaned towards me menacingly and hissed in my ear, 'Because they killed everyone else.'

I cleared my throat, which had suddenly become very dry, and squeaked, 'Thanks.'

Confused by the commotion, Rosa had already turned away and taken another question from a different part of the room.

Soon it was my turn to perform. The only appropriate number that came to mind was one made famous by Mahalia Jackson called 'In the Upper Room', a powerful gospel song that would make the angriest of men turn gentle and calm and think about God. Surely even the Louis Farrakhan guys will like this one, I thought to myself, and I sang my heart out.

They didn't.

The rest of the room loved it, though, and there was a lot of shoulder-slapping and the like going on, but I never got a chance to ask Rosa if she'd enjoyed it. Besides Deepak and his family, she was the only one I was singing for that night. But the path to Rosa was blocked by two well-tailored, brightly coloured – maybe a bit too brightly coloured – suits with shoulder pads so sharp they could kill a man with one blow. These guys hadn't liked me from the get-go.

I never got to speak to her again. We went back to the hotel. I was a little sad, but I decided it would be better not to step outside my hotel room again that night, just in case I bumped into my two new sharply dressed friends.

Fresh Flowers
on the Bridge

I see them often. Flowers tied
to telegraph poles and trees,
next to small crosses that reflect
the beams of my car's lights as
I speed down the highway.

Usually, I am too busy fighting off sleep and trying to make it through a long drive alive to really think about them for too long. But every time I see these tributes, my heart hurts. There is always a pain, deep, deep down. Someone has left the world in a twisted wreck. Snatched away before their time. A blown tyre or a millisecond of sleep sending them careering to a fiery end.

Often, I weave my way on down the road afterwards then ... *whoosh*, the sound of the screaming engine of a sixteen-wheeler hammering out of nowhere on the two-lane highway snaps me back to reality. I swerve back into the safety of my own lane one more time, narrowly avoiding the same fate. At least for now.

I have done this so many times. In fact, it seems like I've spent much of my life driving up and down the east coast of Australia strapped into the suicide seat of a dodgy budget hire car, trying desperately to make it to the next show on time. It's a wonder I haven't died out there on the highway.

On one particular day a while back, a different scene unfolded. I had not been driving all night. I was leaving the Southern Highlands, heading for Sydney, a drive that I had done a million times. It was broad daylight, and there was no cross, just a small bunch of flowers tied to the rail of a bridge on the Hume Highway. Thirty metres or more below the bridge was the Nepean River. It was nearly dry at this point and large rocks blocked its course, making it almost impossible for what little water there was to flow.

The flowers were just a flash of colour. Something that drifted through my peripheral vision at 110 kilometres an hour. But I saw them. And my heart sank. No car could have crashed off the bridge at this point, as the road was straight and wide. This was something else.

I had to concentrate on driving, and soon all my questions about the flowers were gone from my mind, lost in the sound of my tyres bumping as they hit the cats' eyes by the side of the road. Later that night in bed, though, I thought back to that moment. The whole thing had lasted only seconds, but I remembered the bridge, the flowers, the distance from the bridge to the ground, and how these scenes had quickly shot through my head like the preview to a horror movie. I lay there asking myself what had happened. Did someone jump? Or was someone thrown from the bridge?

It was clear I would probably never know, and soon I drifted off to sleep. But for hours afterwards I tossed and turned and every now and then I'd wake up in a sweat with the image of those fresh flowers tied to the bridge still flashing in my head.

Each time I drove to Sydney after that, I noticed the flowers still tied to the railings. But after a while I realised that they weren't always the same flowers. They were being changed, and changed often. Sometimes once a week, sometimes every few days.

That realisation broke my heart. This was the place where someone who was deeply loved had left the world. And I felt like I knew why he or she had left. I'd felt like quitting this life many times before myself. This world is a hard place to live in, and there is no easy way out. But I knew if I'd gone, I would have only left pain and unanswered questions behind me. So I had to stick around as long as I could and work it all out.

I have no idea who it was that departed that day, but I know that the pain of that great loss has not got any easier for their loved ones. In the last year I have driven over that bridge so many times, and I still have no answers. And judging by the fresh flowers that appear every week, I'm not the only one.

Illiterate
in Two
Languages

The car was packed, the kids
were on board. Around eleven
in the morning, we set off from
our home in Aix-en-Provence
in the south of France.

It was 1994. A few years earlier my record label, Mushroom, had opened an office in London and decided it would be beneficial for me to be within striking distance of the European music scene. The idea was that I would live there and play whenever I could around Europe, in the hope of selling some albums and winning over a few new fans. Rather than stay in northern Europe, where the weather was cold and wet, Jane and I had decided we wanted to live somewhere warm and beautiful, and it doesn't get much more beautiful than the south of France. We found a two-hundred-year-old shepherd's house surrounded by wheat fields in that idyllic part of the south of France. Life there was good.

We took the whole family: our daughters Mahalia, then aged twelve; Eliza-Jane, nine; and Elly-May, five; and son Jackie, then eight. It was a great time for us, and we all loved France, its food, history and culture, although I did struggle with the language. I managed to learn just enough French to become officially illiterate in two languages.

On this particular day, we were on our way to play at a big rock show in central France. Leaving the pretty backroads of Provence, we turned onto the highway and ran the gauntlet of French autoroute drivers. Our car was motoring along at what seemed to me like breakneck speed, but somehow other cars were flying past us as if we were standing still. While it was chaos on the roads, inside our car it was a happy, calm space. Jane, myself and the four kids had turned the interior into a little piece of home, filling it with pillows, food, toys, music and laughter. The car wasn't flash, not a rock star's car. But then here I wasn't a rock star, I was a dad. It was a nice, safe car. A Renault Espace. A people mover. The sort of car a French football mum would drive, with lots of seats for all the family.

My family were sitting in the back, singing along to The Carpenters' greatest hits, Jane belting out 'Close to You' while acting out the words in a sort of seated dance and blowing kisses at me between lines. There was a time when, if I'd had to listen to The Carpenters, I would have thrown myself under the wheels of the car. But by this time I'd learned to love them. If Jane loved them, then so did I. The kids were still a little too young to be bothered by the choice of music. They had the odd fight with each other, but besides that they were as happy to be on the road as we were, having done long drives like this since the day they were born. This is what we do. We tour.

The gig was in a place called Clermont-Ferrand. I'd never heard of it, but as it was one of the only shows we would be playing in France, I was looking forward to it. Though we'd been living in France for a few years by this time, much to our disappointment most of the gigs we were offered were somewhere else – somewhere like Germany. Now, I like Germany a lot, and I like the German people. But I'd played so many towns in Germany. Towns that even the Germans didn't like. Towns that were once rotting behind the Iron Curtain and were still crumbling and falling down around your feet, as a result of either the Second World War, simple neglect or the constant battering from the wind and rain that only a northern European winter can bring.

So it was good to be playing in France, it was a novelty, and I was hoping Clermont-Ferrand would be something different, some place beautiful, a place with the smell of coffee and fresh baguettes and pâté de foie gras wafting through the platan-lined boulevards. I was a little worried, though, because we were booked to play at a bikers' festival. But so far I had never seen any scary looking bikies in

France. 'Les 'ells Angels' didn't really sound that frightening in a French accent.

So, on we drove through the French countryside listening to Enya, James Taylor, Bread and America and all the other favourites that the family had for long drives. Most of my playlists didn't suit family outings. But every now and then AC/DC would sneak their way onto the stereo and I would burst into song.

'I'm on a—'

Bang. The music would stop and AC/DC and myself would be quickly silenced. Then the reverb- and echo-laden tones of Enya singing in Gaelic about getting a beauty treatment somewhere would fill the car. 'Ah-ah-ah-ah-ah-ah …'

The countryside changed with every kilometre we travelled. Big fields of yellow sunflowers turned into even bigger fields of purple-blue lavender that went on as far as the eye could see. Then they too would disappear and be replaced by long straight lines of vines. Church steeples could be seen in the distance, standing like guards overlooking beautiful villages. Chimneys and spires jutted up through the mist as it settled over small stone houses and the surrounding countryside. It all looked so appealing. But to get to one of these villages meant leaving the autoroute, and that could be dangerous, as there was always a good chance we would get lost. So we never stopped. We just drove on, singing along to The Carpenters.

By early evening, we were approaching the outskirts of Clermont-Ferrand. It didn't look too pretty. We had to get to the hotel as fast as possible, as my crew were waiting to borrow our car and go on ahead to the show. They'd arrived with the band on a tour bus and the idea was for me and my family to sleep at the hotel and then travel that last few kilometres with the band. Meanwhile the crew would make sure everything was up to scratch for when we arrived, ready to rock, the next day.

We pulled into the driveway of the hotel with 'Calling Occupants of Interplanetary Craft' blasting out of the speakers. Karen Carpenter could sing the phone book and it would sound great, and sometimes I'm not sure she wasn't.

The crew were standing outside, waiting for us. They seemed to be ready to go. But once I got out of the car I saw they looked more confused than workmanlike. You see, this was technically a day off for them, and the crew, led by their faithful leader, Sneaky Pete, were as high as kites.

They always tried to keep the fact that they were stoned a secret from me, especially on show days.

'No, I definitely only smoke after shows, Jimmy,' Sneaky would tell me, with eyes that looked like he was slowly bleeding to death. 'I am a professional, mate, and so are the guys who work with me.'

I would look around and the crew would be eating bars of chocolate and looking at the ground so as not to catch my eye.

'Yeah, yeah. Whatever you say, Sneaky.'

They knew that this was a very serious job we were doing and that if they were stoned and anything went wrong, I might kill them. Well, that's what they thought. I wouldn't really have killed them. Not all of them anyway. Maybe just maimed a couple of them.

On a day off, though, it was a different matter: they could do whatever they liked. As long as they weren't arrested or killed. And this was, technically, a day off.

As well as being my long-time production manager, Sneaky was also a dear friend. He was a charming young guy with an easy manner and an infectious grin. He wasn't tall, but what he lacked in height he made up for in personality. He was smart and friendly and very well mannered, unless you messed with him. Then he could turn. Or so I heard. I never saw it.

The crew helped remove the bags from my car, but there were still stuffed toys and whatnot lying on the back seats.

'We have to go, Jimmy. We want this gig to be perfect. That's what we do, us professionals.' Sneaky was trying to impress me. But he didn't know how to start the car.

I leaned in the driver's window. 'The key goes there, next to the steering wheel. And you put your foot on the brake while you put it into gear,' I said, pretending to give him a bit of a hard time.

'I know. I know that. I was just getting settled in,' he said with a laugh.

He and the crew set off on the twenty-minute drive to the gig. As they sped off into the darkness, I could clearly hear 'Please Mr Postman' ringing out of the car stereo. I cringed. I had forgotten how white The Carpenters could sound. And I wondered how far the crew would go before they realised what they were listening to.

We took the kids inside, checked in and went to bed.

Next day we arrived at the festival on our bus and the security was tight. Big, hairy, tattooed blokes in leather, with no sense of humour.

'Leave this to me, guys, I'll sort it out,' I said to the band. I'd met security guys like this at festivals at home. I knew how to talk to them.

I jumped out of the bus and walked over to them. 'Hello, gentlemen. We are the Jimmy Barnes band from Australia and we have to be on stage in just under an hour. So it would be good if you would let us in.'

They wouldn't budge. They just stared at me as if I was trying to sell them something they didn't want. Then Jane jumped out of the car. 'Bonjour, messieurs, nous sommes Australiens et mon mari s'appelle Jimmy Barnes. Il va faire un concert ici cet après-midi.'

The gorilla on the door suddenly became very charming and smiled and said, 'Alors, madame, entrez-vous – enchanté!' He signalled for us to go through.

We jumped back in the bus and headed backstage.

'Well, ah guess ah sorted zeez guys out,' I said in a bad French accent.

As we pulled in, there was Sneaky, acting like he owned the place.

'Excuse em waaaa!' he was shouting at a local stagehand. 'For fuck's sake. I told you, that box goes over there, you stupid bastard. You're not listening to what I tell you. Don't you understand English?'

The stagehand looked up and simply said, 'No.' In French.

'Well, read my lips or something. We have a show to do here.'

Sneaky walked over to the bus.

'Is everything going okay here, Sneaky?' I enquired. It didn't look like it was.

'I am all over this,' he replied confidently. 'My French is better than I thought.'

I knew he was bullshitting me. I found out later that Sneaky and the crew had arrived the previous night even more stoned than when they'd left us. They'd smoked pot the whole way there and could hardly see by the time they got to the gate and tried to get through the same security we'd encountered. Sneaky was acting like he was the boss and being very pushy. None of the crew had noticed that The Carpenters were still playing on a loop. The security guards had, though, and they had a good laugh about it. How could they beat up such small people, especially if they were listening to music like that and had all those cuddly toys? It wouldn't be a manly thing to do.

'And where could we get something to eat around here?' Sneaky had demanded. 'And no fucking snails, okay?'

The head security guy's patience was running out by this point and he wasn't going to even try to talk to these foreigners. So he'd grunted, snarled at them and waved them through. The crew had then got to work.

Less than one hour before show time, we were using the tour bus as a dressing room, the driver having backed it up next to the stage. The band and I were all at the front of the bus getting ready and the kids were at the back watching DVDs. Or so we thought.

I suddenly heard a lot of yelling and screaming coming from the predominantly male audience and I walked to the back of the bus to check on the kids. From the back window they had a great view of the stage, where, right at that moment, a wet T-shirt competition was happening. The kids thought it was hilarious. I quickly shut the curtains.

We hit the stage and played loud and hard and very fast. The crowd loved us and we loved them. Afterwards the crew packed up the gear and we prepared to leave. As we were driving out, the band that was to follow us, a French punk-funk band, were starting up. They had a new album out and they apparently had thought that it would be a good publicity gimmick if they strapped themselves into the bowl of a big pink, Perspex, see-through cement mixer in their underwear and drove through the audience, playing as they turned around and around in the mixer.

It could only end in tears. As we slowly manoeuvred our bus through the crowd, their worst fears were surely realised when the cement mixer broke down and they were left hanging upside down. By that time, the sun was way hot too. So there they were, in the middle of five thousand crazed French bikies, in their underwear and unable to keep playing. As we left, we could see the crowd shaking the mixer. Trying to tip it over. We were glad to be finished and on our way out.

A Broken
Homecoming

After writing books about growing up in Elizabeth and the impact it had on me, I decided it would be best to wipe everything about the place from my memory.

What purpose could it serve for me to keep any of it? I thought of it as like the end of a fight. Well, a fair fight anyway. Elizabeth and I could dust each other off, shake hands, turn and walk away from each other and move on. Life would continue in Elizabeth, and I now had a new life to live. A life far from the streets where I used to run wild as a child. A life as far as possible from the dark paddocks where I had hidden from my worst nightmares. Elizabeth was the past, and it would, in time, grow dimmer and dimmer, until it was gone. Faded away to nothing. Not a trace left. Then I could get on with enjoying my new, much happier life.

That was my plan. But plans don't always work out, do they?

In September 2016, I was in Adelaide for a *Working Class Boy* show in the Barossa Valley. Now, if anyone else was offered the chance to go to the Barossa Valley, they would think that they had been given a great gift. This is an area that not only grows delicious produce and turns it into gourmet meals for passing connoisseurs to devour, it's also one of the great winegrowing regions of Australia – a green, fertile patch of heaven on the outskirts of Adelaide, where the well-to-do take up hobbies like making wine or raising horses on neat little farms. But all I could think about was that I had to drive through Elizabeth to get there.

I'd hired a top-of-the-line Holden. That seemed appropriate, but strange. Cars like this were no longer going to be made in Elizabeth. Three years earlier, General Motors had announced that all manufacturing in Australia would be phased out by the end of 2017. Like me, the brand felt broken. Soon the best-loved Australian cars would be made somewhere in Europe or Asia.

I could still feel the hold the town had on me. I knew that when I drove through it, it would be like a whirlpool dragging me down into the cold, dark depths of my past. I could already hear the Sirens singing their songs, calling me towards the rocks and certain death. Just the thought of being there made me feel like a weight had been laid on my chest, and I struggled to breathe.

Obviously, I had not shaken hands and walked away from Elizabeth. It would always be there to haunt me. Unless I could get some closure, find a way to let it go.

I headed north out of the city with plenty of time to spare. I had the bright idea of stopping by some landmarks that were important to me in Elizabeth and metaphorically kissing them goodbye. On this final journey to my hometown, I had my Jane with me. Jane always sees things clearer than I do, and the world always seems a better place to her than it does to me. She would help me make sense of the feelings that lay dormant inside my heart, the feelings I feared might explode and destroy me. Maybe she could make the pain go away. Poor Jane, I never thought about the pressure that I and my past placed on her.

The Main North Road hadn't changed a lot since I'd last had to drive out that way. A few new estates had popped up, one or two of them around lakes that must have been artificial because I had walked the length of that road a thousand times as a child in the blistering heat, and there were never any lakes to be seen. Believe me, if they'd been there, I would have dived headlong into them.

This was probably the cheapest land that General Motors could have bought in South Australia in the late 1950s, and so it was here they'd decided to build a town for their workers.

Right on this land that nobody wanted. The soil lacked nutrients and was too dry and hard. It was good for growing nothing. Especially families. As we drove into Elizabeth, now officially part of the much larger 'City of Playford', I identified trees I'd seen planted fifty-odd years earlier, when I was a child. They weren't much bigger and still seemed to be struggling to survive. It was impossible for anything to take root here. Everything was stunted.

I pointed out a few landmarks to Jane, who clearly wasn't impressed.

'Coming up on the right is the drive-in we used to sneak into with our mates and make out with chicks.' I smiled at her.

She tried to smile back, but her heart wasn't in it. Where my teenage haunt had once stood, there was nothing but an empty paddock. It looked like the drive-in had been knocked down and the land cleared, to build more houses. Who knows? We didn't stop. We didn't even slow down. It was gone.

'There goes the nightlife in the town, because there wasn't much else to do when I lived here,' I remarked.

The next attraction was Steve Prestwich's house. Steve and I had gone on to become brothers in Cold Chisel, but in those really early days we hadn't known each other. I only remembered the house because of a drunken party we went to nearby. A local doctor and his wife had gone away for the weekend and left their teenage daughter and her friends to mind the place in their absence. Big mistake. The daughter was a friend of ours and me and my mates had decided we were going to have a party at her house and anybody who wasn't afraid of us was welcome to come along too. The house was a mess by ten o'clock and we decided to leave before the cops turned up. As I left, I bumped into Steve's brother Laurie. One or two of Steve's brothers hung around our gang. They were trouble just like me.

We didn't chat much. I just said hi as I was leaving and he was arriving. 'Hey, Laul, how are ya goin'?'

Laurie could be a bad bastard, but we got on all right.

'Yeah, great Jim, like. That's me Ma an' Da's house right there,' he said in his thick Liverpudlian accent, which oozed past his prominent Prestwich front teeth as he pointed a few doors down. 'So I don't have far to run when the cops or the parents turn up. Ha! See ya, ace.' Then he headed into the party looking for something or someone to turn upside down.

Jane wasn't really that interested in where we'd run amok. She wanted to see where we'd lived and gone to school. And where we'd hidden when we were too scared to go home. The important stuff. The very same stuff I was avoiding.

We drove past the former Elizabeth High School, now Playford International College, which looked very different from how it had been in my day. It was after hours and the place was empty and silent, like a river that had dried up. Obviously you needed the kids there to breathe life into it – as we had done, playing football and fighting with each other, the boys trying to impress the girls, all the while struggling to keep our lives together, at least as long as we were in school. At the end of each day, we ran as far from the place as our legs would carry us, the voices of the teachers calling us to come back or walk slowly fading in the distance. We never listened to them.

On we drove until we hit Elizabeth West. Parts of it were worse than even I remembered it being. Overgrown and crumbling. Some houses had weeds so long you could hardly see the windows or the walls.

There was something about Elizabeth that gave me the same feeling I got when I drove past the Colosseum in Rome. It was nice to see it and it was full of history, but I never wanted to go inside. I'd fought and nearly died there so many times. And there were way too many ghosts for me. Too much suffering and pain had been endured there. Too much blood spilled.

We carried on and went and stood for a moment opposite the house my family had lived in, at 45 Heytesbury Road. I couldn't stay there very long, it was too much to take. In a matter of seconds, a million questions that could never be answered ran through my head, and I didn't want to think about them anymore.

'I've seen enough. Let's get out of here,' I said to Jane.

We drove on, saying very little to each other. But then, as we cruised slowly around the streets I'd run through as a child, I felt a strangely familiar feeling I hadn't experienced for a long time. I'd been a misfit for most of my life. I didn't belong anywhere. But this place was part of me. It had bashed me and beaten me and turned me into the person I am today. Suddenly all that pain and fear I used to feel was, for a brief moment, gone. I shut my eyes and I could still hear the laughter of old friends. Friends who went through the same shit as me. Friends who, like me, had nothing – nothing but each other.

I'd been running from Elizabeth for years and trying to wipe it out of my mind for good, even writing books about it in an attempt to let it go. But here I was, and in some strange, fractured and scrambled way, it seemed like home.

The day had turned into a homecoming. A broken homecoming, you might say. But, still, a homecoming.

I had to get away before I admitted that to Jane. I didn't want her to know I still felt a connection to this place. So we drove on in silence, into the green hills of the Barossa Valley, on to another show where I would talk about how I had finally escaped my past.

Follow Your *Leader*

It was in the late nineties, just after we'd moved back to Australia from France, and we were missing all the friends we had made in Provence.

So much so that we arranged to meet a gang of them in Thailand for a holiday. We had it all planned. We'd take them up north to Chiang Mai to do some trekking. Joel and Cristel, Elizabeth (better known as Zaza), Claude and Brigitte, and Dominique – they all loved the outdoors and a good walk.

Jane spoke perfect French and very good Thai. I spoke very little French and very little Thai, just enough to get by, and my English was questionable. We thought it would be good to bring Jackie, my son, who was only eleven at the time, and he spoke French very well too. Our friends naturally spoke French and broken English. But Jane was the pivotal point here, as she could speak to us all in one language or another. Because my use of any language was not great, I tended to jump between all three. If I was speaking to a Thai person and I hit a wall in Thai, my brain would immediately jump to French, confusing whoever I was talking to, not to mention myself. I still do this when I am travelling. Recently I was in Mexico and I was speaking in broken Spanish, Thai, French and English all within one sentence, and all with a Scottish accent. And I wondered why they didn't understand me.

Anyway, just as we were set to leave Australia to meet our friends for this fantastic trip, we got a call from Jane's father, who was in Melbourne, recovering from a kidney transplant. We had recently gone to Thailand and accompanied him and his entourage to Melbourne for the operation. That journey had been quite a saga in itself, and if I tell you the story, you'll see why we *really* needed a holiday.

Jane's father, Khun Suvit, was a wealthy Thai businessman. He lived on a fantastic golf course in Bangkok called Navatanee and his house was bigger than the clubhouse. I was never

Jane's father, Khun Suvit, with Mahalia in the mid-1980s

sure what he did, but I knew he was well connected. At one time he owned a shipping line and he brokered major deals between the Thai government and all sorts of businessmen. Let's just say he knew how to get things done. I had a lot of respect for Khun Suvit because he treated me with respect. He was always polite, warm and generous. In fact, he was generous with everyone. He loved his daughters and, like me, had a particular soft spot for his eldest daughter, Jane.

When he reached his sixties, his health declined and his kidneys began to fail. The time quickly came where he was on dialysis and was placed on a transplant waiting list. Then a donor became available and he decided he wanted the operation to be carried out by the best specialists in the world, who at that time were in Melbourne.

So it was decided that Khun Suvit would travel there to have the transplant and as I mentioned that we would go and escort him and his entourage from Bangkok to Melbourne. When I say *entourage*, I mean it in every sense of the word. There were about twenty of them, including nurses, doctors, other specialists, the donor, and Jane's stepmother, Khun Chawee, who was one of the nicest people I'd ever met. Then there were the maids and a few cooks who travelled everywhere with them, as well as Khun Suvit's driver, Piek. I'd known him since I first met Jane's father. He was a tough guy, but always nice to us. I wouldn't want to mess with him, though.

A few of Khun Suvit's friends came along too, including a golf buddy – though there didn't seem much likelihood of them playing golf – and another guy who caught my eye, who seemed to be a high-ranking military officer. He wore a massive white-gold ring with the design of some sort of temple on it, maybe Angkor Wat. It looked way too big to be a ring and more like it should have been the emblem on the bonnet of a luxury car. It had been given to him by a leading member of another Southeast Asian military force. I wasn't sure why he was coming, but I did know he cooked one of Khun Suvit's favourite dishes, so maybe that was it.

We all met at Khun Suvit's house and travelled in convoy to Bangkok airport. Khun Suvit, his wife and selected friends travelled in First Class along with his most trusted doctor and a nurse. The rest of us were either in Business Class or Economy. We checked in about forty bags and I was tasked with keeping all the luggage tags. It seemed I was the tour manager. God help us all, I thought.

I had good reason for thinking that. I've worked with a few tour managers over the years and I know what they have to do. They spend days and days setting up and checking every detail of a band's tour to make sure nothing goes wrong. Then they spend the rest of their time changing everything the singer wants to change because he's had a big night or a fight with the other guys in the band.

'I know it's expensive, but I don't want to travel with the band anymore. I just don't like them. So I want you to book me my own plane.'

This sort of request would totally stress out the tour manager. 'But do you know what it costs to get another plane?' he would reply.

'Do *you* know what it will cost to get a new singer or a new guitar player? Because if I have to travel with him, I might just kill him.'

This of course is just a fictional exchange to show you what could possibly go on between a band and their tour manager.

I, for one, never fought with the other band members or the tour manager. I was always hard-working and easy to get along with. As sure as I am riding this camel.

Now back to the story. I had no idea what was in all those bags, but there were no issues on departure and we all settled down for the flight. Jane and I had arrived in Thailand only that morning and were having to fly back that same night with everyone else. So we were exhausted and couldn't wait to get some sleep. We'd have to be sharp when we landed to get everyone safely through Australian customs – I knew the officials there would not be as easy-going as their Thai equivalents, who gave the impression that they worked for Jane's dad.

Sleep was out of the question, though. Throughout the flight I was repeatedly called up to solve problems in the First Class area.

'They want to take my bag off me for take-off, but this one never leaves my side,' Jane's stepmother said. I pleaded with the hostess to let her keep it and thankfully she agreed.

'The food is cold. I'm not eating it,' the doctor moaned.

I got him something hot.

'I need chilli with this dish and, anyway, I ordered fish. Whole fish. Whole fish with big lips,' Jane's father complained.

I wasn't sure if he wanted to eat it or dance with it.

Eventually they all relaxed a bit and I was only called back up every fifteen minutes or so. I guess tour managers never get any sleep. Not the ones I know, anyway.

As we arrived in Melbourne, I realised it was baking hot there and that the suit I'd worn to look the part for Jane's father – pretty smart, if I may say so myself – might have been a mistake. And there was no time to change.

Instead of disembarking en masse, we were made to wait and then walk one by one past some kind of drug dog. Now I have to tell you if we'd had any drugs, I would have taken them all by now. But we hadn't. So it wasn't a big problem, but it did slow us down, and meant I immediately broke out in a sweat.

Being so tired and carrying so much responsibility on my shoulders, I went into hyper-drive and became manic. I walked about twenty kilometres an hour faster than everyone else in the party. I'd walk up to a door and hold it open, only to turn around and find that the others were still about a hundred metres behind me. I'd have to close it, walk back and then race to the front and hold the door open again. This happened over and over.

By the time we got to customs, I was soaked with sweat. I couldn't keep track of everyone and I could hear the odd argument breaking out between one or two of our party and the customs officers, but miraculously we all made it through and into the baggage hall. I checked the luggage tags and everything was correct. How the fuck did that happen? I wondered.

Outside we herded most of the party into waiting limousines. Because there were more of us than we'd been advised, we had to send a few of them in taxis to the hotel. But it wasn't a problem.

We were all staying at the Hilton Hotel, down the road from the MCG. On our arrival, the porters quickly took our bags and stacked them on trollies ready for delivery to our individual rooms and I collected all the keys. Jane and I then escorted Khun Suvit to his suite. As soon as we got there, Jane's stepmother said, 'Where's Doctor ——?' (I can't

Yes, Sir, Whatever You Want, Sir I was much more aerodynamic after my haircut in Thailand. 'Just need a faster boat now.'

Hold My Hand Diving in the Maldives. If I keep really still, maybe that shark won't notice me ... 'Er, Jane ... help!' *(Hannah Anderson)*

Big Jim That's me with three crazy horses. Noel Watson, my martial arts instructor, aka 'Crazy Horse', is riding Jane's horse, Two-up, and I'm on Big Jim.

Big Jim A scene from my 'No Second Prize' video, starring Big Jim and yours truly. Looks like we're getting ready to hold up that train.

The Yakuza Driver Jane and me on the slopes at Niseko. 'Where the hell did Don go? I could swear he was right behind us last time I looked.'

The Yakuza Driver Après-ski, Japanese style. Don, me and Jackie outside the smallest door to the coolest bar in Niseko, Bar Gyu+ *(courtesy of Don Walker)*

Sneaky Pete Young Peter McFee was like one of the family. He loved our kids and they all loved Peter. There was nothing sneaky about him.

Warp Speed Wayne I was glad the motorbike ride was over and I'd now be getting my revenge. 'Come with me, Wayne, we have a song to sing.'

The Golden Buddha What a beautiful statue. It takes your breath away just being in the same room as it. Jane and I visit this temple every time we go to Bangkok.

Follow Your Leader On the trail in Thailand. 'Darn, where are those elephants?'
I had to make a trunk call to find out. *(courtesy of Brigite Mennillo)*

Big Enough Appearing as the 'big cowboy in the sky', in Kirin J. Callinan's video
for 'Big Enough'. When I start screaming, everyone leaves town. *(Video directed and
produced by Danny Cohen; Director of Photography: Sherwin Akbarzadeh)*

You Ain't from Around Here Working with the legendary Memphis Boys (left to right: Gene Chrisman, Bobby Wood, Reggie Young and Mike Leech; not sure who the old guy in the middle is). It doesn't get any better than this. *(Pierre Baroni)*

You Ain't from Around Here Doing a photo shoot in Nate's Bar, upstairs at Earnestine & Hazel's in Memphis, with Philippe Klose (top left) and Pierre Baroni (bottom left). Earnestine & Hazel's used to be a bordello and was the inspiration for the Rolling Stones' song 'Honky Tonk Women'. *(Ginger Light)*

Money for Bones
'Can somebody get these guys a drink?' My boys went everywhere with me, and it was 'Access All Areas' for them at every gig.

Money for Bones Oliver at a protest against the detention of refugees on Manus Island. He always stood up for the oppressed. At front right is our dear friend and publicist Rina Ferris, who makes me work way too hard (but we love her).

Money for Bones Charley Drayton, Oliver, myself and Snoop Dog writing some lyrics in the studio. 'How does this sound, boys?' 'Rough!' *(Robert Hambling)*

Money for Bones The dogs were always much calmer than me on the golf course and always had a great time driving around. Wish they could have told me where my ball went; it would have saved me a lot of time.

Alligators The Royal Bangkok Sports Club, where I learned to play golf while horses raced around the track. They were the only thing faster than my swing.

The Sweet Taste of Success Jackie enjoys sitting on soccer legend Craig Johnston's shoulders, while his dad tries unsuccessfully to attract his attention.

The Swan The beautiful bird that dropped into our home in Aix-en-Provence in the south of France. I'm sure he (or was it she?) could sense a kinship.

Into the Spotlight My youngest daughter, Elly-May, in one of her many capes. She's always been a shy little thing. Don't know where she gets that from.

Good to Be Chieftain Alaistair Saunders from the Brigadoon committee kindly guided Mr and Mrs Chieftain around the Highland gathering.

The Covid Chronicle Writing this book in our cabin on the Eastern & Oriental Express in Thailand. It's a tough gig, but somebody has to do it.

The Covid Chronicle Part of the fun on the Eastern & Oriental Express is getting dressed up to the nines for drinks and dinner. Jane at least looked breathtaking.

The Covid Chronicle The alleyway diner in Bangkok's Chinatown, Uncle Chai's favourite place for fish-ball noodle soup. Spot the scary *farang*.

The Covid Chronicle A regular feast by the sea at our apartment in Hua Hin. 'I wonder what Jane's having?'

The Covid Chronicle On our way from Bangkok to Chiang Mai. I'm not taking any chances. 'Damn! Where are my gloves?!'

The Covid Chronicle Back home in the Southern Highlands, social distancing in matching pyjamas. I'm thinking that we might need a bigger table.

Home Great to be back in my own place. I'm starting out on the small pipes, but it won't be long till I'm on the big ones and driving the neighbours crazy again.

remember his name now. Sorry, doctor.) And she looked at me as if I should have known.

But I didn't have him on my list. He had to have been one of the late additions.

'I don't know where he is, but I'll find him,' I said as confidently as I could, given how many miles I'd travelled in the previous twenty-four hours. Meanwhile my suit was starting to look a little shabby.

'How could you lose a doctor?' Jane's father asked, looking me up and down.

I excused myself, straightened my tie and went to look for him.

Jane followed me out. 'You must find him, Jimmy, they're going crazy in there. He's a doctor!'

I was frazzled by then. I looked at Jane and said, 'There were twenty-odd people, and I'm using the word "odd" carefully here. How do I know who's a doctor and who's not? Was he wearing a white coat? Did he have a stethoscope around his neck? No, I don't think so. I don't know him. I don't know who's who. So he could be anywhere.'

Jane stared at me. If she could have slapped me there and then, she would have. It's true I was getting a little hysterical.

'Settle down, Jimmy. Just see if you can find him.' And she walked back into the suite, which, by the way, took up a whole floor. It occurred to me that the doctor might be in there somewhere, lost.

But when I went down to the foyer, there he was. He had just wandered off. I went back up to give them all the good news and arrived just as the bags were being delivered. Within seconds, Khun Chawee cried out, 'Where is my small hand-luggage bag? All the bags are here but that one.' Somehow the bag that was never to leave her side had not turned up.

'I thought I'd be safe in the hotel, so I gave it to the porter to carry,' she told me with a worried look on her face.

Jane took me aside and said to me quietly, 'Jimmy, my father likes to use cash, not cards. And there was a lot of cash in that bag. A lot.'

'How much is a lot?' I asked, starting to feel unwell.

Jane shook her head. 'I don't know, but a lot. Better find it.'

I ran downstairs to the head porter and asked, 'Were you given a small white hand-luggage bag? It didn't make it up to the room.'

He looked at me and smiled as if nothing was wrong. 'Don't stress, mate. It'll turn up.'

But I was at the end of my rope and if I wasn't careful I might be hanged. I snapped back at him, 'It fucking better, mate, or I will be visiting you again very soon and I won't be as nice.'

In the meantime the whole party had come back downstairs to accompany Khun Suvit to the hospital.

'Have you found the bag yet?' Jane's stepmother asked.

'I think we know where it is,' I lied, 'so don't worry. It will be here when we get back.'

We headed out and into the waiting cars. The hospital was only three or four kilometres up the road, so we were there in no time. As I jumped out of the car, I noticed that the temperature had risen even faster than my blood pressure and it was now about forty degrees.

After being checked in, Jane's father demanded a better room. I understood where he was coming from. Private hospitals in Thailand are really good. You don't get rooms, you get apartments with hot and cold running nurses. And food delivered when and as you want it. But we were in Australia, so we'd have to settle him down.

I was about to explain when I saw Jane looking at me. 'Jimmy, why don't you go out and sit in the waiting room. You look stressed.'

She was right, so I went out and took a seat. I hadn't noticed before but we were in the head injuries section. I didn't know why Jane's father was there. Maybe because the rooms were better. Anyway, I was sitting quietly, trying to gather my thoughts, when a patient, who, judging by the bandages around his head and the bruising on his face, had experienced a major cranial trauma, took one look at me and said, 'Geez, Barnesy, you don't look so good, mate. Are you all right?'

Catching a glimpse of my reflection in the window, I realised he was right. I looked shocking.

'I'm all right, mate. Big night.'

I headed to the bathroom, threw some water on my face and straightened myself up a bit before returning to Khun Suvit's room. By then it was time to take Jane's stepmother, one of the doctors, a nurse and one of her father's friends back to the hotel. Jane would stay behind and settle her father.

I rounded them all up and herded them downstairs to hail a taxi. It was only when I was loading them into the cab that I realised we wouldn't all fit. It had been a big day. I was left standing on the kerb.

'Don't worry,' I said, 'I've told the driver where to go. I'll follow you in another cab and meet you at the hotel.'

As the cab drove off, I suddenly remembered that I hadn't given them any Australian dollars. I'd have to get there before them. I looked around for another cab but there was none in sight. And at eleven o'clock on a fiercely hot Saturday morning, it was going to be hard to find one. So I did the only thing I could think of. I ran. Fast. Dodging my way through the heavy traffic on Victoria Street.

At one point I looked up and saw Jane's father's friend sitting in the cab stuck in traffic, just as I ran by. He was looking straight at me. I kept running and arrived at the hotel thirty seconds before the cab. As it pulled up, I stepped forward and opened the door, looking by now like I'd just had a shower in my three-piece suit. Jane's stepmother, the doctor, the nurse and the friend all studiously ignored me and walked into the hotel and towards the lift.

I followed after them slowly, thinking that at least now I really could have a shower. But just as I approached the lift, I saw Khun Suvit's military pal standing outside the bar, waving at me. I walked over slowly.

'Jimmy. Do you drink vodka, by any chance?'

He was smiling, so I thought 'Why not?' and followed him into the bar. On a table were two of the biggest vodkas I'd ever seen. He slid one over to me. It appeared I had made a friend. He downed his in one gulp and looked to me to do the same. Which I did.

'Shall we have one more?' he asked mischievously. I declined politely and walked out of the bar just as Jane walked into the hotel. Before I could open my mouth, she looked at me and said, 'You smell like a homeless person. Go upstairs and shower.'

It was one of those days. I was walking towards the lift with my shoulders slumped, when suddenly the porter ran up to me, smiling. And carrying a small white piece of hand luggage.

There is a God, I thought.

I took the bag to Jane and she loved me again and the world seemed good once more. After that, the tour party all turned out to be very friendly and we had a lovely time with them all before flying back to Sydney. Jane's father's operation went well and when he got out of hospital he was sent to the hotel to recover and remain close by. And that's when we were given the okay to go on holiday.

*

But then … We were packed and ready to go to the airport the next morning for our flight to Thailand when Jane received the call from her father. He was experiencing complications and wanted her to return to Melbourne.

Our French friends were already en route from France to Thailand. What would we do?

'My dad needs me, Jimmy. You'll just have to carry on with the trip and guide them around Thailand.'

I was stunned. 'But, but, I don't speak French,' I said.

'That's okay,' Jane replied as she repacked.

'And they don't speak great English,' I moaned, swallowing hard and trying not to break down.

'That's okay too,' Jane calmly said, folding her blouse into her suitcase.

'And none of us speak Thai!' I whimpered, with obvious alarm in my voice.

'Calm down, Jimmy. Jackie speaks fluent French, you speak enough Thai to get by and they know a little English. It will all be all right. Trust me. Just go and have a great time.'

And with that we went to bed and Jane slept like a log and I lay and looked at the ceiling for most of the night.

Next day Jane left for Melbourne and Jackie and I set off for Thailand. I studied my French phrase book for most of the trip. It didn't help.

We arrived in Bangkok and met up with our friends. Despite the communication issues, it was great to see them again. Cristel, a maths teacher, and Joel, an architect, were one of the first couples we'd met in France – in fact we rented their place for a while – and it was at sumptuous dinners at their house that we'd met the others. Claude was a jazz musician and had invited me to sing at many a jazz show in Aix-en-Provence. At first my jazz repertoire was very limited, but with a bit of coaching it wasn't long before I had a set of songs that I could sing at any party. Claude's wife, Brigitte, and Zaza were both French teachers, which initially put me off trying to talk to them in French – I thought they'd hate hearing me butcher their beautiful language. But eventually Brigitte said, 'Jimmy, it is time you made an effort, so I won't speak to you in English anymore.' And she never did, leaving me to rely partly on sign language and mime. Dominique, or Doe as we all called her, was a dermatologist, and there was a good chance her services might come in handy in the jungles of Thailand. This little group of friends had taken us into their homes and hearts when we moved to France and have been part of our lives ever since.

We all checked into a smart hotel somewhere near Patpong Road. It's a wild red-light area and we'd thought it might provide some entertainment for our friends on their first night in the country. But, as it happened, they were all too tired and needed to rest for the next day's adventures. So

Jackie and I went out to gather some provisions for our trip. I'd booked an overnight train to Chiang Mai, but I wasn't sure what the food or the train would be like, so I wanted some extra supplies for our friends in case it was all really bad. I found a deli that sold fantastic French cheeses and baguettes and bought those along with some pâté de foie gras and, of course, some great French Bordeaux. Only the best for the gang.

Then I pulled Jackie aside and told him my plan. 'We'll put all our great French wine and food in a cooler bag with ice and, at the right moment, we'll take it out and surprise them. So, mum's the word, right?'

Jackie, having just returned from France, took everything literally. 'Why is "Mum" the word? She's not here.' He was cute.

'No, Jackie, it's got nothing to do with Mum.'

He looked puzzled. 'Is Mum meeting us on the train?'

I scratched my head. 'Son, just forget I mentioned Mum. I'll let you know when to break out the food.'

Jackie nodded. 'So Mum and the food are a surprise,' he said, smiling like he'd just got it.

'Yeah, that's right, son.' I would explain later, though I knew he would be disappointed. He loves his mum.

Next day, after a little sightseeing around Bangkok, we arrived at the train station with our friends in tow. Jackie was my French interpreter and I did my best to speak some of the worst Thai ever heard.

The train wasn't the most comfortable train I'd ever been on, but we were assured that later in the night the seats would convert into beds of some sort. At least I thought that's what they'd said.

A young Thai porter walked through the train selling beer and snacks but nothing much else. Soon I could tell that the girls in particular were sick of beer. I gave Jackie the nod. He pulled the food and wine from under the seat and announced in French that the party had begun. I'm sure that for a second he also looked around for his mum.

I won't try to transcribe any of the conversations that followed in French and Thai, so you'll just have to imagine them. Suffice to say we all had a great time eating, drinking and singing as we travelled north.

Next morning, bleary-eyed and not particularly well rested, we arrived in Chiang Mai, where the tour company running the trek had booked us a hotel for one night. As soon as we got there, I could tell they were trying to get us accustomed to roughing it. Thank God Jane wasn't there because she would not have stayed, and even I was by now used to five-star accommodation, so this place was a bit of a shock. It was maybe a one-star hotel and that star did not burn bright; in fact it was dead. Our French friends were happy, though. As long as there was an adventure ahead, they never complained. So we agreed to stay put. We explored Chiang Mai during the day and met for dinner early that evening. We had to get to sleep early, as we were leaving before sun-up to start the trek.

Come the morning, we were bundled into minibuses and driven out of town. After forty minutes or so, we reached what seemed to be the starting point of the trek. It must have been, because we were asked to leave the bus. Either that or this was a really shitty tour.

Three days of trekking had sounded like hard work to me, so I'd secretly booked elephants to carry us for the first few hours. Sure enough, within minutes of us arriving, we looked up to see four massive beasts coming over the hill, swaying as they walked slowly towards us and trumpeting as they came to a stop. I thought this had been a great idea and that everyone would be thrilled, but Zaza was not impressed. A beautiful soul, Zaza was not as much of an adventurer as the rest of the gang and the idea of riding on an elephant scared the shit out of her. As soon as we climbed aboard, she broke down and cried. It was clear she was not going to go along with us, and we could not leave her behind.

Fortunately I was sharing an elephant with Zaza and I'd brought a secret weapon to deal with just this sort of emergency. Before Zaza could climb off and start trying to talk us out of riding the elephants, I lit up a very strong joint and passed it to her, hoping it might loosen her spirit. Zaza was a bit of a hippy and within minutes she was calling the large pachyderm her best friend and stroking his head while whispering to him in French.

So Zaza was happy, we were happy and the elephant was happy too. Onward and up the mountain we went. Every time the elephants lurched and rolled, Zaza let out a girlish squeal. By now, all our friends were loving every moment of the trip and so was I.

The next section of the climb was quite steep and it was coming up to the hottest part of the day. An hour or so later, we reached the first stop and we all climbed off the elephants and bid our huge banana-eating friends goodbye. It was time to start trekking.

We walked along quietly, enjoying the breathtaking scenery as we gasped for air in the late-afternoon heat. It was hard work, but it was beautiful. Just as the sun was starting to go down, we walked into a small hill-tribe village.

'This is where you will sleep tonight,' our guide said to us as he pointed to a group of small huts that were raised off the ground. There was no running water unless you wanted to run and get it yourself, and there were no lights, beds or blankets. Luckily, the guide gave us sleeping bags – as we found out later, it gets very cold in the hills of northern Thailand.

There were a few other small groups of tourists staying in the same village and we all built a fire while our guide cooked us something simple but delicious to eat. By this point we were so hungry we could have eaten the elephants. We had a few drinks and sang songs from our home countries – French songs, Italian songs, Swedish songs and, of course, Australian songs. Following a bit of coaching, the guide even had us singing in Thai. Before long, we were all laughing and singing songs about elephants while trying our best to imitate them.

Next morning we left the camp and headed up into the mountains. The scenery was incredible. Massive trees and colourful mountain flowers everywhere. No matter where you looked, the view was spectacular. We walked on all day until we reached our next campsite. I don't know if the guide had gone out of his way to find us a private spot we didn't have to share, but we set up our tents next to a secluded waterfall in a beautiful little valley. It was perfect. As the sun set, we realised it was going to be even colder that night. A light mist washed across us every now and then from the waterfall as the wind swirled around the camp, but as the night grew darker it settled down and we all sat speechless around the campfire. There would be no singing tonight. We were all too tired. Our trusty guide whipped up something to eat and we all climbed into our sleeping bags. Silence soon enveloped the camp. Every so often, you heard the odd snore or groan from a weary traveller, but otherwise it was dead quiet.

In the middle of the night, I woke to Jackie's voice. 'Dad, I don't feel good.'

I grabbed a torch and reached him just as he vomited all over himself and his sleeping bag. It was pitch dark and no one else woke up, so I got some water, cleaned him up and re-dressed him. Then I bundled him up into my sleeping bag. Soon he was fast asleep again, while I sat in the dark, freezing and wondering what to do. I took the torch and rummaged around the camp until I found an old blanket. I put on all my remaining clothes and curled up in a ball under the blanket and tried to stay warm.

'Dad?' Jackie's voice again broke the silence of the cold, clear night. 'Dad, I feel sick.'

This time I didn't even manage to turn the torch on before I heard him vomiting. I unwrapped myself and found him crying, covered in what looked a lot like what we'd eaten the evening before. I carefully washed him and calmed him down, then dressed him in my remaining clothes and wrapped him in my blanket. He was asleep again in minutes. I was now down to my underwear, with no blanket, and freezing cold. Somehow, though, I survived the night and Jackie, thankfully, slept like a baby until morning.

As soon as the sun came up, I washed some of our clothes in the river and lay them on the rocks. By the time we'd eaten breakfast and broken camp, it was hot again and the clothes were dry. Jackie was too weak to walk, and too sick to let anyone else near him.

'I want you to carry me, Dad,' he moaned. Though he was only eleven or so, Jackie was already a big guy, so this was quite a prospect. The guide, who was much stronger than me, offered to help, but Jackie would not have a bar of it. It was me or no one.

So I borrowed a sarong and tied Jackie to my back and we walked for four hours to get out of the jungle. When we emerged, I was nearly dead. It was so hot and dry and I was completely worn out. Then, just down the track, I saw what looked like a power line. I walked towards it and found that it *was* a power line and that a smaller line ran off it at an angle towards the ground. And, as I got closer still, I saw that the smaller line led to a small shack that must have been a shop and just outside the shack the line connected to an old-style Coke machine, the type where you have to pull the bottle up and out of the slot.

I'd never been so happy to see a Coke machine in my life, and to this day it remains one of the greatest things I have ever seen.

The Coke was ice cold and I drank two bottles in as many minutes as we waited for a car to pick us up. And miraculously, right then, Jackie came good. Funny that.

It all turned out well. Jackie and I bonded like never before, and the French gang had a great time. Zaza was able to go home and tell her friends that she'd ridden an elephant through the jungles of Thailand.

Khun Suvit's operation was successful and in no time he was back in Bangkok. He lived for another ten years or so, during which time we all got to see more of him and he got to know his grandchildren. He lived out his days in his house on that beautiful golf course in Bangkok, where, in his lounge room, he had a grand piano, drum kit and guitar amplifiers and held regular sessions with musicians. He loved to sing and he and I even went out to some of his favourite haunts from his younger days and sang old songs by Matt Monro and Frank Sinatra. He was a crooner and I wasn't, but we still had a good time.

Big Enough

As you may know, I have a reputation for being a screamer. I can get defensive about it, but most often I just laugh and go out of my way to scream even more.

The thing is, I'm a soul singer and soul singers have been known to scream from time to time. Anyone who listens to Wilson Pickett or Little Richard would know that.

One day Jane said to me, 'Why not make a little something special for all those people who call you a screamer?'

I laughed and replied, 'What did you have in mind: ear plugs?'

Jane had mentioned this idea over the years, but this time I knew she was serious. 'Let's make a screaming Jimmy alarm clock,' she said.

The merchandising company thought she was mad, but Jane persevered and, sure enough, when we made them we sold out of them instantly. Even my kids and grandkids thought the alarm clock was funny, so we made more. Now people all over Australia have Jimmy Barnes alarm clocks in their houses. They are funny … at first, but after a while they can drive you crazy. My grandkids leave them buried under piles of toys and then in the middle of the night they go off, scaring the shit out of everybody in the house.

I must admit, I never really thought I'd be made into an alarm clock. Just like I never thought I'd ever become a meme. The truth be known, I didn't even know what a meme was until I became one. This is how it happened.

Back in early 2017, Elly-May, my youngest daughter, asked me to sing on a track that a friend of hers was recording. In fact, Elly-May and EJ, our number two daughter, had both become friends with this guy, Kirin J. Callinan. Kirin is a singer and performance artist from Sydney, who had already gained a reputation for being an extremely wild young man. It seemed Kirin could not go on stage, or anywhere else really, without taking off his clothes. Kirin is talented, and he likes to challenge people. I am not known for being an exhibitionist, but I have caused a bit of trouble in my time, so I tried not to judge him.

Before I agreed to sing on his record, I thought I'd better meet him. The opportunity arose when our family and Kirin were among those invited to the wedding of a good friend in New Zealand. At the reception, Kirin turned up in a kilt. A mini-kilt. And I couldn't help noticing that he was wearing nothing underneath it. Now this is all well and good if you are in traditional Scottish attire. I myself often wear a kilt and understand that you are not supposed to wear underwear with one. But Kirin's kilt was really short and as he swanned around the party it kept blowing in the wind. I am a bit of a prude and I tried my best not to be offended, but it was difficult. And of course all my children and their friends, as well as a lot of older family friends, were at the wedding.

That said, I seemed to be the only one offended by Kirin's exhibitionism. Everyone else seemed to just look the other way and laugh. 'There goes Kirin again,' I heard one or two of them saying. You'd think that up in the hills of New Zealand it would be too cold for streaking. But not for Kirin, it seemed, so I just kept out of his way.

Next time we met was at our house in Sydney when Kirin came to hang out with Elly and stayed for dinner. Once again he was dressed in a kilt, with a waistcoat but no shirt, and a three-cornered pirate's hat. Funnily enough, this type of hat used to be called a cocked hat. Appropriate, given Kirin's reputation. But at least this time the kilt was full-length and there was no wind blowing in the house. So I got the chance to chat with him without swinging at him.

'Okay, who put my kilt in the tumble dryer?'

He was a good young fellow. Very funny and smart and he knew what he was doing. So I agreed to sing on his record.

'What song do you want me to sing on, Kirin?' I asked over dinner.

'Oh, it's a little dance song of mine called "Big Enough". I think you'll like it. I'll get the song to you tomorrow and you can do it at your leisure.'

I laughed to myself. I thought it was pretty funny that this guy, who was evidently at ease in his own skin, had a song called 'Big Enough', and I couldn't wait to hear it. I asked him exactly what he needed me to do.

'Well, Jimmy, it would be great if you could do one or two of your famous screams on it. That's all I really need. If that's okay.'

How hard could that be? I thought.

'No worries, bring it over tomorrow and we can do it,' I suggested.

'Unfortunately, I'm going to America tomorrow,' he said, with a smile. 'Can I just send you the bit I want you to scream on, and then you can do it and send it back to me?'

'No problem. Do that and I'll scream like one of Hannibal Lecter's dinner guests.'

Next day I received the relevant part of the song by email. I passed it on to my son-in-law Ben, Mahalia's husband, to line up in the studio, ready for me to scream. Ben is a good engineer and producer and I trust his taste. He has played all sorts of music from jazz to hard rock, so I knew he could handle this.

That night, he came out of the studio and said to me, 'Er, have you heard this track he wants you on, Jimmy?' He looked worried.

'No, but let's give it a go.'

Ben wasn't sure about it. 'It's weird music, man, I—'

'Put it up and I'll scream and we can send it off,' I said. 'It doesn't matter if we don't like it. As long as he does.'

I went into the studio. The song did sound kind of strange: a cross between house music and Euro pop. But I decided to give it a go. Ben started the track and I screamed my lungs out for one pass.

'How does that sound, Ben?'

Ben still looked uncertain. 'All right, I guess. Shall we do it again?'

I looked at him and said, 'Why? Let's leave it, it sounds great.' And I walked out of the studio and never heard the song again until it was released. The track sounded good. It wasn't rock, but it was good.

A month or so later, I received a call from Kirin. 'Hey, Jimmy,' he said, 'the American record company love the song. Will you be in the film clip?'

I thought he was pushing his luck here, but I agreed to do it, purely because I liked his spirit. This guy was always in trouble with everyone, but he just kept doing things his way, and I admired that.

A week later, I got a call from the director of the clip.

'Hello, er, Mr Barnes—'

'Jimmy,' I said.

'Yes, right, er … Jimmy, can you come to the studio and film with us? It will only take an hour.'

'Sure,' I said.

'Oh, and by the way,' he added sheepishly, 'do you have any cowboy clothes?'

I couldn't quite see where country clothes and Euro house/pop music crossed paths, but I just laughed and said,

'Have you seen any of my clips from the eighties? All I had was cowboy clothes.' I'd drag a few things out of mothballs, I told him.

So I headed down to the studio and wore various outfits and hats and screamed for him. Then next thing I knew I was getting calls from people in America wanting to talk to me and invite me on shows, even *The Tonight Show* in America. What the fuck was happening?

Much to my surprise, I found out that Kirin's song 'Big Enough' had gone viral on the internet. Over a million people had already watched the film clip and for some reason a lot of people were making memes of my screaming. It appeared I had a new career as a screaming cowboy. Memes of me were inserted into scenes from *Jurassic Park*, *Platoon* and every other blockbuster movie you can think of. I popped up screaming in clips from *South Park* and dozens of other cartoon series. I even made it into a *Game of Thrones* meme. And to cap it all, one person made a ten-hour version of me screaming. Who the fuck sits around putting together ten hours of me screaming, never mind actually watching it? It was crazy.

Soon, between Kirin's clip and all the memes, I had been watched by nearly a billion people on YouTube. I have worked in the music industry for forty-five years and I've spent a lot of time trying to break into new markets, including the American music market. But nothing else has given me anywhere close to the exposure that Kirin's song gave me.

It did have its downside, though. One of the things I loved about not being famous outside Australia was that I could travel the world freely without being bothered. Only very rarely did I get stopped on the street in Asia or Europe, for instance, unless it was by an Australian tourist who had recognised me. But on my last trip away I was in a small back street in Chiang Mai in northern Thailand when I noticed a group of young boys staring at me. They must have been nine or ten years old. I was standing next to an elephant at the time feeding it a banana, but I could tell that it was me they were staring at and not the elephant. I looked away and shuffled my feet uncomfortably, but they kept looking at me and then started smiling and waving. Finally one of them worked up the courage to come over and talk to me. He held up his phone and played a clip of me in my big white cowboy hat, screaming, in the middle of a *South Park* episode, and he said, grinning from ear to ear, 'This is you. You are the big cowboy in the sky.'

I quietly nodded and he asked if I would sign his T-shirt. After I'd done so, he asked politely, 'Can you scream for us, please?'

'I'd better not,' I replied apologetically, 'I might scare the elephant.'

Anyway, despite these minor inconveniences, being famous as a screamer is a good problem to have. In fact, Jane now wants to make a 'Big Screaming Cowboy' alarm clock, and people keep asking if I will be making another appearance as the big cowboy in the sky. I'm not sure, though. It seems to me the world isn't quite big enough for two of those film clips. And my house certainly isn't big enough for two of those alarm clocks.

And in the *Blue Corner* ...

As a young guy, I loved Bruce Lee movies. I watched the *Green Hornet* television series and thought Kato was cool. Then I saw Bruce's early movies and loved them too.

Nothing could stop Bruce. No one pushed him around. I would have loved to have been in control of my life like he was. But by the time those movies were on my radar, it seemed too late for me to start martial arts. You see, already in my early teens, I'd lost the discipline to stay focused on anything for very long, and I felt like I didn't care about much at all. I didn't care if I passed at school. I didn't care if I was too young to drink, I was going to do it anyway. I didn't care if taking drugs was bad for me: I wanted to take them all the time. I didn't care if people tried to hurt me, because I didn't feel anymore. I didn't care if I lived or died. I'd lost hope.

I still used to watch Bruce's films and dream of what might have been, and I learned how to fight. But not like Bruce. It was always fight or die where I came from. I was pretty good at it too. Well, I'm still here, aren't I? But often I didn't know who I was fighting for, or why. Bruce only fought as a last resort. He fought the bad guys to save his family. In my life, the lines between the bad guys and the good guys were blurred. I didn't know who was who most of the time. I'd put my trust in someone then I'd be let down. This happened time and time again. Eventually, I felt I couldn't trust anyone. I could only depend on myself. And that worked for a while, until the day came when I realised that I could no longer trust myself to do what was right. I had become just like everybody else in my life. Flaky and unreliable.

I managed to live with that for a while, partly because I had nothing to lose and no future really. Then I had a chance meeting with a bunch of guys who weren't like me. They hadn't grown up like I had. They had plans. They had dreams. They were normal. In 1973, I joined Cold Chisel and my life changed.

We were nearly all still in our teens and looking for a way to take on the world. And we became a team. Even, dare I say it, a family. After that, for a long time, I had hope again. But that hope slowly disappeared too. Mainly that was because everything that happened to me as a child I'd just pushed to the back of my mind, pretending it had never happened. Yet it was still there, waiting to be dealt with. That's another story, and one some of you might have read already.

Throughout all those years, though, my respect for and fascination with martial arts stayed with me. It was all part of a dream of mine. If only I could be like that. If only I could be disciplined and focus long enough to sort things out. Life might then be good.

Many years later, touring with Cold Chisel in the early 1980s, I met a guy called Noel Watson. His mates from his karate club called him Crazy Horse, because he *was* crazy. He was like me in a lot of ways. I'm sure his early life had been tough too, and just as I'd taken up singing to save my life, he'd taken up martial arts. After years of trying to cope with life, we met and immediately saw a bit of ourselves in each other. We became mates. Just hanging out and drinking and chatting. Noel had to work as a bouncer, but I got the impression he didn't want to punch things and people for a living anymore. It didn't make him feel fulfilled. I was much the same. I didn't want to just get drunk and fucked up and jump around on stage anymore. It wasn't enough. I wanted to be in control.

So Noel started teaching me martial arts. Well, trying to teach me martial arts. I wasn't the best student. I remember accidentally knocking one of his front teeth out one day while he was showing me a move. I thought I was going to

It's amazing how accommodating people are when they can't breathe.
(courtesy of Channel 9)

die after that. Noel taught Jane karate too. She was good. Noel used to say that she was deadlier than me, and I'm not sure he was kidding. I know Noel learned things from us too, like that there was more out there than just fighting. He spent a lot of time with my family and I could see that he gradually changed as he did that more often.

I took Noel with me on the road and he travelled with me for ten years, sometimes touring with bands like ZZ Top, all over America. We never came close to getting ourselves killed the whole time. He had my back and I always had his.

Despite all those years of working with Noel, I didn't become an especially accomplished martial artist. But the training did help me gain the discipline and mental strength I needed to eventually deal with all of my shit. And Noel went on to find a beautiful Hawaiian girl, Tina, and fell in love. Tina could see the real Noel. Not the tough guy who could handle anybody. Not Crazy Horse, one of the boys. But the decent, strong, loving, reliable human being who was always there, hiding inside that tough exterior. They moved to her home in Hawaii and Noel is no longer a bouncer. He doesn't have to beat people up anymore.

I owe a lot to Noel, and I wanted to write this as a way of thanking him for what he gave me as well as an introduction to a couple of stories about my involvement with the martial arts world.

The first one happened when I'd just started my martial arts training. At that time, Noel worked for the Bob Jones Corporation, a company set up in the 1960s to teach self-defence and martial arts and provide security for public events, including concerts. Bob Jones was the owner, the big guy, the *sensei*. I knew him from way back, as he had worked on the doors of a lot of the clubs Cold Chisel played at. Those clubs could be wild places and you could easily get yourself into trouble, especially if you were a young, drunken troublemaker like me. Many a night, Bob or one of his guys saved me from getting beaten up. He kept an eye out for me and spread the word among his doormen to keep an eye out for me too. I don't know why. Maybe because John, my brother, had jumped in to help him out of some tough spots and he was one of his mates, or maybe just because he liked the band. Later I also got to know Bob through his work as a bodyguard. I saw him minding big overseas acts like Fleetwood Mac and Joe Cocker.

One night Bob invited Jane and me to be his guests at a world-title kick-boxing fight at the Sydney Entertainment Centre. On arrival, Jane and I sat in the front row, ringside, right next to Noel and the highest-ranking black belts in the style. This was a room full of big hitters, literally. So we sat down quietly.

Jane was not really happy to be there. She thought the whole martial arts thing was a load of macho bullshit, if the truth be known. But she'd come along to be supportive and to keep me company.

The first fight was introduced by a very loud American voice. 'In the red corner, representing Canada, put your hands together for ...'

I can't remember the name, to be honest, but he was obviously good because all the black belts sitting around us shouted, stood up and clapped their hands.

The Canadian threw off his silk, slightly Liberace-looking red dressing gown, threw his hands in the air and began kicking an imaginary opponent and making the meanest

faces he could pull. The crowd went nuts. They all loved
Liberace.

The tension started building. You could have cut the
testosterone in the air with a knife. Though if you'd pulled a
knife on any of these guys, you would have been dead meat
in seconds.

Then the American started shouting again, this time
stretching out a few of the words for dramatic effect.
'Aaaaaand, in the blluuuue corner, coming all the way from
Baaaangkokkk, Thailand ...'

Same thing: I didn't know him and can't remember his
name. In fact, I had no idea who anyone was. But, again,
he must have been great, judging by the applause he got.
And this guy was a lot cooler. He did a ceremonial Thai
dance around the ring, stretching and bowing as he went,
and asking the spirits for help at each corner of the ring as
Thai music played over the PA system. It was a ritual I'd seen
in Thailand when I'd gone to watch fights there. Jane's uncles
always got a kick out of taking me to a stadium to witness
young boxers beating the hell out of each other.

After the dance was over, the Thai fighter removed
the flowers that were draped around his neck and the two
combatants walked to the centre of the ring for a last-minute
reading of the rules, never for a second taking their eyes off
each other.

'Right, you guys,' said the referee, 'listen here. I don't
want any biting, kicking, gouging, scratching or elbows. You
got that?' And then, after a pause, 'Oh, sorry, I forgot, this is
kick boxing. Do whatever the fuck you like.'

Actually, I don't really know what the referee said, but
soon the fighters were back in their respective corners waiting

for the bell. The Canadian, according to all the guys sitting in our row, was the favourite, but the Thai guy was a dark horse.

'These guys look small but can they kick,' one of the black belts said to me. 'Don't write him off. He could kill this other guy. You never know.'

Ding! The bell rang, and the two fighters walked into the middle of the ring and touched gloves. Very polite. Then the Canadian fighter spun around and hit the Thai guy with a swinging back kick, square on the chin. *Boom!* The Thai boxer flew across the ring and landed flat on his back, right in front of Jane and me. His eyes were open, but he was out cold. He looked as if he was dead. A doctor came running into the ring to check.

At this point, Jane stood up, turned to all the black belts around us and, in a voice that could peel paint and make a man wish he'd never been born, screamed, 'You are all a pack of animals. He's dead! He's dead! You are just a load of losers!' And then she walked out of the place at high speed.

I looked at the black belts, smiled nervously and signalled with a jerk of my head that I'd better be going too. 'Guys, thanks for having us, but, er …' And I turned to walk out.

They looked afraid. I was sure I heard one of them say, 'Please keep her away, she scares us.'

Noel kept an eye on the black belts as I left. I'm sure he would have thumped anybody who looked sideways at us. I ran to catch up with Jane, who was already at the main doors. Not a successful night out.

*

Not surprisingly, it was many years before I was invited back to a martial arts display. This time we were offered tickets to see a demonstration by a group of Shaolin monks. Once again, it was at the Entertainment Centre, only this time it was during the day. I was in the middle of recording the album *Heat* at Festival Studios, just around the corner, so it was close. But Noel was away in Hawaii and Jane of course refused to go. The only person I could persuade to come with me was the studio engineer, a fellow named Rick Will. Now, Rick, a young guy from America, was the biggest hippy I'd ever met. He wore beads and tie-dyed T-shirts and smelled of essential oils. His hair was very long and he looked rather feminine. He was a great engineer and a sweetheart, but also a bit of a softy. Even so, I thought he'd cope with the show.

'Rick, it will be like watching an episode of *Kung Fu*. "Walking on rice paper, Grasshopper" and all that,' I said to him.

Eventually he agreed to come along and keep me company. 'Dude, as long as it's not violent,' he said. 'I can't handle violence.'

'There will be almost no violence,' I lied to him. 'I promise.' I looked at the ground as I spoke.

When we walked into the arena, half of the audience started scowling at Rick and his beads. He just didn't fit in with this mob who had come to see somebody's blood spilled. I could tell what they were thinking: If this is a bad show, at least we can punch out the rock star and the pansy he's with.

Funnily enough, I hadn't been given ringside seats and none of the guys from the club were sitting anywhere near us. But the room was full of martial artists of all sizes, young and old, waiting to be blown away by the skills of the monks.

The lights went down and an announcement was made. 'Ladies and gentlemen, please watch carefully as our Chinese master hangs lead weights from needles inserted in his chest.'

Rick turned to me, white as a ghost. 'Dude, I can't stand the sight of needles.'

I looked at him. 'Probably best you don't call me dude in this crowd.'

I turned back to the show. The master took out a long needle and held it to the light for the crowd to see. Suddenly Rick's head dropped onto my shoulder. He was out cold.

Was I imagining this? Was I really sitting in a stadium full of black belts with this hippy's head on my shoulder, looking like two love birds at the movies?

I tried to get him to wake up. 'Rick. Rick. Wake up.'

No response.

'Rick, dude, you've got to wake up,' I whispered desperately.

But he was gone.

Some of the animals around us began to stare and I knew it was time to leave. So I grabbed Rick under the arms and dragged him out of his seat and into the aisle and started heading towards the door, bumping my way past the hoons who were watching us as we made our way up the stairs.

'Fucking pussy!' one of the meatheads snarled.

'I'll put him outside and I'll be right back for you,' I said with a scowl. But although I managed to get Rick onto his feet at the door, he was too wobbly to leave on his own and I didn't go back in.

'Come on, Grasshopper, I'll take you home,' I said to Rick as I threw him into a cab. Another successful night out watching fights. I was really missing my old mate Noel. If he'd been there, Rick would have stayed at the studio smoking pot and playing Ziggy Marley records, and Noel and I would have been in the front row having a good time. Instead I'd had to carry a hippy on my shoulder while running the gauntlet of a crowd of bloodthirsty, crazed karate killers.

I haven't been to any more martial arts exhibitions since then, but Noel and I catch up whenever I pass through Honolulu and sometimes he comes back to Australia to see all his old mates and kick up his heels. He looks happy and at peace and he's a quiet man these days. But he'll always be dangerous. He is Crazy Horse, after all.

Ear Today ...

'Hey, Dumbo. Come here
and get your boots on.'
John, my brother, was by the
door, ready to go to football
training. I refused to answer.

'Hey, has someone ordered a taxi with the doors left open,' John continued, 'cause there's one right here.' And he pointed at me and laughed.

I was used to this kind of thing and would try not to respond.

'Hey, Dumbo, flap over here quickly or I'll give you a good slapping.'

On it went.

I had a lot of serious problems to deal with as I was growing up, so being teased about my rather prominent ears – it was true, they did stick out a lot – wasn't that big a deal at first. But it did start to get to me as I got older.

When I was a kid it was mostly my big brother and sisters who teased me, but when I reached my teenage years others started picking on me too. Most girls thought I was cute, in a Disney sort of way, but boys laughed and made jokes at my expense. Of course, if anybody my own size had a dig, I would swing at them as quick as look at them, and my ears were the cause of numerous fights as I grew up in Adelaide – though I got good at fighting for many other reasons too.

Then I left school and was able to grow my hair, and all that was left behind. My ears were forgotten about, hidden underneath waves of brushed fuzzy locks. Once I stopped combing my hair, they were constantly concealed by thick unkempt curls for about ten years. And I was happy.

But I didn't want to keep my hair long all my life and in 1979 I decided to change things up a bit. In a moment of madness, I cut my hair short again. Suddenly, there I was, on the front pages of newspapers, ears sticking straight out like a wingnut. The headbands that I brought back from Japan to wear on stage, bearing slogans like 'Death before dishonour' and 'Fight for freedom', didn't help me at all, as they just pressed what little hair I had left flat against my head, drawing even more attention to my ears.

All the embarrassment that I'd endured when I was little came rushing back at me. As a child I'd cringed when it was school photo time, but this was much worse. Now my head was on national television and on the covers of music magazines. A few times while making film clips, I was asked to put tape on the back of my ears to stop them glowing when the light shone through them. This was a whole new level of embarrassment.

I refused to let vanity get the better of me and just acted like my ears didn't stick out at all. If anybody said anything, I punched them. At times I cut my hair even shorter so that people would say something – I wanted to fight.

This went on for a long time. I grew my hair long then had it shorn off at regular intervals. If my ears started to bother me, I grew it back. No problem.

My Jane loved my big ears and that was all that mattered. Our kids loved my big ears too. They would fold them and pull them and play with them.

'Oh, I love your floppy, flappy ears, Dadda,' Eliza-Jane would say, not knowing the damage these floppy, flappy ears had done to me. Still, I could put up with my ears as long as the people who loved me liked them.

In the mid-nineties, we moved to France to begin a new life. God knows I needed a fresh start at that point. I was going through a time of change that would carry on for years to come. As part of that change I decided it was time to fix my ears once and for all. For my fortieth birthday I would have my ears surgically pinned back. This was not like having my lips plumped or my cheekbones lifted to make me look younger; it was a procedure that was readily available and could in one fell swoop eliminate a source of a lot of grief for me.

Jane wasn't convinced. 'I love your ears, Jimmy,' she kept saying. But I was adamant and made an appointment to see a doctor in the south of France.

I remember walking into the doctor's office and suddenly feeling a sense of relief, especially when he told me it was a simple operation.

'*Oui*, Monsieur Barnes. Thees, eh, 'ow you say, operation, can be done right 'ere. No need for going to *l'hôpital*.'

This was exciting; I couldn't wait to be rid of those pesky ears. The doctor didn't speak great English and my French was atrocious, but we seemed to be communicating quite well. I turned to Jane to see if I was understanding everything right. She looked concerned.

'Would you like to have a general *anesthésie* or a local *anesthésie*?' the doctor asked. At least I thought that's what he'd asked.

'Does it matter? I can have either anaesthetic – is that what you're saying?'

The doctor just smiled reassuringly at me without responding. I looked at Jane again.

'I think he's saying it would be better if you had the general, Jimmy,' she whispered.

But I'd already made my mind up. He'd said I could have either, so why would I want a general? The local would be quick and, hopefully, painless.

'I'll just have a local then, if that's okay,' I announced.

Jane shot me a disapproving glance. Now she was really worried. 'Are you sure about this, baby?'

'Yes. No problem. I'm doing it.'

As I always do when I decide to do something, I'd dived in the deep end. I knew this behaviour had got me into a lot of problems in the past, but I still couldn't stop myself. I arranged to return the following day for the procedure.

Next morning I got up and took the two Valium tablets the doctor had given me and we headed for the surgery. Now I have never been very good with downers, and the Valium knocked me sideways. It didn't calm me down as it should have done; in fact, it had the opposite effect. By the time we arrived at the doctor's office, I was stumbling into walls and laughing about it while Jane tried to steer me in the right direction and stop me getting hurt before I'd even had the operation.

'Hold on to my arm, darling, and I'll get you across the road.' Jane reached for me, but I was already moving. 'No, Jimmy, the doctor's is this way. Yes, that's right, over here.'

Finally she got me into his rooms and sighed with relief. 'Sit down and sit still and I'll fill in the forms for you.'

But I kept jumping up and walking around. I was out of control.

Then the doctor took me into his office. Jane stayed in the waiting room – she couldn't bear to see me cut up.

The doctor said, 'If you sit here, I will give you the *anesthésie locale*.' Then he tried to inject me with the anaesthetic. But I was still wagging my head from side to side like it was on a swivel.

Over the course of the next forty-five minutes, the doctor tried desperately to cut and stitch my ears between bouts of me leaping about.

'What does that do?' I'd say as I swung round to look at something on his desk.

There could be just about anything hiding in this hair.

'*Mon Dieu. S'il vous plaît, Monsieur Barnes!* If you could just keep very, very still, I am trying to—'

Suddenly my head turned the other way.

'*Merde!* I will have to start again. Er, 'ow you say: keep still, please!'

This went on for the whole operation. By the time he finished, I had a bandage wrapped tightly around my head, over my ears and under my chin. I looked like a rabbit or van Gogh in his famous self-portrait – quite appropriate for the south of France. The doctor was totally rattled and couldn't wait to get rid of me. Happily, I'd felt no pain at all.

But not long after I got home, the local wore off and then I was in a world of pain. There must be a hell of a lot more nerves in my ears than I'd realised, I told myself. Of course, the fact that I hadn't been able to keep still the whole time the surgeon was operating hadn't helped either.

I was in pain for about two weeks and then, once the swelling went down, I was ready to look in the mirror.

I loved it. My ears swept back against my head just like those of a normal person. I had wanted this for as long as I could remember. Gone was the cause of so much torment in my life.

I'd decided early on that I wouldn't make the procedure common knowledge, but nor would I keep it a secret. If anyone asked, I'd explain. But no one seemed to notice, which amazed me. Some people realised something was different, but they couldn't put their finger on it.

'You look younger,' I remember one interviewer saying to me. 'Have you had a face-lift or something?'

I looked him straight in the eye. 'Don't be fucking stupid. Do I look like I've had a face-lift?' I wasn't lying, but unless he could work out what I'd done, I wasn't going to tell him.

In fact, no one has *ever* asked me outright about my ears. If they had, I would have happily spoken about it.

A few years after the operation, I was sure that my ears were changing shape. They started to stick out again. They were fighting back. But it turned out to be only just a little.

Many years on from my troubled and tormented childhood, I feel much better about myself. Am I at peace? The simple answer is yes. Does it have anything to do with my ears being pinned back? I'd have to say no. It's more to do with the fact that after sixty years of pain and struggling, I have learned to live in my own skin. And if that skin still had ears that stuck out, I'm sure I would be happy living with them as they were.

Sometimes one of my family – usually Jane or Eliza-Jane – will try to turn my ears inside out, and fail.

'I miss your old ears,' they'll say.

I haven't told anyone this, but I miss them too.

A Curse
on You

'Hey, driver, pull into that bottle
shop just down the road there,
would you please, mate?'
The driver turned off the music
and looked at me in his mirror.

'I can't understand a word you're saying,' he said. 'Where do you want me to stop? A "bottle shop" did you say?'

Maybe they don't call them bottle shops over here in Los Angeles, I thought to myself, or maybe he's a bit thick. I wasn't sure.

'Yeah, the bottle shop. You know, where you buy booze. Vodka. Alcohol. You know what I mean? There's a place just up here on the right.'

I wondered if I'd said that properly. Was I slurring my words? I didn't think so. But it was five o'clock in the afternoon, we'd been recording since about ten o'clock that morning and I'd started drinking and snorting cocaine not long after that, so I knew I might be a little hard to understand. It had been a big day. No, a big week. Fuck it, it had been a big life, and I didn't know how long I could keep going anymore.

It was the late 1990s and I was back in Los Angeles, recording with my good friend and producer Don Gehman. Once again, I wasn't in the best shape. It seemed like every time I turned up in LA to work with Don I was smashed. Poor Don, how did he ever get anything worthwhile done with me? How did he put up with me?

'Yeah, there it is,' I said to the driver. 'Next to the fortune-teller.'

I'd seen this bottle shop on La Cienega Boulevard quite a few times and had been meaning to stop by. I remembered it partly because of the fortune-teller's place next door, which looked like something from Coney Island. In its window, dark curtains with tassels flanked a table covered with a mirrored cloth and topped with a crystal ball. It was mysterious in a cheesy sort of way and had caught my eye and my imagination. But right then I was more interested in the bottle shop.

We pulled into the little strip mall and I fell out of the car. It was a stretch limousine, so I must have looked like Dudley Moore's character in the movie *Arthur*. I picked myself up and staggered into the shop.

As soon as the door closed behind me, it all went strangely quiet. The outside noise, the LA traffic, the hustle and bustle were suddenly gone, muffled by the heavy drapes that covered the walls. The smell of incense filled the air and I noticed the lighting was very strange for a bottle shop. Candles burned softly in each corner of the room. I couldn't see bottles anywhere.

Then, as if on cue, I heard the sound of violin music softly playing as a woman appeared from behind a velvet curtain. With a red silk scarf tied round her head and her dark olive skin, she looked like she could be related to Little Steven, the guitarist from Bruce Springsteen's band. She was dressed in a soft, flowing, flower-print gypsy skirt and a blouse that was too low-cut for a woman her age, and she was draped in jewels and her fingers carried too many rings. She shuffled forward slowly, as if she had an injury, and seemed to be almost a hunchback. I could hear the tinkling of her necklaces as she moved, keeping time with the violins.

She drifted closer, staring at me with eyes that burned.

I mumbled, 'Steven, is that you?'

It was then I realised this was definitely not the bottle shop.

'Sorry, I think I used the wrong door,' I said as I quickly backed away from her.

'Wait, darling, wait. There is something wrong with you. Something very bad is happening in your life.'

She didn't have to be a fortune-teller to work that out. I looked like a wreck and smelled like a brewery.

Silk head scarf, olive skin, jewellery. 'Steven, is that you?'
(Peter Coates – Inside Edge Photography)

'No I'm fine. I just need to buy a bottle of vodka, that's all.'

She reached out and grabbed my hand. 'Wait, just talk to me for a minute. It is very important that you don't leave this place.'

At this point I noticed she spoke with some sort of Eastern European accent. Either that or she had just bunged it on – I was sure she'd sounded American a second before.

'Your name, it is coming to me. It starts with a D, no?'

Now I really wanted to get out of there. 'No, it doesn't, but my middle name does. You were close, but no cigar.'

She gazed into my eyes. It was as if she was trying to look into my soul. I hoped that if she could see it, she would tell me where I'd left it. I'd need it the next day.

'Yes, of course it is. That's right. It is a family name, darling.'

Another good guess, I thought. By this point I was starting to enjoy the act. All she needed was a pet wolf. 'Very good, it is a family name,' I said to her.

'But it is so strange. I see two family names. Not first names, but surnames. Does this make sense to you?'

Oh-oh. She was getting close to something. Or was I just taking the bait?

'Yes, I do have two surnames in my name,' I admitted. I was confused. How had she guessed that?

Boom, she had me.

'You have been very troubled since the break-up of your family. But there is more you should know ...'

I started to argue with myself. Should I tell her my name? Ask more questions? I decided not to, and just get the fuck out of there. If it was a con, I was in no state to put up with it. And if she was for real, I was in trouble.

'Listen, I need to go, but thank you for the free session. To tell you the truth, the last thing I need at this point in my life is to take advice from a gypsy from Los Angeles.'

Slowly, a strange smile formed on her wrinkled face. She knew I was hooked.

'I'm not from Los Angeles, darling, I am from Hungary.' Then the smile disappeared. 'If you want to leave, go ahead. But you must know this before you leave. Someone has placed a curse on you and if you don't do something about it, you will die.'

I felt there was a fairly good chance I might die soon too. But that was just because of what I was doing to myself. I turned to the door.

She waved her hand in front of my face as if to hypnotise me. It didn't work. I was too wired.

'Come back tonight at 7.30 and I will tell you all that has happened. And who it is that is out for your blood. It is someone very close to you.' Then she laughed out loud.

I laughed nervously in response. 'I don't think I'll be back, but maybe. You never know your luck in the big city. I'll think about it. Okay?' I started walking towards the door.

'Wait, darling. You must come back this evening. If you leave me one thousand dollars, I will have all the information you need to save your soul when you get here.'

I looked at her again. She seemed even more like Little Steven now – wide-eyed and slightly crazy-looking. But I no doubt appeared much the same, so that was nothing to worry about.

'You *must* come back tonight. It is a matter of life and death. I am going back to the old country, Hungary, my home, tomorrow. So it has to be tonight. Return to me this evening, or I cannot be responsible for what will happen!' Then she held out her hand and waited for me to give her my money.

Now, I had a thousand dollars on me, but I already had plans for that money, which involved some very evil spirits too. And at that moment I had the feeling that if I gave it to her it was simply going towards her ticket out of town. So I turned and walked out.

Outside, I looked at the two shop doors side by side. One to the fortune-teller and one to the bottle shop. I had a hunch I wasn't the first person to walk through the wrong one. And the fortune-teller clearly had a whole act ready for any confused, unsuspecting drunks like me to step straight into.

I went through the other door, now desperate for a drink.

'Do you have spirits here?' I asked.

The guy laughed. 'No, you need to go next door.' He laughed again then paused for a second, waiting for me to get the gag. I didn't.

'No, I'm only kidding. What do you want? Whisky, bourbon, we got it all.'

I grabbed a large bottle of vodka and went back to my car. I'd had enough of comedians for one day.

Then, getting into the car, I started to think back over my run-in with the fortune-teller. It seemed like an obvious con, but I wasn't sure the gypsy was acting. Did she know something for real? I was so coked out and paranoid I'd almost believed her. In fact I'd thought twice about giving her my money.

'Driver, I need to go home. Right now.'

We sped off down the street.

At home I told Jane my story.

'Please tell me you didn't give her any money, baby,' Jane said nervously.

I shuffled my feet uncomfortably. 'Er, no, I never gave her any. But maybe I should go back and see her again.'

Jane looked at me with sad eyes. 'Jimmy, I don't want you to take any more drugs now, please baby. Have an early night and it will all be all right tomorrow.' She kissed me and led me to bed.

Next day I woke up feeling almost fresh and tried to laugh about what had happened, but I couldn't. Sometimes, the world has a way of warning you that you are going too far and that it's time to stop. It felt like my encounter with the fortune-teller, as weird as it had been, was one of those times. I realised then that I really had to get my life together.

The following morning I drove past the shop on the way to the studio and it was gone. Boarded up. She *had* left town. I hadn't seen that coming.

Even today, I shiver a little when I drive past her place. I wish I could drop in and thank her for that show, her advice and her disappearing act. Because she was right: someone very close to me was trying to kill me in those days. And all the evidence pointed to me.

I'm sure she would just hit me up for money again. But it would be interesting to hear what accent she's using now.

Don't Move, *Man*

Cricket is a mystery to most Scottish people. Any game that takes five days is way too long. How could you predict Scottish weather that far in advance?

You'd be lucky if you could say what's going to happen in just a few hours' time. I've been in Scotland in midsummer on days when it has been absolutely beautiful at nine in the morning, and then come two o'clock in the afternoon you're thinking that maybe you should be building an ark, and building it quickly. No, it's just too risky.

Imagine a bunch of Glaswegians on a Thursday sitting around with time to kill.

'Right, boys, let's get a game going, eh. Ah'm no working again till next Tuesday. The weather's good. What'll we play? A game o' cricket?'

'Don't be fuckin' stupit, Jimmy. The weather will only be good for aboot ten minutes. Hey, and by the fuckin' way, how did you get a job like that?'

'Ah work for an Englishman. They do this every weekend. Nothing gets in the way of their cricket.'

'Well you're no in England now, pal. And ah'm no playing cricket for five fuckin' days. Are you crazy? Anyway, I don't want to be anywhere near Danny over there if he's had a few pints and he's got a lump o' wood in his hand. He's a fuckin' nutcase. What aboot darts?'

'Aye, that's a good idea. Much safer. Then we can order drinks whenever the barman walks past.'

'Aye, aye, very civilised. Good call.'

I'm like that. I was never interested in playing a game that went on for days, partly because I have the attention span of a fence post. But when I was touring the United Kingdom back in 1988, a good mate of mine, Craig Johnston, talked me into playing a game of cricket for the charity Sport Aid, which was supporting famine relief in Africa.

Craig was a fantastic footballer who grew up in Newcastle,

222

just north of Sydney, and went on to play in the English Football League in the 1980s for Liverpool, where he became a favourite son of most fans. He succeeded not just because he was born with a God-given talent, but also because he was one of those guys who would turn up for training two hours before everyone else and not leave until about two hours after the rest of the team had gone home. He was the hardest-working man in football, and I admired him for that. So much so that I am a Liverpool supporter to this day.

I'd met Craig a few times in Australia and we'd become friends. I remember one night in the early 1980s we were out having a few drinks and he confessed to me that he'd had his hair curled because he wanted to look like me. Who does that? Was he fucking nuts? Anyway, that particular night we were in a bar and, as it happened, I'd just had my hair cut short. We were having a quiet drink when a young lady walked up to the table and said to Craig, 'Are you Jimmy Barnes?'

Of course, you can guess what Craig said. He was a cheeky bastard. 'Er, yeah, I am. What can I do for you?'

He went on to sign my name on her arm – at least I think it was her arm – and he might have even got her phone number. I just sat there quietly, saying nothing. Anyway, back to the story.

'Jimmy, it'll be great. Come and play this cricket match with me,' Craig said. 'We'll have a nice day in the country, a few drinks and a bit of a laugh. And raise money for a good cause.'

'Yeah, all right then,' I said.

It wasn't until we were driving to the Hampshire County Ground at Southampton that I realised how serious the game was.

'So who are we playing against?' I asked.

'The Australian Aboriginal cricket team,' Craig replied casually.

Now, all the young Aboriginal guys I knew were very good sportsmen, so I realised at once that we were going to get hammered and that I would be way out of my league.

'And who's going to be on our team?' I asked anxiously. It was clearly not just some mates getting together for a hit.

'Oh, you know, a few musos, a few cricketers and a few other sports people. You'll love them.'

What had I got myself into? 'Which musos and which sports people?'

Craig was a bit cagey about this, but I eventually prised it out of him. 'Bill Wyman from the Rolling Stones, David Essex, myself and a few others.'

Some of them, I knew, were very keen cricketers. Unlike me.

'And which real cricketers?'

'Oh, you know, Clive Lloyd, Steve Waugh, people like that.'

People like that? Clive was already a legend and while it was still early days for Steve, he wasn't far behind.

'Craig, you know that I've never played a game of cricket in my life? Ever.'

Craig had an answer for everything. 'It's all for a good cause and you'll be fine. I'll look after you.'

Eventually, Craig explained that the match was being held to highlight and support a tour of England by a group of seventeen Aboriginal cricketers, which had been organised to commemorate a trailblazing trip to Great Britain by another team of Indigenous players 120 years earlier.

We drove on in silence until we reached the ground. Of course we were late and everyone was waiting for us. Unfortunately, there weren't enough celebrities there to count me out of the team. I was also told that the Australian Aboriginal XI were all big fans and really wanted me to play. There was no escape.

The game was about to start and we would be batting first. I wandered into the dressing room, not quite sure what to do.

'Excuse me,' I heard someone say to me from the other side of the room. 'Aren't you supposed to be batting soon?'

I looked up and saw Steve Waugh.

'Er, yes. I'm ready.'

He looked me up and down and said, 'You can't go out to bat dressed like that.'

I was wearing blue jeans, a T-shirt and R.M. Williams riding boots.

'I don't have anything else to wear,' I confessed. 'I've never played cricket before.'

That made Steve laugh. 'Okay, put these on quick, mate,' he said and proceeded to pull out a whole kit for me from his cricket bag: white shirt, white pants and white shoes. Then he padded me up so that I wouldn't be killed. 'You'll need these pads,' he said. 'These guys can bowl pretty fast. And you are likely to get hit.'

What? No one had told me this was a contact sport.

'Where am I supposed to put this,' I said, holding up a box. I'd never seen one before.

'Put it over your valuables, Jimmy. You know, your most valuable possessions?'

He looked down. I got his drift. 'Fuck, this is serious,' I muttered.

Steve laughed. 'Yep, this is a serious game, Jim.'

I walked out to bat as Bill Wyman came off the field, moaning under his breath. 'Watch out, man, these guys are fucking seriously good.'

He'd been clean bowled for a duck. Just what I needed. I was terrified.

I nervously approached the crease.

'Great to see you here, Jimmy,' one of the Aboriginal team shouted from under his baggy green cap.

'Yeah, great to see you, mate,' said another. A few of them ran up and shook my hand.

'I love "Khe Sanh", it's my favourite song,' one said.

They seemed incredibly friendly and it was really nice of them, considering they were the opposition. But it would take more than a few how-do-you-dos to make me feel comfortable.

The bowler went to start his run-up. Was it really necessary to go back that far? Couldn't he just walk up and bowl?

He charged towards the wicket at high speed and – *boom!* – the ball hit the pitch, skipped, spun, flew just past my valuable possessions and demolished my wickets. I was out first ball.

But, as I turned to walk away with my head hung in shame, the bowler shouted at the umpire, 'No, mate. Not out. It was a no ball.'

The official laughed and replied, 'Okay, if you say so. Not out.'

The next ball was a lot gentler. Any slower and it wouldn't have made it down the pitch. I swung at it, clipped it and ran.

The ball flew high in the air then came down right where one of the fielders was standing. I was gobsmacked when he dropped it – he could just about have swallowed the thing. Clearly he was being kind too.

Looks like I know what I'm doing, but where's the ball?

I'd made a run and was safely at the other end. The fielders were all smiling, the Aboriginal guys seemingly as happy as me.

I can't remember who the other batsman was at this point, maybe David Essex. Whoever it was, I think he was clean bowled by the very next ball. I stayed in for a while at the other end as further batsmen came and went but then another wicket fell with the last ball of an over.

Oh shit. Now I'd have to face the bowler again.

As the next batsman walked onto the field, the crowd roared. I looked to see who was coming out to help me. Even I recognised Clive Lloyd, the 'Big Cat', West Indies legend and one of the greatest batsmen in history. He was the main drawcard for this event and now I was batting with him.

I was hoping to get just a touch on the ball and make a single run to the relative safety of the other end so that Clive could do his thing, but when I tried to run after nudging the first ball away, Clive could see he might be run out and told me to get back to the crease. He didn't look happy. After a couple more close calls, he held up his bat – it looked like a toothpick in his big hands – pointed at me and shouted, his voice booming across the whole cricket ground, 'Don't move, man! Unless I tell you. Okay?'

This was not a request, it was an order and there was no way I was going to disobey the captain of my team in front of this crowd. 'I'll do my best,' I said and laughed nervously.

Clive scowled and shouted, 'This is not funny, man. Just don't move!'

The next ball came in and I swung and missed. Then I hit one in the air that the Aboriginal team graciously dropped, but when I did the same again one of their fielders finally held a catch and I was out, much to the approval of the crowd.

As I trudged to the boundary, someone shouted, 'About time, you mug!'

I quickly looked up but couldn't see who'd spoken. Just as well, as I did have a big piece of wood in my hand and off the field I knew how to use a weapon like that. The spectator didn't know how lucky he was.

When I got back to the sheds, there was Bill Wyman, still angry, still moaning, still fuming about getting out. 'How come they were so nice to you?' he asked.

'They like me, I guess,' I said with a shrug. 'But at least your daughter got to see you play.'

He didn't look too happy about that and mumbled something about it being his wife, not his daughter.

Eventually the Big Cat's shoulders must have got sore from carrying the whole team. We were all out for not enough and the Aboriginal Australian XI chased down our total without breaking a sweat. I knew Clive had thrown in the towel when he asked me to bowl what turned out to be the last few balls of the game. Despite the best efforts of our proper cricketers, we'd been totally outplayed by the visiting team, who had won over a lot of new friends and admirers. Bill Wyman wasn't one of them.

When I gave Steve Waugh his gear back, he smiled and said, 'You did well, Jimmy, for a first-timer. Good on you, mate.'

He was being too kind. I'd been lousy. But at least I had played a game with some of the best in the world and survived. It was clear my cricket career was officially over, but I was happy.

Luck, Who *Needs It?*

Things seem to have a way of blowing up in my face. Everything is going well and then ... *boom!* It all falls apart.

Yet I have survived so many times when the whole world around me has exploded. When I was a child, our family was destroyed by violence and abuse. Everything we had and every one of us was left shattered and broken, but I somehow ended up still standing. Even though I'd been facing the blast, I remained alive, emotionally scarred for life but physically unhurt. In my teenage years, my friends got into fighting in gangs and taking hard drugs, and I jumped in head-first with them. We drove around the streets looking for trouble and most nights found it. Off our heads on whatever we'd taken, we'd drive at high speed, fleeing other, bigger gangs. Not all of us made it through. Some were lost to the violence. Some were wrapped around poles and disappeared in fire and twisted metal. Some died in the gutter from drug overdoses. But I escaped and went on to join a band that became the biggest musical act in the country.

Strange, don't you think? You might call me lucky, but I'm not sure about that. You might say I'm tough, but that would definitely be pushing it. I think maybe I was born unlucky, but over the years learned to surround myself with very lucky people. I am alive, in other words, because of the luck of those around me. I should be dead, but the people closest to me deserve to be alive. So here I am, still kicking after all these years.

There have been times, though, when I've come too close to the blast even for my liking. In October 2002 my family came with me to Bali for a few shows at the Hard Rock Hotel in Kuta. I'd never really wanted to go to Bali: it just didn't appeal to me. If I want to escape, I go to Thailand with Jane. But this was work, so we decided to combine it with a holiday and take the kids too. They were all older teenagers by then, except for Elly-May, who had just turned thirteen. The first few nights, the older kids went out to the Sari Club then came home and slept like logs. But the next night, instead of going out, they all came to play in my band.

Towards the end of the show, we could see the audience leaving in droves. I knew that the band weren't playing that badly, so I ran outside to see why everyone had left. The hotel section of the Hard Rock, which was directly next door, had been burning to the ground as we played. If we hadn't all been performing that night, we might have been asleep in bed. I ran into the burning building, pushed my way past the firemen and made it to our room and grabbed our passports just before the place collapsed.

Later that night, the older kids and the rest of my band went back to the Sari Club for drinks. We moved to another hotel, as there was nothing left of ours. Because it was on the far side of the island and a long way from the action, Mahalia, EJ and Jackie and the band decided to fly back to Australia the next day. Jane and I opted to stay on with Elly-May, partly because we'd been invited to a friend's place for dinner the next night. Elly-May wasn't happy because she'd wanted to go shopping, so we promised her that straight after the dinner we'd go downtown to the market at Kuta and let her buy some gifts and trinkets. But during the dinner she misbehaved and we ended up taking her straight home.

As we drove back to the hotel, we could see bright flashes, like explosions, on the horizon above Kuta, then flames and smoke reaching into the dark night sky – right where we would have been if we'd gone shopping and where our older kids and the band would have been partying if they hadn't returned home. As we learned later, two bombs had been set off in Kuta's busy nightclub district by terrorists, killing more than two hundred people, including eighty-eight Australians, and injuring over two hundred more. Fate, or luck, had stepped in and saved us.

This put me off Bali forever.

'I'm never going back there,' I announced to Jane one day.

Jane replied, 'Don't worry, baby, neither am I.'

We'd made a pact.

But a few years after that eventful night, my agent, Frank, rang me. 'Yeah, listen, some bozo is starting a new airline that flies from Perth to Bali—'

I cut him off. 'Don't want to go.'

Frank persevered. 'Hear me out. They want you to do one show in Bali and they want to pay you a fucking fortune. Just in and out. You don't have to stay more than one day, I promise.'

I made it clearer. 'Frank, I don't want to do it. I don't want to go there again. I don't care what they are paying, the answer is no.'

Frank wouldn't give in. 'Look, I want you to sleep on it and I'll call you tomorrow.'

'Frank, we can sleep on it all you like, but it's not happening.'

I hung up and it was never mentioned again. Then, months later, a good friend of ours telephoned me and said, 'I see you're playing in Bali for the launch of this new airline.'

I couldn't believe it. I rang Frank. 'I told you we weren't doing the show for the airline in Bali, in no uncertain terms. And now I hear they are advertising me as the headliner.'

Frank had an answer for everything. 'No, mate, you said that you'd sleep on it and you never rang me back again, so I assumed you wanted to do it.'

I was blunt. 'Frank, I said no. I meant no. I am not doing it.' I tried not to shout.

'Well, it's going to be hard to cancel this close to the show. It's happening in three weeks. You'll have to do it this time and just bite the bullet.'

I could tell Frank thought he had me trapped. But I turned on him. 'I don't give a fuck, I'm not doing it. You bite the fucking bullet.' And I hung up.

Three weeks later, on 1 October 2005, the night we would have been playing the show, and right where we would have been staying at Jimbaran Bay, a second lot of bombs went off. Twenty people died and more than a hundred were injured.

And the bombs didn't stop there. In 2015 I took Jane and the family with me to Thailand for a charity show. Our kids and some of their partners were part of the band, and we had three grandkids with us too: Ruby, Bella and Dylan. The youngest, Dylan, is the son of Elly-May, who had grown up by this time and married Liam. Dylan was still in his pram.

The charity had booked us all into the Erawan Hotel, the place where Jane and I had stayed when I first went to Thailand. Only now it was all new and modern. One evening we decided to go to a restaurant that was on the other side of the main road from the hotel. To get there we would have to go down in the elevator and walk to the street crossing then past a small temple on the corner called the Erawan Shrine, a little place where people went to make a wish for themselves or on behalf of a loved one. But we could see it was going to be difficult to squeeze past the shrine with Dylan's pram, as there were roadworks nearby. So we took another route, which was longer but easier with the pram.

Stunned after the bomb went off in Bangkok, 2015

As we headed off in that direction, there was an enormous explosion. A bomb had been set off in the shrine, killing twenty and injuring more than a hundred people. If we had gone that way, we would probably have been blown to pieces.

You know, now I think about it all again — surviving a brutal childhood, running wild in my youth, driving across the country in trucks and cars that were basically wrecks, risking my life night after night consuming copious amounts of drugs and alcohol, and surviving three terrorist attacks — perhaps I got it wrong. After all, I'm still here, with the best life in the world. I have a beautiful wife, amazing children, grandchildren and even great grandchildren. I am still doing what I love for a living, and getting better at it every day.

Yeah, I take it all back. I *am* lucky. Very, very lucky.

Studio
Ghosts

Every room has its ghosts, its
stories and its own energy.
You can't build that into a room.
It has to exist as a result of
things that happened there.

Recording studios are like that too. Each one has a different feel, and different ghosts. And strange things happen in studios, for no apparent reason. One minute everything is working perfectly, next minute it's all falling apart. Things disappear at odd times, sometimes for good, though often they reappear somewhere else just when you need them. Some studios suit certain people, while others don't. I've recorded in studios that just felt bad to me. The room didn't like me and I didn't like the room.

Trafalgar Studios in Sydney was one such place for me. I know other musicians who were perfectly at home there, but when I recorded at Trafalgar I always felt something was about to go wrong, and sometimes it did. We recorded the first Cold Chisel album there. That was my first taste of working in a real studio, and it was a bad experience for a lot of reasons. For one thing, Trafalgar was small, and I didn't like being in confined spaces: I felt closed in, trapped. I had this urge to escape and get as far away as I could. Plus, it was not a comfortable space and I didn't like the sound of the room. To make matters worse, there was a weird feeling about the place – maybe it was ghosts in the room – and I could not relax. Consequently, when I had to be there, I got smashed. It was the only way I could deal with it. And I couldn't wait to get out of there every night.

I think that first taste of Trafalgar forever tainted the way I related to that studio. Even though we recorded 'Khe Sanh' during those sessions – a song that really set our careers rolling, a song that people still cry out for more than forty years later, a song that means so much to so many Australians – I never grew to like it. Some of the ghosts that disturbed me there belonged to the room, others I brought along with me, but they still haunt me to this day.

I recorded the vocal for 'The Things I Love in You', from our 1998 album *The Last Wave of Summer*, at Trafalgar, and I remember finishing the song and feeling physically sick. I'd drunk a bit, but it was more than that. It was the space. I felt I had nowhere to get away from the intensity of the lyrics. I was in a little box of a room, screaming from deep down in my soul, and I had nowhere to run to. I don't think I ever went back there after that, and the experience affected me so badly that whenever I hear that song my stomach churns. I can only put it down to studio ghosts.

Many of the world's best studios have ghosts, some friendly and some not. When I walk into a studio, I can usually sense them. If it's a good feeling, I stay. If it's not, I leave. In mid-1987, I went with Jane to Woodstock in upstate New York to record at Bearsville Studios. At the time I was halfway through an album that was being produced by Jonathan Cain. We had struck up a friendship on the previous album I'd made, called *For the Working Class Man*, for which Jon had written the title track. For this new project, he and I had written a bunch of songs together, but there were two additional songs I'd written with a guy called Desmond Child. So, during a break from recording the album with Jon at Record Plant in Sausalito in San Francisco, I flew to New York and drove up to Woodstock to put down the two tracks with Desmond.

Bearsville Studios was founded in 1969 by Albert Grossman, a giant of the music world, and his wife, Sally. Moving from folk music in the sixties to more mainstream rock in the seventies, Albert had at various times managed Peter, Paul and Mary, Bob Dylan, Janis Joplin, Todd Rundgren, The Band and Gordon Lightfoot, and many of these acts had written and recorded at his studio. As you probably know,

Woodstock is famous for the major music festivals and other arts events that took place there in the late 1960s and when I went there it was still home to thousands of hippies, and a very peaceful part of the world – a bit too peaceful for my liking. But Bearsville was great. As soon as I arrived, I could tell why so many fantastic records had been made there. The rooms felt amazing: big, old and musty and full of fabulous vintage equipment, but also slightly spooky. They had stories to tell, some of them possibly dark and disturbing, and you could imagine that those stories somehow bled into everything that was recorded there.

The studio was out in the country and surrounded by fields, so there weren't many distractions. And we were only there for three days, so we didn't have time to sit around doing nothing. Desmond is an incredibly talented songwriter and producer, a little eccentric, I guess, but I liked that. He was right at home among the hippies, the brown rice and the lentils.

The songs we were to cut were 'Walk On' and 'Waitin' for the Heartache'. Both are big songs, demanding and emotional. Whether or not they sounded like my kind of songs was debatable, but I'd have to sort that out later. Desmond liked his singers to sing everything pure and sweet, and although these were not qualities I was known for, we managed to hit on a compromise: pure but not quite sweet. I tried to be as sweet as I could, but I felt that there had to be something tortured about these songs if they were going to work, partly because of the subject matter and partly because of the studio. By halfway through the first day, I was still having trouble settling into the place, so I started drinking. By the time we finished, I was well on my way to being tortured too.

Towards the end of the night, Sally Grossman turned up. She was a strong, funny, entertaining woman. But there was a sadness about her that I could feel. I knew she had a million stories to tell about Bearsville, and I wanted to hear them all. She told me that Albert had died the year before and she still missed him terribly – that was why she was so sad – and that the studio was the place where she felt closest to him. She could feel his spirit there. I'd wondered why she had come over so late at night. It was like she was driven to be there.

A bunch of us sat around and drank vodka and smoked pot. Occasionally, I'd sneak out and have the odd line of cocaine, but it clearly wasn't the drug of choice around Woodstock – too aggressive – so I kept it to myself. By the end of the night we were tired and ready to sleep, even me, surprisingly enough. So Jane and I said goodnight and we left for our accommodation, which was on the same property but quite a way from the studio. In the middle of nowhere really, and all around it was pitch black.

I didn't get a lot of sleep. I'm not that good with darkness. It scares the fuck out of me, so I was restless and kept waking up. It felt like the whole place was haunted. All through the night there were bumps and noises that didn't sound like farm animals to me. I was up and down, checking the door was locked, and I kept the lights on most of the night.

The next day, after we'd finished work, we had a few drinks with Sally again and she told us more stories about the studio.

I had to say something about the accommodation. 'Hey, Sally. That place is a bit special, stuck out there in those big empty fields. And it's very dark out there, isn't it?'

Sally's eyes got a bit of a glint in them. 'How did you guys sleep?'

I'd thought she'd never ask. 'Not that well really. There were a lot of noises and I was sure I heard someone or something at our door a few times in the middle of the night.'

Sally sat upright. 'Did you guys shut your door?'

I looked at her and laughed. 'Fuck, yes. And locked it.'

Sally shook her head. 'Didn't anyone tell you about your room?'

Now she had my full attention. 'What about our room?' I asked.

'That accommodation wasn't part of the original property when we bought it. And it wasn't until after we bought it that we heard the stories.'

I let out an audible gulp.

'Rumour has it that some farmer killed his wife in that very room with a knife. If you look at the door, you'll see marks where he stabbed the knife into the door as he was trying to get to her.'

Christ! This place was like *The Shining*. I definitely wasn't going back out there now.

'But don't worry. If you leave the door open, he just goes away. It's a bit odd of course, but many musicians find it inspires them to write while they're staying there.'

I was silent for a second. 'Are you fucking serious? I got inspired to run. And I'm going to nail that door shut tonight.'

Sally looked concerned. 'I wouldn't do that,' she advised. 'It's better if you just stay calm and leave your door open. Then everything will be fine.'

I shook my head. 'On second thoughts, I'm not sleeping there at all. Let's give that room to one of the band.'

Sally was disappointed. 'But it's the nicest room and you're the artist, so you should have it. Don't worry, the ghosts around here are not dangerous.'

But it wasn't *that* nice a room. Not nice enough to be killed in. I sat back, poured another drink and said, 'I think that the band are playing so well that one of them should have that lovely room. I'm staying right here in the studio. There are no windows and the doors are two feet thick. By the way, can I lock this place?'

The rest of the recording went well, but I never went back to the accommodation.

*

Next day, Desmond asked me if I'd mind if another artist he was working with came to stay for a day or two. Desmond was in demand. He'd recently co-written big hits like 'Livin' on a Prayer' for Bon Jovi and the Aerosmith smash 'Dude (Looks Like a Lady)', so now artists were lining up at his door, begging him to work with them. Without a break, he planned to go from one session straight to the next, an album for Bonnie Tyler, eventually called *Hide Your Heart*. As he was finishing my tracks, he and Bonnie would start on hers.

I didn't mind at all. Bonnie is a great singer, a gravel-voiced, Welsh belter, and I enjoyed listening to her sessions. Plus she was a very cool person, easy to talk to and down to earth, so we got on very well and sat chatting between sessions.

During one of those breaks, Desmond came through and said to the two of us, 'Hey, you guys. Would you do me a big favour? I'm writing songs for the new Cher album and I need to get someone to sing the demos. Would you guys do that for me? It won't take you long.'

We were happy to help, so he pulled out a few tunes for Bonnie to sing and a few for me to sing. I had to laugh, I'd never thought that one day I'd be singing Cher songs.

The song I remember best was called 'Just Like Jesse James'. Bonnie and I sang the demo together. Afterwards I completely forgot about it, until I heard the single on the radio about a year or so later. It was a smash hit and all the melodies that we'd sung, and our phrasing, were still there on the record, only with Cher's voice singing them. It made me laugh when I heard it, and I felt like I was another invisible studio ghost haunting a famous song.

Desmond went on to produce hits for everybody. He is probably one of the most talented people I have ever worked with and I would work with him again in a heartbeat. And Bearsville's studio rooms did have a great feel, just like Sally said, and the results sounded amazing. But by the end of the third day I was happy to escape the ghosts of Woodstock and get on a plane back to San Francisco and Sausalito. I had a record to finish.

*

Record Plant in Sausalito had a history too. Sly and the Family Stone had recorded some of their great records in the very rooms I found myself in. I learned that in one studio Sly had had the control room redesigned not as a separate booth but as a pit in the middle of the room. He wanted to be surrounded by the music. There was a big bed in the control pit too, all covered in red velvet. In fact, when we

Record Plant, on the dock of the bay. Now, there's an idea for a song. *(Alamy)*

worked there, some of the walls were still covered in that same material.

The pit looked like it should have been part of a bordello rather than a studio and from what I heard, the studio was like a bordello much of the time. Copious amounts of drugs were consumed there in the early seventies. Acid, weed, coke, heroin. Sometimes all at once. Often someone would have to wake Sly up to sing. One story goes like this. The group were recording 'Family Affair', one of the greatest songs ever recorded. Sly was passed out cold on the floor and they needed him to sing, so they gave him a shove and woke him up. He stood at the microphone and swayed, then, according to legend, sang the song in one take. Listen to the recording. I think it sounds true.

I also heard that at that time the studio had huge, industrial-sized bottles of nitrous oxide placed outside and the gas pumped into masks that were strategically positioned around the room, so that performers could grab one and trip out whenever they wanted to. And I thought I was bad. How the fuck did they get anything done? Mind you, in saying that, making some records is like pulling teeth, so it seems appropriate.

Clearly the place would have seen its share of overdoses and heart attacks, and maybe that's why I never really felt safe in that studio either – I'd come close to the edge many times too. There were definitely ghosts in the machines there. The engineer, Jim Gaines, had worked at Record Plant since the sixties and he seemed to know them and be at peace with them. But I wasn't.

Jim told me a great story about working at the studio with Otis Redding, one of my favourite singers. He said that Otis and his guitar player and songwriting partner, the great Steve Cropper, were making an album and some record company executives came in to hear a few of the tunes and see how things were going. This is always a stressful time for artists. Everybody has an opinion, and often ones you don't want to hear. One of these guys, in his wisdom, said, 'I like the album, but I don't hear a single.' If I had a dollar for every time I've heard that, I'd be much richer.

Otis and Steve walked out the back of Record Plant and onto the dock outside – the studio was right on San Francisco Bay – where they sat in silence, listening to the waves as they washed against the pier. They wondered what they could write a single about, then after a few minutes, as they looked across the water, it came to them. 'Sitting on the Dock of the Bay' went to the top of the US charts and gave Otis his first big hit. Sadly he was killed in a plane crash just a few weeks after the session finished and never got to enjoy his success. Did that have something to do with the studio? I wasn't sure, but Jim Gaines thought it did, and he'd have known, as he'd seen it all there: the good, the bad and the ugly.

Not long after returning to Sausalito, I had a fight with Jonathan Cain and I walked out of Record Plant and never went back. I told you the place wasn't good for me. In fact, it was such a big fight I had to leave America completely and I never worked with Jon again. He went on to bigger and better things. Well, bigger anyway. He married a girl who happens to be the spiritual adviser to Donald Trump – yes, Trump really has a spiritual adviser – and that means Jon gets to play piano for Trump now. Jon used to work with a lot of great soul singers, and I wonder if Donald sings. I fucking doubt it, and am glad I'm not there to find out.

With Michael Hutchence, one of the ghosts haunting Rhinoceros
(Tony Mott)

Anyway, I took my tapes back to Australia and finished the record, *Freight Train Heart*, in Rhinoceros Studios in Sydney. It was a smash hit and arguably one of the best records I've ever made. I said these guys were good writers.

Rhinoceros had its ghosts and stories too. It was in the same building as ASIO – in fact ASIO was on the floor below the studio – so the building certainly housed secrets. On the floor above the studio there was a regular gathering of Pentecostal Charismatic worshippers. A few times I walked out on the wrong floor to find them speaking in tongues. It was spooky. Luckily I was usually so smashed that I was listening in tongues. The noises they were making sounded like gibberish to me, but my record probably sounded pretty bad to them too.

There were definitely ghosts in the building, though, and I felt them every time I was there. Some good friends who'd run wild with me in that studio didn't make it through. Life was too tough for them. And I'm sure their spirits still prowled around inside those walls at night, screaming and looking for action. Just like we used to do in the good old days.

Where's the Baby?

The Germans love rock music. Always have and probably always will. And Germany is one of the few places where bands can go and play no-frills rock 'n' roll.

Germany was one of the biggest markets for Cold Chisel outside Australia and we toured there a lot. The German tour I remember best was one we did in 1983 with a fellow called Roger Chapman. He'd been the singer of the legendary English band Family but was by then working as a solo artist. He was very arty but he was a good guy and his audience loved our band. We were falling apart and couldn't stand our band by then, so we were glad somebody liked us.

Cold Chisel played thirty-odd shows all over Germany, opening for Roger. Unfortunately it was the tour that put the final nail in the coffin of Cold Chisel and we broke up just after it. But it remains memorable for other reasons too. One is that when we started the tour, Jane and I were new parents with a little baby, Mahalia, and we had never travelled anywhere with our baby before. It was to be a steep and gruelling learning curve for both of us.

On arrival in Germany early one morning, we rented a VW people mover to get us to where the tour was starting. We'd put Mahalia into a baby capsule, that wonderful invention that combines a cot and a baby seat in one. It wasn't the easiest thing to carry around, but it worked. We strapped her and the capsule into the car and headed down the autobahn. If you've never driven on an autobahn before it can be a bit of a shock. The Germans like to travel very fast, often driving at about two hundred kilometres an hour. I enjoy that speed too, but it was a little foggy, I couldn't really see all that well and I wanted to drive safely for Jane's and Mahalia's sakes. So there we were in our people mover, with our new baby, driving at one hundred kilometres an hour or so while Porsches and Mercedes-Benzes flew past us like we were standing still, beeping their horns and frantically gesturing at us to get out of the way.

'Aren't the Germans lovely, Jimmy?' said Jane. 'Look, there's another one waving at us.' Jane always sees the best in people.

'I'm not sure they're waving, baby. You don't wave with one finger up.' I smiled at her and grabbed a cassette tape from my jacket pocket. I'd made up some mix tapes for our drives and I had a particular one in mind for our first German trip. I slipped it into the cassette deck, cranked it up and the sound of Kraftwerk filled the car. It was perfect for these roads, and with this haunting industrial techno music as a soundtrack the countryside flowed past like a German film clip.

I liked it. But clearly Jane wasn't sure about my choice. I could feel her starting to wriggle in her seat. I turned the music down.

'This is a bit intense and I'm feeling tired. Why don't we pull over and get a cup of coffee and take a break?' I suggested.

'Yes, that would be nice. Maybe I can find some rice to eat,' Jane said, licking her lips. She always likes to eat rice, wherever we go. I thought that she might be out of luck this time. There wasn't much chance of finding rice at a German truck stop. But I just smiled at her and found an exit and pulled up outside the restaurant.

'Don't forget the baby, darling,' Jane reminded me.

'Hey, I'm all over this fatherhood stuff,' I said with a laugh. I grabbed the capsule where Mahalia was sleeping, like a baby of course, and we headed in and found seats. I placed Mahalia on the far side, tucked under the table so that the waitress wouldn't spill anything on her and none of the big German truck drivers would stand on her. I studied the menu, where the only things I could understand were 'sandwich' and 'coffee'. No sign of any rice.

'There's a lot of cold meat here and shitloads of bread if you would like that, my love,' I said to Jane. 'But I definitely don't see anything that sounds like rice.'

I could see Jane was disappointed. We were both exhausted after our plane ride and our first traumatic encounter with the autobahn.

But after some food we began to feel better, and my eyes even started to adjust to the cold, misty morning light. Soon we were ready to take to the highway again.

We paid the bill and jumped in the car. Fired up by my coffee, I was feeling more confident and it wasn't long until I was driving at a record-shattering (for me) one hundred and fifty kilometres an hour. And I was almost keeping up with the traffic.

As we hurtled along, Jane looked at me and smiled. 'Mahalia is such a good baby, isn't she? So quiet.' And she turned to check on our daughter.

Suddenly the sound of Jane screaming pierced my eardrums. 'Where's the baby?!'

We looked at each other in horror. We'd left her at the truck stop. And we were now at least ten kilometres down the autobahn.

'Fuck me! I thought you had her!' I yelled.

By this point Jane was crying hysterically. 'You carried her into the place and I thought you'd bring her out too!' Looking back now, it's funny how each of us blamed the other, when in fact fatigue was the real culprit. 'Quick, turn the car around!' she screamed.

I don't know if you have ever tried to turn around quickly on an autobahn, but it is not fucking easy. There were no exits for twenty kilometres or so.

'Don't worry, baby,' I said feebly. 'She'll be there, waiting for us.' I was trying to console Jane. But inside my head I was freaking out. And then I let slip, 'What if someone has taken her?'

That wasn't going to make Jane feel any more settled. I had to shut the fuck up.

'You were supposed to put her in the car while I paid the bill,' she said.

'I never knew we'd made that arrangement,' I replied. But it had to be my fault. Everything was my fault. I was the untogether one of the two of us and I knew it.

At last I found an exit and turned around. From there, I drove so fast that it felt like the car was about to explode, its engine revving like crazy and screaming loudly – in German of course. That was a good thing because it almost covered up the sound of Jane screaming at me.

When we reached the truck stop, I hadn't even fully stopped the car before Jane jumped out and ran towards the restaurant. I parked and followed behind her.

There was Mahalia, exactly where we had left her. No one had noticed she was there. She hadn't even woken up.

Jane pulled her from the capsule and held her tightly to her chest. I thought to myself, 'I wish she'd do that to me.' Mahalia hadn't even missed us. I was the one who was stressed. I needed a cuddle, and another coffee. I'd have had something stronger, but it was still only nine in the morning.

Then Jane leaned over and gave me a kiss and we all had a little group hug. Life was good again.

You Ain't *from Around* Here

In 2016 I decided to go to Nashville, Tennessee, to make a new record with producer Kevin Shirley. That record would be called *Soul Searchin'*.

Kevin and I have made about ten albums together and I always love working with him. On this new record I would get the chance to sing with an amazing bunch of musicians, including The Memphis Boys. They'd backed Elvis on 'In the Ghetto' and 'Suspicious Minds' and had also played with Joe Tex, Dusty Springfield (on *Dusty in Memphis*), Bobby Womack, B.J. Thomas, The Box Tops and Neil Diamond, to name just a few. They were legends and had appeared on some of my favourite records of all time, so I was very excited.

I decided that we should all fly into Memphis first, just to get a feel for the place before going on to Nashville. You know, eat some Memphis soul food, soak up the atmosphere and take a few photos at some of the great old Memphis landmarks. We also planned to visit the Reverend Al Green's Full Gospel Tabernacle Church in the city and experience a bit of Southern preaching. As you probably know, I'm not particularly religious, but I will occasionally visit an African-American church in the US because the music is such a big part of their gatherings – I've always thought that music is the best way to connect with your soul – and I'd heard wonderful stories about the services at this one. Of course, Al Green is one of the greatest singers of all time, and if we were lucky he'd be there that day giving the sermon.

Travelling with me were Jane, our friend Pierre Baroni and his girlfriend, Ginger Light. Pierre has an encyclopaedic knowledge of soul music and has helped me with every soul record I've ever made. His collection of soul recordings, all on the original forty-fives, is the biggest I have ever seen. He's also a brilliant photographer and an amazing human being, utterly unique. I could think of no better person to visit this church with. Ginger, a DJ who plays clubs in Melbourne,

'Really, Kevin, have you turned on my microphone or not?' *(Robert Hambling)*

is also pretty special and knows a lot about music too. She looks like a cross between Dusty Springfield and Ginger from *Gilligan's Island*. Also accompanying us was Philippe Klose, a German photographer and cinematographer who was filming our travels. He had done a lot of work for Kevin Shirley, and Kevin wanted the entire trip documented.

Jane was so excited. 'Oh, I hope Al is there. Do you think he'll sing?' she asked Pierre.

'He always sings. That's his thing. But it will be an interesting sermon, so be prepared. He's famous for going off on rants. Sometimes he picks on racists. Sometimes he picks on politicians. Sometimes he picks on people in the church. You never know where he'll go. Depends on his mood.'

I was ready for anything just as long as he sang.

On arrival we made our way into the church and sat down in the second row. People were looking at us as we walked in. I could understand why. Compared to the rest of the congregation, dressed in their Sunday-best, church-going outfits, we, in our mainly black rock 'n' roll clothes, looked like the Addams family.

Al walked in and the whole church stood up. Just for a second, he seemed to look our way and smile.

'Brothers and sisters,' he began, 'this world is a beautiful place. But we want to keep it like this, so …' And then he burst into song: 'Let's stay together … Yeah, we oughta stick together …' It was soulful and beautiful.

From then on, the sermon was punctuated by Al singing lines from his many hits. All were in context too: whatever he was preaching about at the time, the song fitted perfectly.

In between songs and preaching, he occasionally seemed to glance, smile or wave in our direction.

Jane was so happy. 'He's smiling at me, Jimmy.'

I assumed he was just being friendly to what was clearly a group of visitors.

On he went. 'In this world where we are getting pulled further and further apart, love is being lost. Swept away in fear and hate—'

Jane gave me a dig in the ribs. 'He just waved at me again. Isn't he sweet? Maybe it's because we're the only people here who aren't black.'

But I was too caught up in Al just being Al and breaking out into song at any given moment to give that any further thought. It was so great.

'How will we get through this time?' he asked us. 'What will it take to keep us all together? Tell me what will it take to keep us all together, children? I ask you.'

He was working his way up to fever pitch again and I had an idea of what was coming.

'Looovve and Happiiinesss' he sang, his voice as soft as silk as he dragged out each syllable to cries of joy from the whole congregation as he reached a crescendo, then he glanced our way again and appeared to give another little wave.

Jane whispered to me again, 'He's waving at me.'

This went on throughout the sermon: Al shouting, singing, sweating and crying and, every so often, waving to Jane.

At one point Al called out, 'Where is the Lord at this time when we need him most? I ask you, where is the Lord?' Then he answered his own question: 'He's right here with us! "Heeerre IIII aaaamm, baaabbyyy!" The Lord is here with you and with me right now.' And he let out a little scream – 'Oowww!' – and half of the women in the audience nearly fainted.

Most of the sermon was really beautiful, though some of it was a little on the cheesy side and some of it was out and out dark. At one point about halfway through, he took off on a tangent, ranting and raving about tattoos being the Devil's work and the Devil's writing. I think he'd spotted a few people in the audience with tatts and didn't like the look of them. He obviously thought their souls weren't going to be saved and it had triggered his anger. But he got his message across effectively, and overall the experience was magical.

After about forty-five minutes, the sermon came to an emotional end. People were standing, shouting, clapping their hands and walking up and down the aisles calling out to the Father, the Son, the Holy Spirit and anyone else who was listening, 'Lord, my time has come. Take me with you. I said, take me with you!'

Finally, the Reverend Al said to everyone, 'Come on, line up y'all, and come see me for a blessin'.'

Jane was by now ecstatic that Al had been acknowledging her throughout the service and she couldn't wait to meet him, so we both joined the queue.

When we got to the front, Al looked at Jane and smiled, and Jane smiled back. Then he said, 'Hey, girl. You ain't from around here, are you?'

Jane replied shyly, 'No, Reverend.' I think she might even have blushed.

Then the Reverend blessed us and we went back to our seats. Jane could not stop smiling and on the way out of the church she turned to Pierre and said, 'Did you see Al? He kept looking at me and smiling and waving.'

Pierre laughed. 'No, he wasn't waving at you.'

Outside Al Green's church in Memphis. Somebody save me! *(Pierre Baroni)*

But Jane was adamant. 'He was, the whole way through and—'

Pierre cut her off. 'I'm sorry to tell you this, but sitting right behind you guys was a very famous old singer, Bobby Rush, and his family. That's who Al was waving at. They're good friends.'

Jane was clearly disappointed and not entirely convinced. 'Oh. I was sure he was waving at me because I was the only Asian in the congregation.'

I looked at her and kissed her. 'If I was Al and it was my church, I would have waved at you, baby.'

And we walked outside, all now a little closer to God – and Al – and drove on to Nashville.

Money
for Bones

Today I dragged myself out
of bed. It's the first time in
two days that I've been able
to face the world for more
than ten minutes.

I've had my head buried in a pillow to stop the noise of my crying from driving everyone in the house mad. My nose is red raw and my eyes are bloodshot. I look like I've been on a coke bender for a week. But this is not some drug-induced psychosis – God knows, I've seen a few of those in my time, but those days are long gone. This is pain. Real pain. Even worse than the pain I felt when I had my chest opened up and my heart repaired. This feels like my heart has been ripped out. It's the saddest time of my life, and everything hurts.

You see, two days ago I helped my darling little schnauzer, Oliver, leave this world. My best mate, Oliver was nearly sixteen years old and he was suffering. His kidneys had failed and he had to be on a drip – it was the only thing that was keeping him alive. He lay on his bed, unable to lift his head.

Normally, Oliver lit up every time I walked into the room. He'd done that for the previous sixteen years. But now he was just too sick to move. He couldn't even wag his little tail. I looked into his eyes – the same eyes that had stared lovingly at me for as long as I have known him – and I knew that it was his time to leave. I wasn't ready for it, but he was. I had been through this eight months earlier with his brother, Snoop Dog, and it had nearly killed me then too. The only thing that had kept me going was that Oliver was still there and needed me.

But before I go into any more detail about those heartbreaking days, let's go back, back sixteen years or so, and I'll tell you about the Schnauzer Brothers. That's what we called them. That or just 'the boys'. Our boys.

*

'We really want a little black schnauzer. We saw one in the park and they look so cute,' we told the breeders. The same breeders that Jane's sister Jep and her husband, Mark – you guys know him better as Diesel – had bought their little dog from. Rufus was the best dog we'd ever met. He was smart, cute and loving, and we wanted a puppy just like him.

'As a matter of fact,' Alison, the breeder, said, 'my dog is about to have a litter of pups, and we are expecting a few little black ones. The father is black and the mother is salt and pepper. We'll just have to wait and see what comes out.'

We got the call two weeks later. There was one black puppy, and he was ours. I had already picked a name: Snoop Dog. But we would have to wait eight weeks until we got him. The whole family was extremely excited. The time passed quickly and the big day came. The dog was to be delivered on a Saturday morning.

Now I've had dogs all my life and was as keen as the kids, but I didn't expect to be so affected by what happened next.

The doorbell rang and we rushed to open the door.

'Are you ready to take your puppy?' Alison asked. Alison was a slightly eccentric dog lover who always arrived with a pack of adorable schnauzers in tow.

'James, go to the car and bring in the pups.'

James, her husband, was equally eccentric and equally enthusiastic about their dogs. He returned with a basket of what looked like balls of wool. On closer inspection, I realised they were puppies. James picked up a small black baby schnauzer and handed him to Jane. He was adorable.

My boys with their brother Rufus, and Mark. Man, we miss these guys.

'Hi, Snoopy,' I whispered as I walked up to him. My eyes kept darting back to the basket. 'Do they all have homes?' I asked. I had an odd feeling about the other puppies.

'All of them except this one here,' James said. There in the corner of the basket, away from the other puppies, was the little fat guy of the litter.

'He does now,' I said and grabbed him. 'What will we call him, kids?' I held up the little grey puppy in a scene reminiscent of *The Lion King*.

'Oliver Twist,' Jane said. 'He doesn't have a home. He has to be Oliver Twist.'

And as easy as that, we became the proud parents of two beautiful little dogs that would change our lives forever.

I soon realised these puppies were the smartest dogs I had ever met. I'd always had bigger, fiercer-looking dogs – Rottweilers, bull mastiffs, even German shepherds – but none was as smart as these two.

Thanks to Jane's love and attention, they were toilet trained within a matter of weeks. On hearing the slightest whimper from the boys, Jane would jump out of bed, scoop them up and take them outside before I'd even opened my eyes. It didn't matter if it was pouring with rain or freezing cold, Jane would still go out in the middle of the night with the puppies. Her maternal instincts were as strong with them as they'd been with the kids.

We all loved the boys and they became irreplaceable members of the Barnes family. They went everywhere with us. They came on tour and travelled in the car. I found hotels that let them stay. If they didn't like the dogs, I didn't like them. There were a few places that didn't normally permit kids, let alone dogs, to stay, but they allowed us to bring the boys every time. Kims Beachside Retreat, a great boutique beach resort in Toowoon Bay up on the Central Coast of New South Wales, welcomed my boys like they were their own. In all fairness, Kims let us bring the kids too when we weren't supposed to. It probably helped that the owners are Scottish. We would rock up at all hours of the day and night to eat comfort food and swim or walk on the beach with the dogs and kids in tow. The place felt like it was our own. We would arrive for a quick holiday and there in the fridge would be lamb bones with ribbons tied around them and the boys' names on the plates, which made the kids a bit jealous – no bones or ribbons for them. Kims will never be the same without the boys.

One hotel in Brisbane even had the pastry chef make all sorts of dog treats and biscuits for the boys. The room we stayed in there had been Queen Elizabeth's room when she was in Brisbane. It was a big apartment with a grand piano and a balcony big enough for a royal reception. It was also large enough for me and the boys to hang out on and watch the river roll by on a sunny day. There would always be a basket full of bone-shaped treats on the table when we arrived.

The boys even came to rehab with me, and if they hadn't I don't think I would have made it through. I told the staff that the dogs had a three-can-a-day dog food habit they had to kick. Actually, my dogs never ate canned dog food; I made that up. Fresh chicken and rice and seaweed were on the menu for these guys. Only the best. They were gourmet dogs.

Over time, Snoopy became more Jane's dog and Oliver became more mine, though we loved them both equally. Snoop was needy and nervous and felt safe with Jane – a lot like myself when I think about it – whereas Oliver, from

Mossy was ready for his close-up when Snoopy popped up.
(Robert Hambling)

day one, would follow me around. He would sit and stare into my eyes and grunt and purr like a cat. I had never met a dog that liked to stare into anyone's eyes. He really was special and he loved me. That might have been because I used to sneak him toast with thick butter and jam every morning. Snoopy would be up and out in the kitchen first thing with Jane, but Oliver and I would stay in bed drinking coffee and eating toast. Just as I do, Oliver liked a lie-in. Both boys would sleep on our bed, but when Jane turned in for the night Snoopy would jump down and sleep on his own luxurious cushion. Oliver, though, seemed particularly drawn to high-thread-count Egyptian cotton sheets; he would doze at the foot of the bed until Jane was asleep, then he would snuggle up next to me with his head on my pillow.

When I had open-heart surgery, Oliver sat on my bed with me the whole time I was recovering. He knew I was in pain and he was guarding me, making sure no one hurt me again. One day I was asleep and a dear friend of ours, Tony Mac, came over to visit me. Tony is a gay Glaswegian; in fact, Tony was the first gay Glaswegian I ever met. We are still good mates. He came into the darkened room and walked over to my bed and placed his hand on my shoulder to wake me. As he leaned over to kiss me on the cheek, Oliver leaped at him and bit him on the hand. I woke up to the sound of Tony shrieking, 'That fucking dog is homophobic. I was only goin' to gie you a wee kiss and he mauled me.'

I had to laugh. 'He was just defending my honour, ya durrty ol' queen,' I said in my broadest Glaswegian accent.

Tony managed to laugh about it, but he kept his distance from Oliver from then on.

Snoop and Oliver witnessed every aspect of our lives. The good, the bad and the ugly. They saw me at my best and at my worst. They sat with me while I sang and made records with some of the best musicians in the world, including Cold Chisel. They watched me cry as I wrote my first two books, and never left my side.

It was always hard to go away and leave them. And it got harder as the years went by. Whenever I pulled out a suitcase to pack for a tour or to go overseas, the boys would jump into it and sit and look at me with big sad eyes. 'How could you do this to us?' their faces would say as they climbed out of the case then turned their backs on me and faced the wall.

'Listen boys,' I would plead. 'I don't want to go away, but I've got to go to work.'

'You're deserting us. Why can't we come with you?' It was funny how I always knew exactly what they were thinking.

'I'm going out to make money for bones,' I'd say. That's what I called touring: making money for bones.

Even when Jane and I were both away, the boys were never left in doggy-care places. One of the family would always come to the house and look after them. They all loved them too. And when I staggered home feeling the worse for wear, there they would be, by the door, waiting: the Schnauzer Brothers. Howling and barking with their tails frantically wagging as I came in. They were always happy to see me. They always loved me. No matter what I had done or said. Pure, unadulterated, beautiful love. (I need to take a break to breathe for a second.)

They came to rallies with us to protest against the cruel treatment of humans by humans on Manus Island. 'Let them

I always consulted the boys when writing my books.

be free, you bastards,' I was sure I heard them bark at the politicians ignoring the cries of the crowds outside Parliament House in Canberra. If I'd let them off the leash, I'm sure they would have bitten one of them. But they hadn't had their shots for that sort of poison. Even the Schnauzer Brothers couldn't stomach that.

They were at the weddings of our children and the funerals of our friends. They were the first to greet our newborn grandchildren when they came to our house. They cried with me and I'm sure I could see them smile with me. They were part of our family.

But sadly, dogs don't live anything like as many years as humans. Perhaps the world is too cruel a place for these loving souls to stick around too long. All too soon, Snoopy's jet black coat started to turn grey and Oliver's eyes dulled a little. Then their hearing started to go. The boys were getting old.

Jane tried to prepare me for the inevitable. 'Now, Jimmy, my darling, the boys won't be here forever—'

'Of course they will. My dogs aren't going anywhere,' I'd snap back. Whenever anyone mentioned anything about the dogs dying, I could feel my eyes start to water and a pain shoot through my heart. A pain I'd never felt before.

'Baby, I'm just trying to let you know that one day—'

'I don't want to think about it. They're not going without me. Come on, boys, let's go for a walk.' And we would leave the house before Jane could finish.

A few more years rolled by. Long, beautiful years. Jane and myself and the dogs, we had each other's backs, we were happy together. I'm sure there were times when the dogs stopped Jane and me fighting with each other. They were there for us through thick and thin.

But gradually Oliver got slower and Snoop started to sit and stare at the walls.

'Poor old Snoop, he looks lost,' Jane finally said to me one day. 'We should take him to see Karina.'

Karina was our vet. We first met her when she was working at the North Shore Veterinary Hospital in Sydney and looking after Rufus, Jep and Mark's schnauzer. When Rufus was just a few years old, he was running across the floor in our house when he suddenly sat down and couldn't get back up. It turned out he had blown a disc in his back and would never walk again. The veterinary team suggested Jep and Mark should buy a set of wheels and a harness so that Rufus would still be able to get around. So that's what they did, and from then on Rufus was as happy as he had always been. Everybody at North Shore loved Rufus, especially Karina. So when we got our own schnauzers, we knew who to go to. Karina was skilled and caring. More importantly, she loved our boys. So I trusted her. But I could feel myself panic at the thought of something being wrong with Snoopy.

Sure enough, Karina came back with bad news. Snoopy had brain cancer.

'Well, he can have chemo,' I spluttered. 'It works for humans. It's got to work for him.' Later, I cried and held on to Jane as we lay in bed.

Jane whispered, 'It might not work, though, so you've got to be prepared for that.'

'Don't talk in front of him. He'll hear you,' I said getting out of bed, picking him up and holding him. 'It's got to work.'

Snoopy had seven rounds of chemotherapy until the day came when Karina helped me make the hardest decision of my life. I trusted Karina and we had already made a pact when Snoopy had first got old and sick.

'Karina,' I'd said to her one day, 'when it's time to say goodbye to my boys, I need you to tell me. Because I won't be able to make that decision.'

Karina had promised me she would tell me when it was time.

Snoopy fought on for weeks, but he got steadily worse. He wasn't eating and he became slower by the day. Finally, Karina said, 'Jimmy, it's time. If you wait too long, he will start having fits and it will be too much for him or you to take.' She had already explained this and I knew I couldn't put it off any longer. I didn't want him to suffer. The time had come.

The family gathered to say goodbye, all taking turns to hold him and cry. Poor Snoopy must have been sick of people weeping all over him. Karina came to the house and we sat out the back in the sun and Jane and I took turns holding our darling Snoopy in our arms. Jane would hold him then I would take over as she began to cry.

Karina gave Snoopy the first injection. I had a lump in my throat that would not go away. He looked at me then he relaxed. The needle had calmed him down. His eyes half-closed and his little tongue hung out of the side of his mouth. I held him even tighter.

'Look at the beautiful flowers, Snoopy. This is your house. The Schnauzer House.'

This really was the Schnauzer House. Jane and I had bought this place in the country so that the little puppies would have somewhere to run free. It became so special to all of us, and it was ours because of the boys.

Karina put her hand on my shoulder. 'It's time, Jimmy.'

She placed the second needle into the drip before I could even think.

'It's done. Just hold him and he will slip away slowly.'

Tears poured from my eyes and rolled down my cheeks and onto Snoopy's face as I kissed him. I felt his breathing slow down and finally stop. A gaping hole that would never be filled opened up in my heart. Snoopy was gone. I held him as Jane and EJ both cried out loud. I didn't want to let him go. Jane brought out a soft blanket and we wrapped him up so he wouldn't be cold. It was over.

Karina took our little guy away and said she would make sure he would be looked after. She would bring me his ashes.

I climbed into bed and I thought I might never get up again. But Oliver needed me. While I was lying in bed crying, he was still there, waiting for me to reach out to him. He had lost his brother after all.

Eventually I got up and we went for a walk. The neighbours all asked me where Snoopy was and I was sure I saw a few of them shed a tear as I told them he had passed. When we got back home, I climbed into bed again with Oliver and slept for days. At one point I woke up to Snoopy bounding into the room and jumping onto the bed. He leaped onto me and I held him. It was so beautiful. But then I woke up and he was gone. In that dream he'd come to tell me he was all right. And that I had to be there for Oliver.

I got out of bed again. Life went on, though it was not the same. Oliver seemed to know how I felt and he never left my side. The only time we were apart was when I was on tour or had to be away for other work commitments. He was too old to travel anymore. His touring days were over. But he lived

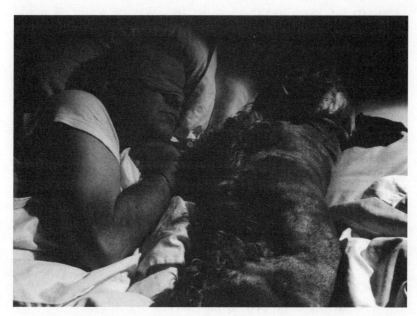

What I wouldn't give to wake up next to this guy, Mr Oliver.

on and was there for me for many months. Always happy to see me. Always ready to wag his tail and lie down next to me and stare at me lovingly. He continued to eat toast in bed in the morning, even though he wasn't supposed to. We liked to lie there watching television. It was our secret. Our walks got a little shorter every day. But he was still happy.

Then I went away for a week and a half for a holiday with the family. As was usually the case, I couldn't wait to get home to my boy, and the whole time we were away I made video calls to our friend Claudine, who was staying with him, so that I could see him (he loved her too). Claudine always said he was fine, and he seemed well. But she told me later that he had been struggling; she just hadn't wanted to worry me.

At the end of the holiday we flew back into Sydney at six in the morning and drove straight to the country to see our little guy. I got out of the car and ran to the door, calling, 'Oliver! Where's my boy?'

There was no sound. This was very unusual. I looked around the kitchen. There, on the far side of the room, in his bed, lay Oliver. He couldn't even lift his head.

'My darling little boy, what's wrong?' I called.

I held him. He was clearly sick, very sick.

'Let's get him to the vet quickly,' I said to Jane.

I carried him to the car and Jane sat in the back seat holding him. We drove all the way back to Sydney. As I drove, I called Karina. 'He's not well,' I said to her. 'He can't even wag his tail.'

She was calm. 'Come straight to me and we'll do some tests.'

I put my foot down and sped the whole way.

Oliver was put on a drip and blood was taken. His spirits lifted as the fluids went into him, but he still couldn't move. Karina wanted to keep him in overnight, but I didn't want to leave him. I wanted to take him home with me.

'All right,' she said. 'We can set him up at your Sydney place while we find out what's happening to him.'

So we took Oliver home, with a drip still attached to him. Almost as soon as we got there, Karina called me. 'It's not good, Jimmy. His kidneys have failed and he is not in a good way.'

This was the news I had dreaded.

'There's not a lot we can do except keep him comfortable,' Karina continued. 'I think all his organs are shutting down, poor little guy.'

I didn't want to hear that. 'Surely we can do something. He's looking better already,' I said desperately.

'Let's keep him comfortable and on the drip until we decide. You don't have to rush anything. But he needs you to be strong,' Karina advised.

So we set Oliver up on a bed in our lounge room at our house in Sydney. His drip was attached to one of my microphone stands to keep the bag up high. I set up a rollaway bed next to him, and Jane slept on the couch, but we spent most of the time lying on the floor beside him.

Next day the family gathered to farewell our other little boy. They all took turns talking to and hugging Oliver. In my heart I knew he wasn't going to make it, but I wanted to fight for him. He hung on for three days. Each day I watched for signs that he was on the mend. They never came. He could hardly eat or drink. The drip was all that was keeping him going.

'Jimmy, you have to think about him now. He needs you to make the decision,' Karina said softly to me.

I knew she was right. 'Okay,' I managed to say between sobs, 'but can we take him home to the Schnauzer House? I want him to leave us there, not in the city.'

'No problem,' Karina replied. 'Whatever you need to do. I can be there too. We will all go down in the morning.'

I knew I had only one more night to spend with him. But I still hoped for a miracle. That night I prayed to God to help him. Why did I think God would help? He'd never helped me before. I would have to be the one to help my friend.

We arrived at the Schnauzer House mid-morning the next day. Oliver had already been given a full dose of fluids through his drip, so we removed the bag, keeping the cannula in place in case we needed it. I made Oliver some fried bacon – one of his favourite things – and a fresh piece of toast, thickly spread with butter and jam. He ate the bacon; it was the first food he'd eaten in days. Then we took him into his garden (remember, this was the Schnauzer House) for a walk, but he only managed a few steps before he had to sit down.

We fed him the toast. 'Yes, he can eat toast now. He can have whatever he likes,' Jane said quietly.

I had to break it to her then that he'd shared my toast every day. Oliver and I wanted a clean slate.

My heart was pounding, but I was calm. I had to be, for my mate. We walked slowly around the garden for another twenty minutes or so. We weren't alone. I noticed a kookaburra sitting in the tree watching us. He didn't seem scared at all, just sat and looked at us as if he knew what was happening, like he was there to help us get through the day.

Then we took Oliver inside. And we all cried. I carried my little friend into my room and put him on the bed. This was his favourite place to be, the place where he'd spent most of his time. I turned on the television and we lay together on the bed for the last time.

'I'm going to give him something to settle him down now,' Karina said. 'Just so he doesn't get scared.' She injected something into his little leg.

I sat at the foot of the bed and held Oliver's face close to mine. He never took his eyes off me. 'I'm here, son. Don't worry, I will never leave you.' My nose was touching his and we stared into each other's eyes.

'I'm going to administer the last shot now, Jimmy. Don't worry, he won't feel any pain. He'll just close his eyes and drift off.' Karina moved towards the drip.

'I'm here, my darling boy,' I said. 'I'm here.'

He never even blinked. He just kept looking at me. I held his face and looked straight back into his eyes. They never closed.

'He's gone, Jimmy.' Karina touched my shoulder. 'He's gone.'

I couldn't believe it. 'Oh, Oliver, I love you so much. My darling little boy.' I howled like a baby.

It was time for Karina to take him away. I didn't want him to go, even though I knew he had to. So I prepared him. I had a soft woollen blanket in the colours of the Scottish flag and I wrapped him carefully in that. I know schnauzers are originally German, but Oliver was my boy. He was Scottish.

He looked perfect. Like a highland warrior. And he was finally at peace, with no more pain.

I still feed that kookaburra nearly every day.

*

What helped me get myself out of bed today, two days after Oliver's death, was another dream. Just as had happened with Snoopy, Oliver visited me in my sleep. It was amazing. Both of my little guys were running and barking as we walked down the road and to the river. I knew then that they were still looking out for me.

*

Karina comes over, bringing me Oliver's ashes in a beautiful little wooden box, just as she did with Snoopy's. Their names are on the boxes. I put them on the shelf in our room, near our bed, and on top of each box I placed their little collars with their nametags on them. I've also kept a little bit of Oliver's fur from his last haircut so that I can still smell him.

Every night I put my hands on the boxes and tell my boys how much I miss them, and I cry. The Schnauzer House seems empty without them. Life seems empty.

Then one day I'm sitting in the garden and I notice that the kookaburra that was there on Oliver's last day is still visiting. He lands on the tree next to me and I hand-feed him toast and meat. Afterwards, he just sits there, staring into my eyes. He knows I miss Snoop and Oliver. And he reminds me that they are still with me, every day.

I feel them near me, and I hope they never leave.

Alligators

The Royal Bangkok Sports Club
is a prestigious place to hang out
in Bangkok, and it's like an oasis
in the middle of that bustling,
blisteringly hot city.

The club consists of restaurants, tennis courts, a gymnasium, steam baths, massage areas, swimming pools and a golf course, all wrapped up in a horse-racing track. Believe it or not, this is where I learned to play golf, during one of my first trips to Thailand around 1980.

Now, I know golf was invented by the Scots, but it has been refined by the Thais. Playing golf in Thailand is a new experience. For a start, the courses are perfectly manicured. Swarms of Thai greenkeepers cover the course daily, watering the grass and hand-plucking each and every weed. The result is fairways that are perfect, and greens that are even smoother. It's a club rule that every golfer must take a caddy out with them, not only to help them through their game but also to repair any damage done by hack golfers who think that they might be the next Tiger Woods. The Thais are very serious about their golf.

On arrival at the club, you are met by an official who assigns a caddy to you. Your clubs are carried right from the boot of the car until your game is over, when they are cleaned and placed gently back into the boot they came from. Most of my Thai friends have their own special caddy. Your caddy can be a coach when you need one, and a handy scapegoat if you mess up. Some people have more than one caddy – a clear sign of wealth. You can even have one for every individual club if you feel like it. On many days, I've seen groups of ten or so people walking around together: two players, with one caddy each to carry umbrellas to block out the sun (the Thais don't like to be in the sun), two caddies to carry the clubs, two more to advise on putting and, of course, one or two to handle all the betting that goes on at every hole. The Thais love to gamble too.

I was a beginner, so I only had one caddy. His name was Lek. To get me started, he took me onto the driving range and basically showed me how to hit a ball.

I had of course bought myself the best clubs I could find. This is something that all golfers do worldwide. Whether you can play really well or not at all, you never let that stop you spending a fortune on your equipment. The thinking is that if you have great gear, your golf will be better. I had Ping Beryllium Copper hand-forged clubs with specially cut square grooves on the face that helped spin the ball so that you could, in theory, land it just about anywhere you wanted. This was state-of-the-art equipment, the best you could get in the early eighties. The latest technology. In fact, those square-cut grooves were quickly declared illegal. But none of it helped me anyway, because, obviously, I couldn't play golf. Sure, I looked marvellous. I had the best shoes, a cool shirt and fabulous pants. But there was still that little issue of not knowing how to play.

Undaunted, Lek took me through my clubs and found one or two that he thought I might be able to swing properly. Then he pointed at the rest. 'Get rid of these. No need them,' he said to me. 'You waste your money.'

I was ready to join my group. It consisted of a few young guys who were married to Jane's cousins or friends. They had even better clubs than me and they each had a few caddies. I noticed there were also a couple of other men, who were running ahead of the group, like scouts.

'Who are those guys?' I asked my faithful caddy.

'Alligators,' he said casually. I had no idea what he meant.

On this particular day – and this only happened about once a month – there were horse races on the adjacent track.

At such times, the golf course was modified and shortened so that all play took place inside the race course. This meant the round was a few holes shorter, which suited me just fine. But it also meant that at some point we would have to play one or two holes that ran right in front of the grandstand. There could be up to five thousand people in the stands on race day, and as they waited for each race to start, they were often bored, drinking heavily in the sun, and in need of entertainment.

But I would worry about that when I got there. Right now, I just had to get started. Lek passed me the club he felt I could do the least damage with, my five wood, and I waited to take my first shot. It's always the hardest, with all the members sitting around the clubhouse, watching as you go out. And in this case the members were mostly locals from very wealthy families, and they included some of Jane's relatives, so I was nervous to say the least.

My group all hit off. I would be the last to play. As I watched the other players, any confidence I had left drained away. Every other player in my group seemed to know their shortcomings and how to compensate for them. Each ball, even if it flew through the air in a big arc, eventually landed somewhere near the middle of the fairway.

When my turn came, I stepped up, had a practice swing – and dug a hole in the grass.

'Ah, sorry about that. I think there might be something wrong with this club. Are you sure it's right, Lek?' I said as I tried to stuff the grass back into the gaping divot.

'Club good. Your swing no good.'

Couldn't he just lie a little? Make me feel better? Anyway, that was enough practice. I squared up to the ball and swung like a rusty gate.

Whoosh.

I had missed the ball completely.

'Just practising. Nothing to see here,' I joked nervously.

I lined up my shot again.

Crack. The ball sailed through the air. Straight at first, then fading slightly to the right. Well, maybe 'slightly' is the wrong word here. It flew so far right that it crossed onto another fairway, rolled on, then seemed to splash into a pond. I turned to my caddy.

'Good shot,' he said, hardly able to look me in the eye.

'Really?' I replied, but he had walked off without me. It seemed he was a man of few words.

I was covered in sweat already, but I ran to catch up with him, expecting him to fish my ball out of the pond, if we could find it. I arrived roughly adjacent to the spot where I thought my ball had gone into the water and there it was, sitting up on a tuft of grass. You couldn't have placed that ball more perfectly if you'd tried.

'That was lucky. I thought I'd seen it splash into the water. I must have been wrong.'

Lek just shook his head. I had survived my first shot.

As I walked up to the ball and got ready to play my next shot, I noticed the 'alligators' were prowling a few hundred yards in front of us. Was it my imagination or were they wet?

Lek went to give me the same club I'd used previously.

'Don't you think I need a different club for this one?' I asked. 'It's not half as far.'

He looked at the bag and then at me. 'Why? You can't hit other clubs yet. This one good.' And he shoved it into my hand.

I swung again with all the style and grace of a cave man clubbing a small furry animal to death.

'You need slow down. Can't hit so hard yet.'

'People have been telling me that for years, mate, it's not going to happen.'

This time the ball flew left in what golfers call, for a right-hander, a hook.

'Fore!' screamed Lek as my ball miraculously missed the head of a man playing in a group coming the opposite way. I slowed down so that I wouldn't have to face my near-victim. But I could see even from a distance that he wasn't happy.

After a few more shots I made it to the green. Multiple putts followed until we finally finished the first hole.

'What did you get, Jimmy?' one of my playing partners asked. I looked at my caddy.

'Sip.'

'How many?' I asked.

'Sip,' he said again.

'No, how many shots?'

'Sip – ten.'

Yes, of course, *sip* meant ten in Thai. Clearly, I needed to get a better handle on the language too.

I rubbed my hands together. 'That's not bad, is it?'

That was when one of the guys told me that I should have been finished in three.

'Maybe it will take a bit more time until I master this,' I joked.

My playing partners weren't impressed, and as the game went on I only got worse. And soon it dawned on me why they called these guys that ran in front of us alligators. Their job was to jump into the water every time a player hit a ball into a lake, pond or stream, then fish it out and set it up for the next shot. This is a small but valuable service that I have never seen anywhere except Thailand. I would have to tip them when we finished. A lot.

As we walked up to the next hole, I realised to my horror that it was directly opposite the grandstand. A slight cheer rang out as we appeared on the tee. The other boys all hit off to mild applause. Then I marched up. Whenever there's a crowd I always try to look confident, even if I'm not.

Lek gave me the same club. The five wood. The only one I could remotely connect to the ball.

'Are you *sure* this is the right club?' I asked under my breath.

'It the only one you can hit.'

I took that as a yes.

This was going to be bad. I had a practice swing and tore up the turf again. I could hear what sounded like quiet laughter coming from the stand. My knees were shaking. I pulled back the club and – *crack!*

It sounded good, but I couldn't see it. As I walked back to Lek, the spectators roared. My ball had landed on the green, not too far from the hole.

There and then, I made up my mind that golf is always better when you play in front of a big crowd.

I never hit another good shot that day. Luckily, I wasn't betting, so I kept my money. But I did see Lek collect a wad of cash from the other caddies. I think he'd bet on me to lose. I should have got a cut.

Trouble in
Paradise

After Jane's stepfather, John
Mahoney, was appointed High
Commissioner of Kiribati, Jane
and I decided to take a trip there.
If we could find it.

I couldn't work out why John or anybody else would be posted to Kiribati, as it was hundreds of kilometres from anywhere and seemed to be nothing but sand and water. As I learned later, it's made up of thirty-two tiny coral atolls spread over millions of square kilometres of ocean, which these days are on the point of disappearing under water thanks to climate change. What I did know at the time was that the islands had been keenly fought over during World War II because they occupied an important strategic position. I knew this because I watched too much television and I'd seen a program about the Battle of Tarawa on the show *The World at War*. It was one of the most fiercely contested battles of the Pacific campaign, and the Japanese had defended the place until every last drop of their army's blood was spilled. Since Kiribati had gained its independence from the UK in 1979, John would later tell me, Russian and Chinese ships had constantly cruised the area, keeping an eye on the place and looking for an opportunity to build their own bases there – something that continues to this day.

I was intrigued by the history, but our main reason for going to Kiribati was for us and our baby, Mahalia, to spend time with Jane's parents. We decided to make the trip in 1984. To get there we had to fly to New Zealand and then hop from island to island. I'd never been anywhere so remote before. I remember touching down on one island and looking out of the window as we landed on a grass runway lined with palm trees. I felt like I was in an Indiana Jones movie and quickly looked around the plane to see if anyone in the cabin was holding chickens. There were none, thank God. The door opened up and someone dressed in a sarong and sandals and carrying a briefcase quickly got off. Then, in next to no time, the plane taxied to the end of the runway and continued on to the next island. Every stop seemed to take only minutes.

On one of the islands the plane came to a halt next to a small grass hut and I sat staring out the window in disbelief as the locals walked across the runway in front of the plane carrying bunches of fruit. I was expecting them to come to the door and try to sell us something, but it became evident that they were only taking a shortcut across the runway on their way home from or to a market.

Finally, we reached the capital of Kiribati, Tarawa. The island wraps around a coral reef and is about fourteen kilometres long but only two or three hundred metres wide at any one point, so every part of it has ocean views. The sea was flat and clear and bright blue. It looked amazing.

Although it was very hot, every now and then you could feel the soft breeze off the sea brush across your face. I was told the weather on Tarawa was the same almost every day of the year, except when the occasional wild storm came in out of nowhere and then disappeared as quickly as it arrived.

I loved it.

Nothing on the island moved quickly. There were hardly any cars, and the few I did see travelled slowly, avoiding the large potholes in the dirt roads. The people walked at a snail's pace, usually from the shade of one palm tree to the next — almost everyone seemed to spend most of their time sitting under a tree, avoiding the burning sun.

There was one hotel and from what I could see of it, it didn't look very impressive. A bit like a chicken coop with windows. But even that chicken coop had a view of the bright blue ocean.

Luckily, we were staying with John, and Jane's mum, Phorn. They'd had to have their own place built from the ground up, but it was finished by the time we arrived, a beautiful big house facing a sandy beach. Most of the rooms were on the upper floor and the whole house was built on stilts in case of storm surges. But our room was downstairs, on the ground floor, and from it we could walk out the door, straight onto the sand and down to the water's edge, where Jane's dad's beautiful boat was moored. The holiday was shaping up to be a lot of fun.

During the first couple of days we did nothing but relax, eat and walk around the island, recovering from our journey. On the first night we sat and listened to the local children's choir sing as the waves rolled softly onto the beach. The children sounded like angels. I remember asking how hard it had been to teach them to sing so well, and one of the elders replying that they had no lessons. Music was as natural to these kids as breathing. They all picked their own parts and just sang.

For a long time I kept a recording I made that night and I would listen to it and be transported back to the island, back to the sea. Unfortunately, I eventually lost it. But if I sit quietly anywhere by the ocean, in my mind I can still hear those children sing.

Life on the island seemed to be idyllic. It was as if the rest of the universe had just passed this place by and time had stood still. Tarawa was an eternity away from the stress of the modern world. Within a few days, it began to rub off on me and I started to relax.

Then one afternoon John called us up to the living room and said, 'Hey, you guys, why don't you see if you can leave Mahalia at home and I'll take you out fishing?'

Sounded good to me.

'Maybe your mum would like to spend time with Mahalia,' I said to Jane as we all went down to the beach to take a look at John's boat.

But Phorn wasn't too keen. She loved her granddaughter but was worried about being responsible for her. I couldn't understand that, as she seemed to have about four maids. Surely they would help.

I whispered to Jane to ask her again.

This time Phorn completely lost it. 'I'm not your babysitter,' she yelled. 'Don't think you can just dump your child with me and run off.'

I couldn't believe what I was hearing.

'I'm not your slave,' she went on. 'You watch her yourselves.' She was getting really heated, and I was flabbergasted. I could tell that Jane was angry too.

'Are you fucking serious?' Now, I thought I had said this to myself, but I must have let it slip out. Oops.

That got Jane's mum even more worked up. 'I *am* serious. You mind your own child. I'm *not* going to do it.' And she turned and walked back towards the house.

Jane screamed something at her mum in Thai as she walked away. She was fuming too.

At this point my Scottish temper really kicked in and I saw nothing but red. I turned to Jane and said, 'I don't want to be here any longer, baby. Let's get the fuck off this island.'

All of a sudden Jane was surprisingly calm again. Only a few seconds before, she had been yelling her head off. What was going on here?

'Just relax, Jimmy,' she said. 'Mum is worried, that's all. In any case, there's only one flight a week off this island, so we can't go anywhere.'

But I was still furious and wasn't going to calm down. 'I don't give a shit how worried she is. I don't want to stay in her house. I'll check into the hotel.'

Jane tried her best to settle me. 'Just forget it, Jimmy. The hotel is not open at this time of year. We'll have to stay here with the family. The soonest we can leave is in five days.'

I had made up my mind, though. I was out of there. 'I'll find somewhere else to stay. Anywhere!'

Jane just laughed and began talking to her dad. 'Is something wrong with Mum today, Dad?' she asked him.

I didn't wait for his reply but just turned and stormed off to our downstairs room. And there I sat and stewed. I was trapped like a rat. I could sleep under a tree or I could stay in my room. I'd never been good with camping, so it seemed I had no choice. But whatever it required, I wasn't going to be the first to give in.

Where I come from, families don't just fight, they feud. Disagreements can last for years. I had a fight with my mum once and we didn't speak for two years – until Jane insisted I call her. In fact, a Scot can hold a grudge for a lifetime, so I wasn't going to get over this in a hurry. None of this 'kiss and make up' shit. The only kiss that would be thrown around where I came from was a Glasgow kiss. That's a headbutt, just in case you haven't heard of it.

So there I was in our room, pacing up and down, cursing under my breath just loud enough for them to hear me upstairs. Surely one of them would come down and try to calm me down. Maybe even apologise.

No one did. It appeared I was on my own.

After a while I could hear the sound of laughter. Jane and her family were all back in the house and joking and talking as if nothing had happened. I couldn't believe it. I was sure I even heard Jane say, 'Just let him sit down there for a little while and he'll get over it.'

No, I would not! This was so strange to me. How could they fight like that and then forgive each other and be so happy again so soon? I wasn't having a bar of it. I made up my mind that I would continue to sulk in the basement alone. I was going to stay mad until someone apologised, no matter how long it took.

All afternoon, Jane and her family remained upstairs, happily playing board games. I stood at the door, looking out to sea, but not even that calmed me.

As the sun went down that night, I heard Jane's mum shout to her, 'You'd better take Jimmy something to eat, darling.' Soon after, Jane came down the stairs carrying a plate of delicious fish. Freshly caught that day. This was obviously a peace offering. But it wouldn't work with me.

'Mum wants you to eat, baby,' Jane whispered, trying to placate me.

I stood firm, cold as ice. I walked around the room pouting, feeling sorry for myself and throwing clothes against the walls. 'I don't want her fucking food!'

Jane just smiled, left the tray and returned to the warmth of her family upstairs. I picked at the food. Just a little, though. I didn't want them to think I was really eating it.

I kept sulking for about three days, refusing to talk to anyone but Jane. At night she held me and tried to talk me round, then the next day she left me to stew and went off to spend quality time with her parents.

After about three days, I felt like a fool. I had settled down, was starving and had started to come to my senses.

Maybe this was how life was supposed to be. Maybe this was how real families related to each other. It was okay to argue, it was normal. Fight, but then just get over it. Don't hold onto things until it's too late and it's impossible to back down, make peace or forgive somebody.

Yeah, they were right. Life shouldn't be about grudges and feuds. It's too short for that kind of behaviour. Maybe, just maybe, my family had it all wrong.

Surely not?

The Sweet *Taste of* Success

Back when my son was six years old and in the early years of primary school, I became the coach of the school soccer team. The Under Sevens to be exact.

The school, which all my kids attended, was a beautiful little country school in the Southern Highlands. This was long before we started calling the game by its proper name in this country: football. I grew up playing football and loved the game. I refused to call it soccer. It was Association Football. When I was a kid, I would sneak out of bed before anyone else in the house was awake and run to the oval to be the first at training. I would have my boots on my feet from sun-up to sun-down every day. I practically slept with my gear on. Most kids in the area were the same. We played all day long. I got pretty good at it too, but as soon as I joined my first band and became obsessed with music and girls, my football career took a back seat.

Jackie's school team weren't that good, if the truth be known. But they were only little kids. When Jackie first started playing with the team, I would take him to his games and cheer for them. I eventually noticed that they didn't have a proper coach. A different parent took on that role every week. No wonder they weren't winning any games, I thought. They needed someone who knew what they were doing. Someone who had experience. Someone who could motivate them. Someone who could pass on their own lifetime of knowledge to these young boys and girls. But they couldn't find anyone like that, so they got me to coach instead.

I decided I could at least help the kids enjoy the game and maybe even learn something about it along the way. But it was easier said than done. Anyone who has ever coached a team of seven-year-olds will understand. I arrived at the first training session and none of the kids wanted to do anything but wrestle and run wild. I sized up their strengths and weaknesses, which were a little out of balance: the weaknesses

Jack and Clare: best friends and my two best players

far outweighed the strengths. If I could only get them to run around with purpose, I thought. Learn a few skills. Then they might even win a few games.

The school was not like any of the schools I went to as a child. For a start, these kids weren't tough. They were all gentle and happy and only wanted to play for fun. Now, that was not the way most of the great footballers I knew had grown up. For kids in working-class Britain or in poverty-stricken parts of South America and Africa, football offered a way out of their hard lives, out of the poverty and abuse that many of them put up with every day. And if that opportunity came along, they had to grab on to it with both hands and fight to keep it.

These kids were different. They didn't need to escape anything and their parents had already mapped out affluent, privileged lives for them. From this primary school to this high school and then on to that university, eventually leading them to the job their parents wanted them to have. Whether they won or lost a game of football was not going to make any difference. It took me a while to understand this, and when I did I started to relax and enjoy my coaching job.

The first game the team played with me as coach was a massive success. They all ran after the ball enthusiastically, at the same time. They looked like a swarm of bees or ants converging on the ball. No one held their positions. As soon as the other team got the ball, they took it up the other end and scored. But our kids all had a good time and every one of them got to be a part of the game. They did get beaten 14–0, but that wasn't important.

'Mr Barnes, did we win?' one or two of them asked as they ran off the pitch, smiling and screaming.

What could I say? 'Yes, you did win. Well done, everyone. Let's all go to the ice-cream shop and celebrate.'

And with that we would all jump into their parents' cars and hit the town. This went on every week we played.

At the Wednesday afternoon training sessions I would get there and find all the team running around like crazy. It was a challenge to get them to practise.

'Right. Everyone line up over here.'

And they would straggle over and almost form a line.

There was one boy who just couldn't keep still and was constantly running off and crashing into other kids. His name was Dean. Even when he managed to stay in one spot, he seemed to vibrate with energy. Dean was a good kid, but he was wild and I couldn't work out the best way to keep him focused.

'Dean you're not listening to me,' I'd say.

He would run in a small circle and then fall over.

I'd ask the team to perform a drill and suddenly there would be chaos again.

'Dean, pay attention, please.'

Then I'd continue with the coaching while Dean stood and made dinosaur noises and jumped on the back of the player next to him.

'Right, Dean, I think you need to run around the oval once and then come back,' I'd say. And off he'd go at breakneck speed.

While he was gone, I'd try to teach the other kids how to pass the ball. But Dean was so quick he'd be back before too long and disrupting the session again.

I'd look at him and say. 'Okay, Dean, you know what to do.'

And off he would go, running around the oval again.

This went on for most of our training sessions. If Dean continued to misbehave, I told myself, he'd at least become the fittest player in the world.

It wasn't until a few years later that we realised Dean suffered from ADHD. He turned up at our house for one of Jackie's birthday parties and he was the most laid-back kid there. Dean's mum looked a lot more at ease too. She told me about his diagnosis and it all made sense. Poor Dean. I felt bad about making him run so much, though he did love it.

The toughest kid in the team, the captain, the one who was scared of no one, was Clare. A great kid, funny and caring, Clare was a bit of a tomboy and bigger than most of the others. She was the only girl in the team, but she was fast and strong and loved playing football. Her flaming red hair blew in the wind as she ran and crashed into groups of young boys, sending them flying through the air. Clare and Jackie were best mates. They both played the game really well and loved to practise, and they would take every exercise I showed them very seriously.

Despite my efforts, though, the team didn't improve. Every weekend they would get thrashed and then celebrate at the ice-cream shop.

Eventually one of the parents complained. 'I don't think you're working them hard enough. You need to teach them more ball skills.'

I hate parents who push their kids too hard, so I looked him in the eye and said, 'They are only fucking six and seven years old. Give them a chance. Just back off and let them be children.'

But I got word from the school too that I needed to lift my game as coach. So I did just that. I enlisted my dear friend Craig Johnston, who had played for Liverpool FC and was one of the best players Australia had ever produced. He didn't do a lot of coaching clinics for schools as small as ours, but he agreed to help me out because he was my mate. He turned up at the next Wednesday training session with two potential future Socceroos and ran a football clinic. These were the luckiest kids in Australia. It didn't get any better than this.

At the end of the training session I looked at Craig. His hair was standing on end. 'What do you think of my squad, mate?'

He shuffled his feet awkwardly and said, 'They need a lot of work. It might be best if you just let them have some fun. They don't have to win, Jimmy.'

We both laughed.

'My sentiments exactly,' I said, and we took the team out for hot chocolate and cake.

Things went along nicely after that. I don't think we ever won a game, but we all had a good time. Despite some of the parents.

One day I spotted the father of one of the boys who was playing in defence screaming at him, as if he was a professional player, 'Get back, you bloody idiot!'

I hated this sort of behaviour, so I walked his way.

'Run, you bloody lazy kid,' he was shouting. 'Your team is going to lose because of you.'

He was way out of line. It wasn't the first time I'd noticed him pushing his kid, but now it had escalated to abuse. It was nasty. This guy was one of those dads who had never made it as a footballer and wanted to live his life again vicariously

The coaching clinic. Not many teams get this lucky.

through his son. He was bitter and twisted. By the time I reached him, his son was on the ground crying. I couldn't work out why the referee hadn't said something to him.

I turned on him. 'Why don't you shut the fuck up and leave the kid to play his game? Did you hear that word, you moron? It's a *game*. Now back off, or you can try to push me around if you like.'

I was in his face and he didn't like it. Suddenly the referee, who hadn't noticed the father cursing and swearing at his son, was right next to me. He seemed to think I was the one who had been yelling at the kid on the ground. I tried to explain, but he'd made up his mind and he blew his whistle and ordered me away from the pitch. I was on report.

Word got back to the school and I was sacked as coach. It's not cool to threaten parents, apparently. Even if they are arseholes.

The team went back to having a different coach every week and never got the chance to win a game. Every now and then I would wait around and take them all for ice cream.

Unlike most of his team-mates, Jackie had big plans when it came to sport. He wanted to play football for Scotland or cricket for Australia, and if neither of those worked out he wanted to play drums in my band. If he'd had his way, he would have done all three. He went on to be a really good footballer, developing his skills at high school and becoming a great goalkeeper. But Jackie didn't want to play for just any old local team. He had dreams. Dreams of playing in the big leagues in Europe. So he practised and practised.

I had a cousin who was the head coach of Dundee Football Club in Scotland and he offered Jackie a trial at the club. He wouldn't have done that if Jackie hadn't had the talent, though. That's not the way things work in Scotland. You have to earn every break you get. Jackie eventually spent about ten months living in Dundee and training with the first team before he tore the ligaments in one knee, which ended his career. He didn't sit back and feel sorry for himself, but quickly moved on to pursue another passion. He got himself into Berklee College of Music in Boston and became an amazing musician.

I'm so glad Jackie turned to music, as now I have him playing in the engine room of my band every night. A lot of kids think that making music is about becoming famous, which means they're doing it for the wrong reasons. But Jackie knows that you make music because you love it. Because you have to. You don't have a choice.

It was a shame about his football career, though. And mine as coach. Still, we can laugh about it all now. And every so often, after a show, I'll take Jackie out for ice cream. For old times' sake.

Indoor,
All-weather
Golf

The road goes on forever. Well,
it seems to when you're on a tour
of a hundred venues. Day after
day, night after night, till you
don't know where you are.

Eventually you go crazy. I know. I've felt it. I call it road fever. It affects everyone differently, but a lot of the time touring musicians end up doing stupid things just out of boredom. We've all heard stories about Led Zeppelin gluing furniture to the ceiling of their hotel room. Or bands tossing their television sets out of windows into swimming pools. I know these sorts of stories seem far-fetched and may sound like urban myths, but after forty-five years or more on the road I'm here to tell you they are not.

Sometimes boredom isn't the only factor. Sometimes these things happen out of spite. Many hotel managers have it in for rock 'n' roll bands. Certainly, I've stayed in hotels and motels where the management clearly regarded us as second-rate citizens and troublemakers, only after their women-folk and their money, and decided to give us a hard time. One time we were touring and played at Goulburn in New South Wales. The management at the motel we were staying at hated the fact that a band had checked into their precious establishment, and they went out of their way to make sure we wouldn't come back. At first, they were just unhelpful. But as the stay wore on, they became downright unpleasant.

On that particular tour I had Jane and my children with me, so we weren't being wild at all. We played our show and came back to the motel to rest without causing them too much grief. Jane, myself and the kids all climbed into bed and, as was usual for us during the night, all the kids ended up in our bed. In the wee hours, Eliza-Jane, my number-two daughter, who was about five at the time, had a nosebleed and left a bit of a mess on the pillow and sheets. Given this was a 'family motel', we were sure the staff would have seen such things before and would not think twice about it.

We had breakfast and moved on to the next town. I think it was Griffith. When we went to check into the hotel we had booked, they wouldn't let us in. Apparently the manager of the motel in Goulburn had rung ahead and told them we'd had a debauched party with a bunch of girls in my room. I think they thought we had been sacrificing virgins in my bed.

I tried to explain and even took the kids into reception to prove my point, but they didn't believe me. Not one hotel in that town would let us stay. They must have spread the word. I was so angry that I have never forgotten it. If I ever have no money and end up staying in that shithole of a motel in Goulburn again, I will get them back.

I have to confess that I've occasionally retaliated to hassle from hotel staff. One effective strategy was to order a plate of prawns or a large glass of milk and, instead of consuming them, hide them in the roof space above the room or inside the back of the television. No one would notice anything until the band was hundreds of kilometres away. Then they'd get a whiff of a rather bad smell that no amount of cleaning seemed to get rid of. It could be weeks until they discovered the little gift you'd left for them.

As I said, though, most high jinks are the result of boredom. One time we stayed at a hotel in Coffs Harbour. It had just been updated and even though it was a bit tacky, it was clean, and the staff and management were friendly. My room, the Honeymoon Suite, had a large shell-shaped spa bath right next to the bed. I tried not to imagine what had taken place there, particularly as the management had told me that rugby league teams from Sydney stayed and partied at the hotel while they were having training camps. I was never going to go anywhere near that bath. I even wore my thongs in the shower.

After our show was finished, we returned to the hotel to find all the lights out and the bar shut. There was nothing to do. Not even any late-night television. It can take hours after a gig to come down from all the adrenaline. Luckily, we had taken a large bucket of booze back to the hotel and myself and a few of the band decided to have a quiet drink. Well, it started off quiet.

After a while we were desperate for something to do. I was heavily into golf at the time and had taken my clubs on the road with me. I hadn't wanted to leave them in the car in case they were stolen, so I'd carried them into my room and left them next to the bath. To kill time, we started a putting competition, playing for money. I placed a glass at one end of the room and my drummer Tony Brock, my guitar player Jeff Neil and me started putting balls into the glass. We were all quite competitive, so it quickly got rowdy. And the more we drank, the rowdier it got.

After finishing a bottle of vodka, I was keen to make the game more challenging. So I placed the glass on the bedhead and we started unsuccessfully chipping balls towards it. But it wasn't long before we got bored with that too.

'Right, guys. Let's raise the bets and make this more exciting,' I announced. 'I think it's time we started using the driver.'

It all went downhill rapidly from there.

'What's missing here?' I wondered. 'You guys watch golf. What is it?'

Tony looked at me and said, 'Golf was invented in Scotland, right?'

Where was this going? 'Yes, but what's your point here?' I asked.

'If this was in Scotland, the weather would be much worse, wouldn't it?'

Of course he was right, but what could we do about that? I thought long and hard, and then it came to me.

'Okay, guys, the game is changing.' I rummaged around in my golf bag and found my wet weather gear. I put it on then grabbed the bucket we'd used for the booze and filled it with water. 'Now we are playing indoor, all-weather golf,' I proclaimed.

The game went like this. Whoever was taking the shot had to wear my wet-weather gear. When they were in the middle of their backswing, one of us would throw a bucket of water over them. That made it fun! And more difficult – as we were using a driver, none of us got a single ball into the glass. But we did leave a lot of holes in the wall above the bed.

The game went on for hours, and by the time we finished we were ankle-deep in water. The room was completely trashed.

Next morning as we checked out, I took the manager aside and confessed to what we'd done. 'Listen, mate, things got a little out of hand in my room last night.'

He looked at me. 'Are there any bodies?' he asked calmly.

'No, no bodies,' I assured him.

'Well, what's the problem?'

I was feeling very guilty. 'You'd better come and see it before we go. You'll probably want to charge me a bit of money to repair it.'

Off we went to the room. It looked like it had been hit by a tornado.

He took one look and laughed. 'It's not that bad,' he said. 'You should see what the footballers do to the place.'

I shuddered to think. 'You can just fix it and send me the bill if you like,' I said sheepishly. 'Very sorry, mate.'

'No, don't worry about it,' he replied. 'I'll just tell people that you did it and charge them more for the room.'

Thank goodness some hotel managers have a sense of humour. For years, whenever we played Coffs, we stayed with him at his hotel. Though he did ban golf from that day on.

The *Antarctica* Letters

Every year the members of the Australian National Antarctic Research Expedition invite selected guests to a big party at Australia's Davis Research Station.

It's called the Midwinter Festival. But, of course, there's no way that anyone could or would go down to Antarctica in the middle of winter. The place is frozen over and the temperature is minus forty degrees, on a good day. Believe me, I've played to some pretty cold audiences in my time, but not even I'd be tempted.

In any case, rather than accept the invitation, the idea is that you write back to them with your excuses for not making it. You can say anything you like as long as it's entertaining. Obviously they're sick of hearing each other's stories and want some new ones to share while they sit around rubbing their hands together to get some sort of feeling back into them, checking to see if the person sitting next to them still has a pulse, dreaming of Bondi Beach, and waiting six months or so for the sun to come up.

One day I must get down there and surprise them, though I think I'll try it in the summer. It's only minus twenty then.

June 2014

Hi all,

Jimmy Barnes here and, unfortunately, not there. I know that I promised I'd join you, but fate and the elements had other ideas.

I planned my expedition thoroughly while lying in my hammock on the beach in Thailand. If you haven't been there, you're not missing a lot: the coconuts are a tad too fresh, as are the natives. I believe the local girls are extremely fond of heavily bearded men and women. I have found that it's better if I and my group of beautiful assistants soak in as much sun and sea as possible before setting off on an expedition. Better for the morale of the team.

But I digress. I planned to set sail from South Georgia Island. Well, when I say 'I planned', I mean the crew planned – I would meet them much later when I arrived in Antarctica in my helicopter. In a cruel twist of fate, disaster struck the boat halfway. It has been stuck in pack ice now for a month, and as I was bringing the bulk of the provisions with me, things on board started to get desperate pretty quickly. Luckily for the crew, in my cabin there was a large supply of vodka and a little something I'd picked up on my recent climbing trip to Colombia (some of the best walls I've ever climbed, by the way). So they were fine for the first few weeks. They weren't hungry, though they were a tad aggressive. I like my crews aggressive! The last few weeks they've taken to drinking martinis with a twist of penguin – delicious, so I've heard. The first mate ran off with a rather good-looking leopard seal and was last heard saying that the beast reminded him of his wife back home in Double Bay.

So, suffice to say, I'm afraid I won't be joining you for the winter. A damn shame, as I've just spent the last few days getting a good healthy layer of blubber smeared all over me to keep out the cold. What a senseless waste of a good whale.

Oh well, chaps and chapettes, keep up the good work. Let's try to lock in a date for next year, but best do it soon, as other offers are coming in fast. I've been asked to lead a nude attempt on Everest from the treacherous and very, very windy Tibetan side. Sounds challenging, eh, what?

Yours comfortably,
Jimmy 'I laugh in the face of danger' Barnes

PS Sorry I'm late with the letter, but this week we had a family tragedy. My uncle, who drank a bottle of whisky every day for forty-five years, died yesterday. Tomorrow we are going to his house to beat his liver to death with a stick. His wife was so grief-stricken she drank a bottle of varnish. She had a horrible end but a lovely finish.

*

June 2015

Dear team,
As I sit here, the wind is screaming outside my door. It's cold and dark and it doesn't look like it will get better any time soon. I can hear the howling of the dogs outside. The poor bastards haven't stopped doing that for days. Their mournful calls seem to be getting weaker and they sound like they won't make it through another night. They are huddled together, hoping their combined warmth will keep them alive.

My last human contact was five days ago. A group of frightened young Englishmen, carrying all they owned on their backs, were trying to walk out of here. They waved and mumbled feebly as they disappeared out of sight. It was their last chance to make it home to their families, who waited, praying that they would come back alive. We may never know if they got there.

I hear a far-off rumbling like the sound of a thousand drums. Low and constant, it has been my only companion for a long time, and that rhythm is all that's keeping me alive. I haven't eaten in two or three days and no water has passed my lips in even longer. This is hell.

But besides that, Bondi is much the same as when you last saw it. Sorry I can't be there with you all for the winter. I know where I'd rather be, and so do you.

Jimmy Barnes

*

June 2016

Dear team,

I haven't heard from you for a long time. Are you still having rock shows down there and, if so, can I come down? I know I haven't stayed in touch, but, fuck, you guys hardly ever write back. I'm lucky to get a letter once a year. And when I do get them they are wet and smell like seals. But let's not go on about that. I forgive you.

Now, what about those rock shows? I hear it's a bit warmer down there these days. If I'm not mistaken, the other day I saw it was twenty degrees above zero. Fuck. I won't even have to repack after Tahiti. And I guess I'll have to sell my snowshoes. I wonder if you could have them turned into tennis racquets.

I don't know if you've heard, but rumour has it that your research facility is being taken over by Club Med. Don't worry, I have bought shares in the company and I will endeavour to make sure that, after we build the pool, spa, golf course and tennis courts, we'll set aside some space for you to work in. And it will still look exactly as it does today. Except for the sushi bar. Blubber is all the rage in Sydney at the moment. If you want to eat there, I would suggest you book now.

I told the company that there would be no need to buy ice machines. It was the thing that sealed the deal (no pun intended). There is still a bit of ice hanging around, isn't there?

I have posted you some things you might need while you wait for the resort to be built, including bathers, sunscreen and, of course, clippers for your huskies. Too hot for all that fur.

Yours tropically,
Jimmy Barnes

My Girl's Got *Superpowers*

'I don't smell as good as you,'
I said to my Jane one day.
'Sorry, let me rephrase that.
I don't smell as well as you.'
Either way it was true.

My Jane smells better than anyone I have met, and she has the best sense of smell of anyone I have ever met too. It's a heightened sense. I know that it is a curse at times, but it can also be a help. Jane can smell food from a great distance and because of that I know we'll never go hungry. She can also smell whether food is good or bad – she says the smell of the oil that's been used normally gives it away. This saves us from having to walk into bad restaurants. If it's rotten, she knows immediately, and we keep moving.

But that's not her only talent. She can also shop at high speed and from great distances too. As an example, one day in the early 1990s we were driving on the Cahill Expressway heading for the Sydney Harbour Bridge. Jane was sitting happily in the passenger seat gazing out the window. Music was playing on the CD player. Remember those? CDs? The format that would change the world. 'You will never have to buy music twice again,' the ads would say. 'CDs are indestructible.' Great, I always thought, I must buy some of these. Then I'd fuck them up within days of buying them.

Anyway, I digress. We were driving towards the Harbour Bridge when Jane suddenly turned to me and said, 'Did you see the legs on that table up there? Absolutely beautiful.'

I turned the music down, to just below eardrum-shattering volume.

'Pardon me, darling.' I turned and smiled at her and for a second continued to stare as the afternoon sun shone through her thick black hair. She is a breathtakingly beautiful lady. Then I quickly turned back to driving.

'Did you see the legs on that table up there?'

I took a quick look out of the passenger-side window,

trying desperately not to smash into the car in front of me. It's very hard to shop at high speed.

'Er, where darling?' I asked, rather confused. I was confused a lot in those days.

'In the window of that building over there,' Jane replied, pointing to one of the many high-rise buildings that line the Cahill Expressway. I couldn't see the building, never mind the window. I certainly couldn't see a table.

'They were really fine, beautifully crafted.'

I glanced at her legs. 'Yes, they are,' I said.

Jane smiled at me.

'Do you want me to drive there and have a look?' I asked.

'Yes, please, Jimmy,'

We had to go all the way across the Harbour Bridge before we could turn around, so it was a while before we got back to the CBD. We found a parking space then headed into the building in search of an antique shop that seemed to me very hard to locate.

'How do these places sell anything? No one could ever find this place,' I mumbled under my breath as we stepped out on the fourteenth floor.

'Well, I did,' said Jane. 'It's right there.' She pointed to a door further down the hallway.

We walked into the shop and, sure enough, on the other side of the room, by a window that looked out over glorious Sydney Harbour, was a table.

I peered out of the window. Twenty minutes before I'd been on that freeway below, and now here I was, surrounded by antique plates and silver candelabras. And, of course, tables.

I looked carefully at the one Jane had spotted. I'd always thought that if you'd seen one table, you'd seen them all. But now I had to acknowledge I was wrong.

'Pretty bloody good legs on that table,' I remarked.

'I know. That's why we're here,' said Jane patiently.

Before long we were the proud owners of a very old and very wobbly but very nice table, with the best legs in Sydney.

Now back to Jane's other superpower, her sense of smell. I particularly remember one incident way back in the mid-nineties. I've said it before and I will say it again, there are a lot of blanks for me in the nineties, but this episode stands out. We were doing the last show of a tour in a club in the 'Twin Towns', Tweed Heads and Coolangatta, on the Queensland–New South Wales border. As usual, we had a support band playing before us. I don't really recall much about them, except that they had a young, fresh-faced singer and were pretty good. I know that because they made it through the show without getting killed – our audience were pretty tough on support bands. Besides that, the only other thing I remember about them was that they were very polite.

The singer came into our dressing room after we had finished to thank us for the show and said, 'Aw, it's so good to get to play with you guys. You were grouse.' Then, after a pause: 'Your crew have told us that youse are having an end-of-tour party. Maybe we could come to it and catch up for a chat there. If youse wanna.' And then he left the room.

I looked at Jane. She had a look on her face that I know all too well. It's the face that she and her sisters all make when they are doing something they call 'auto-block', a breathing technique that helps them block out any really bad smells.

'You okay, my love?' I asked.

'Did you smell that?'

I looked around the room. The whole band, including me, were soaking wet and must have all smelled bad. I could see the other guys in the band quickly sniffing themselves in case they were the ones offending Jane.

'What? No, I didn't smell anything. What was it?'

'I don't want to be rude,' Jane said, 'but that guy smelled really bad.'

One of Jane's pet hates is the smell of overly scented body spray – the kind often used by teenagers – mixed with strong body odour. It's like torture for her. I can understand that, of course, but because I don't have her keen sense of smell I hadn't noticed it.

Jane leaped up and opened the window to the dressing room. 'We have to get out of here before I'm sick,' she whispered to me with tears in her eyes.

Before long, we were in the car, driving to our hotel for the end-of-tour party.

'I can't believe that you don't smell those things,' Jane said to me with a puzzled look.

'I've spent years touring and hanging out in dodgy dressing rooms,' I replied. 'In fact most of the clubs we've played over the last twenty years have had old toilets for dressing rooms. If I had your sense of smell, I would have had to retire long before now, baby.'

We drove on in silence. I pulled up in the driveway of the hotel and got out of the car. Jane stepped out too and immediately said, 'That singer's here. I can smell him.'

There was a strong sea breeze blowing and we were standing in a driveway that was like a wind tunnel.

'Come on, baby. You couldn't possibly smell anything out here,' I said. Besides, the crew had promised me that they had not given the address to anyone, especially the other band, so I was sure there was no way the singer could have been there.

'I think you are imagining it, darling,' I said, trying to reassure her. 'Anyway, he's not coming to the party, he's not invited.'

'He's here. I can tell,' Jane insisted.

We walked into the reception of the hotel and were given directions to the party. We had to go about fifty metres along an outside walkway then into a large function room. The party was full of record company and radio people. You could always spot them in the old days. They wore satin tour jackets and their pants were way too high. There were also a few of the crew, their families and assorted guests. It wasn't a huge party, but it was reasonably busy. I prepared to settle in for a drink and looked around the room, trying to find a comfortable spot.

My eyes came to a sudden halt. There, on the far side of the room, was the singer and the support band. The singer waved, then started walking through the crowd towards us.

'Shall we go now, baby?' I looked at Jane and then at the door.

'Yes, please,' she said.

And before he could reach us, we were gone.

As we left, I said to Jane, 'You really do have a great nose. And your legs are pretty cute too.'

How Not to *Succeed in* the Music *Business*

In the 1980s in America, a group of independent record pluggers – we called them the Indy Promo Cartel – helped record companies sell their wares.

These guys were the kings of radio. Offer them enough money and they would guarantee that your song would be played by radio stations. They could make or break an artist.

Everyone in the music business danced around the pluggers, doing whatever they asked and paying them whatever they asked for. In turn, many of the pluggers were prepared to do almost anything to gain the goodwill of the radio stations, and a few years later a bunch of them were jailed for supplying hookers, drugs and money to programmers. Maybe I was in the wrong business.

My record company at the time, Geffen, was just like all the other record companies in America, in that it had become dependent on the pluggers. It was the only way record executives knew to break new music. You had to get the pluggers on side or you were fucked.

The plugger Geffen depended on was one of the biggest. For fear of violent retribution, let's call him Harry Stone. Harry was highly respected, above board and extremely well paid. He even had his own convention, a huge weekend of music that was held annually. Every record company sent their best promotion people there, along with any newly signed artists, to go and kowtow at the feet of Harry the great.

Now, bowing and grovelling wasn't something I'd been taught to do. Where I came from, if you wanted something, you took it. And if they wouldn't give it to you, you smashed them. So, when my record company promo guy – with his perfect teeth, extremely well coiffured hair and neat beard – insisted on me going to the convention, I wasn't keen.

'Jimmy, I need you to go and be on your best behaviour,' he pleaded with me.

It's not easy to look tough wearing this much eyeliner.
(Frank Gargani)

I'd just come off the road in Australia and had travelled overnight to LA. With a little help from a few of the other passengers, I'd drunk the plane dry. So I wasn't feeling too helpful at the time.

'Who the fuck is Harry Stone anyway?' I asked in a slightly acid way.

'Jimmy!'

I really wasn't interested.

'Jimmy, look at me. Harry is the most important guy you could meet in the States. If he likes you, your record might get a chance. He controls radio.'

This was like waving a red rag in front of me. 'What? I have got to be nice to some radio adviser if I want any success in this country? Is that what you're telling me? It has nothing to do with the quality of the music or the fucking hard work that we've all done? Or the great songwriters and musicians I've worked with? It all comes down to some bloke with a head that belongs on radio waving his hand – which we have just filled with money, by the way – and giving me his blessing? Is that what you're saying?'

He looked confused. 'Yeah, that's pretty much it.' He was clearly stunned that I had learned so much about the business in such a short time.

'Fuck that. I don't want to go.'

He begged again. 'We need this, Jimmy. And I will be there with you every step of the way.'

I still wasn't happy. 'Doesn't sound like we will be stepping anywhere. You mean we will be crawling?'

He had an expression on his face that suggested he'd heard me but didn't believe what I was saying. 'So, I can count on you then? Best behaviour and all that, okay?'

'Yeah, yeah, yeah. Whatever. You guys will do anything to sell records, won't you?' I'd never liked the music business.

He was already on the phone, organising flights. We were on our way to Florida.

*

I woke up as the plane touched down at Fort Lauderdale. We were picked up by a limo and taken to the hotel where the convention was to be held. As we got out of the car, the driver handed a suspicious-looking package to the promo guy, winked at me and said, 'Have a great night.'

The hotel was vast and luxurious, and every record company in America had booked a huge suite. Smaller showcases would take place in these rooms, bigger ones in the function room on the ground floor.

'That's where you'll be playing tonight, Jimmy,' said the promo guy. 'It's going to be great. Everybody who is anybody is going to be there.'

'What time am I on?' I asked.

'You hit the stage at 6 pm. First up.'

I was worried. It was already 5 pm and it looked like most of the guests were just arriving. I went to my room and got myself ready to sing. My band had just flown in.

At 5.30 there was a knock at the door. 'Hey, dude. You ready to rock. Let's go!'

I headed out and followed the promo guy down to the foyer.

At six o'clock we hit the stage.

There was no one there. Apart from the odd waitress and, of course, my promo guy in the front row, grinning from ear to ear. I was thinking he must have opened the parcel the driver had given him.

By the time we finished the set, maybe two more people had arrived. I wasn't happy. I went back to my room and the band headed back to the airport.

I had of course stocked up in case of emergencies. I had a bottle of vodka and a little something I'd picked up in LA, thanks to a very dodgy friend from South America, and I was in the process of destroying myself when someone tapped on the door. I opened it to the promo guy.

'Hey, Jimmy. That was a great show. Why don't you come down to our suite and meet a few of the other artists?'

I wasn't feeling very sociable. 'There was nobody fucking there. What the fuck are you talking about?'

He was still smiling. I wanted to punch him.

'Hey, calm down, big fella,' he said as he grabbed my shoulder. My head snapped around to look at where he'd put his hand and he quickly withdrew it.

'Listen, man. These things have a way of working out. People are already talking about how good you were.' His eyes were looking away from me, so I knew he was lying. But at least he was trying to cheer me up.

'Okay. What room are you in?'

As he walked away, he shouted back, 'Twelve-fifteen, man. It's the best suite in the hotel. Let's go!'

We walked down the hallway to the elevators. 'Are you sure you want me to meet these people,' I asked warily. 'I'm not the best person to have at one of these things.' I was worried, as I had already destroyed the vodka and put a dent in my letter from Colombia.

'Come on, you'll have a great time. There are some wonderful artists here.'

We wandered through the hotel to suite 1215. The scene was like a birthday party for a real loser. There were lots of drinks and snacks, coloured lights and a big sound system, but no people.

'Hey, rock star, what do you want to drink?' the promo guy asked.

I looked around the room. We were still the only people there. So he had to be talking to me.

'Is anybody else coming or is this it?' I asked. 'I don't like crowds, but this is fucking ridiculous.'

He shuffled nervously around the room. 'Yeah, man, it'll be busy soon. Everyone is on their way here from other showcases. What's your poison?'

If there was something that would have put me out of my misery I would have gladly taken it.

'A large vodka. Unless you have some real poison. If so, give me a vial of hemlock, no ice.'

He laughed awkwardly and offered me a line of cocaine. The party got marginally better.

Then the doorbell rang.

'Come on in,' called the promo guy. 'Everyone, this is Jimmy Barnes from Australia.'

Taking up most of the doorway was a bloke who was the size of a small truck. He walked in with his entourage of two, both of whom were nearly as big as he was. Suddenly the room felt crowded.

'How are you doing, Jimmy?' the guy's voice boomed across the room. When he reached out, I noticed his fist was the size of a leg of lamb. He grabbed my hand and almost broke it. 'My name's Tommy.'

Then I realised I was staring at his forehead, which was covered in scars. It looked like it had been sliced up with a knife.

'Pretty good scars, eh?' he growled. 'You probably don't know this, but I'm a wrestler. And I did these scars myself with a razor blade to make me look tougher. Also, it means I bleed easier when I get hit, so it's good for the show.'

I was flabbergasted. What was this guy doing at a music convention? The drugs had kicked in and I couldn't hold my tongue. 'Why are you here tonight?' I asked as politely as I could.

'Well, you see, Jimmy, the truth is that I'm getting a bit old for the wrestling game and I'm trying to start a new career in the music business.'

I must have looked a little baffled at this point because that's certainly how I felt. I was not feeling comfortable at all in Florida, and this was making it worse.

'So, you're working for the record company, are you?' I said slowly.

'Hell, no!' he boomed. 'I'm a singer.' His face lit up with pride. At least, I think it was pride. It might have been the result of too many steroids. 'What do you do?' he asked.

'I'm a singer,' I said quietly. Every man and his dog at this convention was a singer.

I'd never heard of this guy, and I got the feeling he wouldn't be the best singer in the world. I figured he might be a novelty act, and I felt a bit embarrassed for him.

'What do you sing?' I asked.

He laughed out loud and roared, 'Let me play you a bit of my record. It's brand new and I'm gonna be a rock star.'

He walked over to the CD player, looking like a Yeti that had wandered in from the wild and was about to smash the equipment. But he knew how to work it and before I could even move his record started playing.

It was the worst-sounding piece of shit I'd heard for a while. And I've heard some bad shit in my time. But his two friends were very impressed. The first song finished. He looked at me. 'What do you think?'

I was speechless at first. Then I turned to the promo guy and said, 'If he's taking up singing, then I'm taking up fucking wrestling.'

I said this without thinking of my own safety. That gorilla could have turned on me and ripped my bloody arms off. But he didn't. He thought I was serious. 'Hey, great, well if you need some help with anything, call me, and I can show you a few moves,' he said and gave me a goofy but warm smile. He seemed to think it would be as easy to make a wrestler of me as it would be for him to become a singer. It was at that point that I realised the wrestling I'd watched on TV as a kid was even more fake than I'd thought. Though, as he towered over me, it became clear that I'd need more than a few moves to break into that 'sport'.

He gave me his card and said, 'Call me when you get to LA and we can go to the gym.'

I once again shook his leg-of-lamb hand and, trying not to say anything that would prompt him to kill me, headed for the door.

'I'll be right back. I just have to get something,' I muttered.

Bewildered by the night that was evolving around me, I went back to my room, took all the cocaine I had and washed it down with a large glass of vodka. I felt like I was being pranked. Were these people serious?

I decided to go for a walk around the hotel and see what else was happening musically in the other suites. It had to be better than our showcase.

I heard music coming from a few different rooms but nothing really grabbed me until I walked past a really big suite with its door wide open. I looked in and there was Stevie Ray Vaughan with another guitar player I didn't know. They were just sitting on chairs playing guitars, but they were both amazing. Three or four other guys in their fifties were standing around in their satin tour jackets watching them and rubbing their hands together. They looked like they had dollar signs in their eyes.

I walked in and joined the audience. I had sung with Stevie a few years earlier and was a big fan. So I thought I'd wait until he took a break and say hello. We had a lot of mutual friends.

I nodded politely and listened to the incredible music. They finished the song and there was silence, just for a second. Then one of the onlookers, the biggest and loudest of the group, stepped forward and announced, 'This guy is amazing.' And he started to pat the other guitar player on the back.

Stevie Ray sat looking dejected.

'I think we're going to make this guy a star,' the loudmouth went on.

I should have kept quiet at this point, but I've never been very good at that. I had to throw in my two cents' worth. 'Have you guys been listening to the same two players as me? Because Stevie is incredible—'

The loudmouth cut me off. 'Yeah, I know, but this guy here is a star. He's the best. What feel. What speed.'

'You fucking idiot,' I replied. 'Stevie Ray Vaughan has more feel than anyone I know. He's the one who should be a star.'

The guys in the tour jackets all turned away from me and went into a huddle, trying to block me out. I obviously didn't know what I was talking about. Every word I said bounced back off a wall of satin.

'That's it, guys, I want you all to get behind me on this. We are going to make this man a star,' announced the loudmouth.

'You have to be kidding,' I shouted. 'Who the fuck do you think you are anyway?'

He looked at me, a little confused, and said, 'I'm Harry Stone. And this is my convention.'

I bit my lip so hard I was lucky it didn't bleed.

'Right, I'll see you later then.' I turned and walked out the door.

One more stake had just been driven into the heart of my American music career.

The
Swan

Glasgow Geese. That's what people once called swans in Tasmania, where these beautiful birds were hunted for their delicious meat.

In other parts of the world, they were known as long-necked geese. They were considered a delicacy in England and eaten by the royal family. Of course, those bastards there would eat anything. Oops! Only kidding. I just can't help it. It's in my genes. I get on a rant and the old Scottish prejudices fly out of me like demons flying from a burning Christian. So excuse me, I'll try to control myself.

Swans are considered by many the poster bird for love and fidelity because they mate for life; they are monogamous. And, even though they have these wonderful, strong characteristics – maybe it's because they have these wonderful, strong characteristics – if you smother them in salt and pepper and bake them slowly in a medium oven for one hour then let them rest, breast down, for the same amount of time, they are absolutely delicious. I was told this by a dear friend who can cook anything, fellow Scot and star chef Jock Zonfrillo. Jock is like a brother to me, but even he couldn't get me to eat a swan.

That's because I *am* a Swan. I changed my name to Barnes when I was twelve because my stepfather was a decent man and I loved him. But underneath everything, if you scrape away the name change that's there to protect the guilty, and Mum's remarrying, I'm still a Swan, and I will die a Swan. Consequently, I don't cook or eat those birds.

Apparently swans are hard to kill. Who knew? The feathers are tough, like armour, and very hard to penetrate. Swans don't die easily. I wish someone had told me that long ago. It might have explained why, whenever I wanted to throw myself off a cliff, those damn updraughts would get under my wings and I would end up standing somewhere safer than where I started. Could have saved me a lot of confusion.

I had a memorable encounter with my namesake bird when I was living in France in the mid–1990s, in Aix-en-Provence to be exact. We had rented a beautiful old shepherd's house, or *bergerie*, surrounded by wheat fields. The house had changed significantly from the days when it was part of a working farm, and by the time we moved in it was quite luxurious and even had an indoor swimming pool.

It was a day in mid–December. Winter was setting in. The sky was clear, but the prevailing wind, the mistral, was blowing down from the north, funnelling cold air through the valleys of central France and into Provence. I woke up early and decided to walk outside and feel the cold breeze on my face. It was the best way to clear my head before tackling the day.

As I walked through the garden, drinking coffee, I noticed the doors to the swimming pool had been left open. They had to remain closed to keep the heat in; if not, anybody getting into the pool could freeze to death. I walked over to shut the door and that was when I saw it: a large white swan, swimming quietly at the far end of our pool, having clearly taken refuge from the wind and cold.

I shouted to Jane and she came running down, worried I'd fallen over or had some other kind of accident. 'What is it? Are you all right?' she asked.

I pointed to the pool. 'We have a visitor. Look.'

The swan was barely moving. It looked like it had been battered by wind and rain as it travelled south for the winter.

'I thought they migrated in flocks,' I said. 'Maybe this one had to stop for a rest and got left behind. Let's see if he needs some food.'

We went inside and looked for something suitable for a swan. All the Swans I knew would eat anything they were given. But I guessed the birds were different.

'We could try bread. That might work,' Jane suggested.

'I thought they ate fish or bugs or something like that,' I said, but I really didn't have a clue, so I kept rummaging through the cupboard until something caught my eye. 'There you go. He'll love this,' I announced.

'How do you know it's a he?' Jane said. '*She* looks beautiful.'

I laughed. 'All us Swans are beautiful, in case you hadn't noticed.'

Jane insisted it was a girl.

'Okay, I'm sure *she* will like this,' I said, holding up a tin of clams in brine.

'I'm not sure, but let's see if she'll try that or the bread,' Jane said, heading back out to the pool.

The swan was starving and ate both. And she was so tired that she let me move close to her and stroke her head.

'Look, she knows I wouldn't hurt her,' I proudly declared.

'Let's not give her too much,' Jane advised. 'We don't want to make her sick. I think we should ask a few of our French friends what we should do with her. Maybe we shouldn't be feeding her at all.' Jane is always the voice of reason.

Over the next few days, we started asking different people about our new guest. One afternoon there was a local farmer walking through the wheat fields carrying a shotgun, evidently on his way to hunt. Jane spoke to him in her best French.

'Excuse me, sir. There is a swan in our swimming pool. We were wondering what we should do with it.'

He thought for just a second then gruffly replied, 'Well, I think you should eat it.' Then he laughed to himself and walked away. I'd have to keep an eye on him, I thought. If his hunt was unsuccessful, he might return for the bird.

We were never going to kill a swan and we were certainly never going to cook one, as far as I was concerned. 'We are not eating it,' I told Jane.

'No way. I'm not killing such a magnificent creature,' Jane agreed.

'No, it's a swan. Like me. No one is eating it. That's final.'

Next day, we asked a man selling vegetables in the markets in town and got the same response. Then we decided to ask our good friend Joel, who was caring and gentle.

'He'll know what to do,' Jane said.

'Well, 'ere in France,' said Joel, 'I think if you asked anybody what you should do, they would tell you to eat it.'

I was shocked. *Et tu*, Joel?

But Joel was not finished. 'Personally, though, I don't think it would be a good thing to eat this swan. It would be bad luck. Especially for the swan.'

He was right about that.

So it was decided. The swan would stay with us until she (or he) felt it was time to leave. And if that never happened, she (or he) would become a member of the family.

'He can stay with us as long as he likes,' I said to Joel. 'Come out and meet him. He's so friendly.' And I guided him towards the pool.

'*She*,' Jane said as we walked out.

'Yeah, that's what I said. She.'

We arrived at the pool.

'Look,' I said to Joel confidently, 'he's so calm you can even stroke his beautiful neck.' I reached out my hand. The once friendly swan's head snapped around and he tried to bite me.

'He must be afraid of you,' I said to Joel. 'He's overheard our conversations with a few French people and knows what you all want to do to him.'

Joel smiled at me. 'Maybe. But, then again, perhaps she doesn't speak French.'

Next day the swan was more active, swimming up and down the pool as if he or she was in training, and also a little more aggressive. So we placed some food at one end of the pool and left the bird alone to eat. No one likes being watched while they eat.

This went on for a week. Each day the swan seemed to be swimming harder and faster in our little pool and getting angrier, hissing and flapping his or her wings whenever we approached.

'I'm going to stick my neck out here,' I said one morning. 'I think he's in training for the rest of the flight to Africa or wherever they go for the winter.'

'She,' said Jane.

'Pardon me?'

'*She*'s in training,' Jane replied.

'Yeah, that's what I said. She. She's in training.'

I had been joking, but in my heart I felt it was probably true and that he, or she, was getting ready to leave.

Then one morning we went down with fresh bread and a new tin of clams and found that our new baby, the cygnet of the family, had gone. Not even as much as a thank you or a goodbye. We were sad, but we knew that this was a wild swan and he or she had to fly off and find his or her own kind.

We never really worked out if it was a boy or a girl. How do you tell? The colour of the beak? I don't know.

Whatever the case, in my heart of hearts, I felt that by landing in my backyard – of all the places he or she could have landed in the south of France – this creature had chosen to be with one of his or her own kind. I was, after all, underneath everything I had learned, and no matter how much I had grown, still a Swan.

Into the *Spotlight*

'Come and see my cabaret show,
Dad. You'll love it,' Elly-May
said proudly one day. 'Oh, and
could you please invite a
bunch of your friends too?'

I suspected that maybe I was being used as rent-a-crowd. If I went along and took all my mates, the place would be reasonably full. But Elly-May is my youngest daughter and naturally I would do anything for her (and for any of my kids). Even force my friends to go to a show midweek, when I know they all have work the next day.

'All right, baby, where and when is it on? You'd better give me the times so I can tell all the gang. If you want a crowd, I'll need to give them a heads-up.'

'It's next Tuesday, at eight o'clock,' Elly said casually as she headed for the door. It was Friday, so that wasn't a lot of notice, especially as it was close to Christmas and everybody was flat out. But then again, it was for Elly-May.

Not only is she my youngest daughter, but she's had a tough life. A life full of challenges. She was born small and frail, arriving very prematurely at just twenty-six weeks – three and a half months early. Her odds of survival weren't that good. Not thirty years ago anyway. But she was a fighter from day one.

Being born so early affected Elly-May physically. She had trouble with some of her motor skills and walking was especially difficult. When she was two, she was diagnosed with cerebral palsy. That led to her being fitted with splints and undergoing countless operations and procedures, and enduring chronic pain. Yet all the while she smiled and brought brightness into our lives.

Since then, Elly-May has had to struggle every day just to get by, let alone become the beautiful, accomplished young woman she is now. She's funny, positive and strong, but frail and needy at the same time. She's also very smart and, dare I say it, a little bit manipulative. Let's just say she likes to get

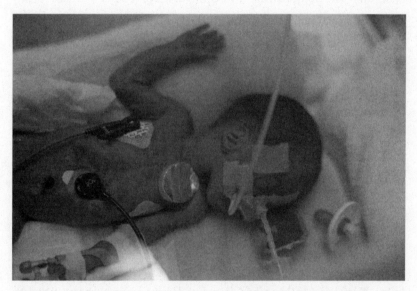

Elly-May's first spotlight was a heat lamp that helped keep her alive.

her own way, and that's not easy in our family, so she has to have a few tricks up her sleeve. And she seems to have trained me to respond to those tricks more than the others. Hence I'm the go-to person when she wants anything. Which is fine because I like to spoil her.

It's not easy being part of our family business. You would think that my success in the music world would smooth the way for Elly. But it is as much a hindrance as it is a help. Ask any of her siblings. People always expect more from the children of performers. Plus she has so much close competition. Her mum, Jane, is amazing. She writes songs, sings and plays various musical instruments – guitar, bass, piano and bagpipes, to mention just a few. Elly's sisters and brother are all high achievers too. Mahalia is a superwoman who can do anything she puts her mind to. She writes songs and manages tours, and she's a great soul singer. Eliza-Jane has the voice of an angel (and the temper of a demon!), can play beautiful guitar and could engineer and produce an album if you wanted her to. She has spent years singing backing vocals with me and with our dear friend Neil Finn. Jackie, my son, topped his year in music at Cranbrook School and graduated from Berklee College of Music in Boston, one of the world's most prestigious music schools, with flying colours. He's an excellent drummer, a very accomplished piano player and also writes songs and sings really well.

These guys don't cut Elly-May any slack, especially if she messes anything up. They want her to be tough. So she's had to fight her whole life to crawl out from their shadows, even just for a chance to sing with the family. It's been harder still for her to do her own thing, develop her own ideas, be herself. That's meant steadily building up her confidence, and the cabaret show she'd been working on really seemed to be helping with that. I couldn't wait to see it.

'What songs are you singing, baby?' I asked. I wanted to know what to expect.

'Oh, you know. A bit of this and a bit of that. You'll just have to wait and see, Dadda.' She smiled and blew me a kiss.

I had absolutely no trouble talking people into coming out early in the week to see Elly's show. In fact, I soon found out that most of our close friends were already going. The word was out. Elly didn't need me to fill the room. She pulled her own crowd. I got the feeling that I was the last to know how good she really was.

Of course I'd seen her sing. She performs with my band most nights, but to be out front, alone, was a new challenge and I wanted her to nail it. I was probably more nervous than she was, but I tried not to let her see it. I'd known for a while that she was working on a show and I'd even seen parts of it, but it was clear that she had refined her ideas since then, adding costumes, props, gags, lights and special effects. She'd even poached Clayton Doley, the piano player from my band. And with Clayton behind her she was confident enough to take the show to anyone.

The venue was to be Elly-May's favourite bar, a little place called Low 302 in Crown Street, Surry Hills. She and her friends had held parties there for years. Elly told me she'd roped in a lot of those friends to be part of the show. One was the maître d' at the bar. Another friend would be the compere. Her cousin James, who plays great guitar and sings, was to be the opening act. Her favourite barman had been promoted to sound guy, but he still had to run and get Elly any drinks she needed during the show. Lucky it was a small bar.

One of Elly's best friends, Mel, who also happened to be the bar manager, would be playing the trombone in the show. And the stage dressing had been assigned to a couple of other friends who are particularly tall as well as beautiful: Grace Garrett, daughter of Peter Garrett, my dear friend from Midnight Oil, and Kitty Callaghan, daughter of Mark Callaghan from GANGgajang. Both also had roles throughout the show, dancing, playing percussion, rearranging the stage props and even escorting people onto and off the stage.

The following Tuesday I arrived at the venue a little early to make sure my friends were well looked after. Grace and Kitty were standing on the tiny stage, sticking stars to the ceiling and pinning up curtains. No need for ladders – a smart move by Elly. I had to laugh. Friends in high places, you might say. Elly was running around giving final instructions to her troupe as they carried costumes from the car. A lot of costumes.

The doors opened and the room quickly filled. Not only with friends but with all sorts of punters. I sat in a corner and looked around the room. I recognised a few big guys from local record companies, as well as singers, guitar players, TV stars, dancers, chefs, actors, bikies and bankers, as well as a few high-profile people from the Sydney cabaret scene. All waiting for the show to start, all waiting to see my baby. I started to sweat with anxiety. I needed a drink.

On my way to the bar, I spotted some fans I'd seen many times in the front rows of my own shows. I nodded as I walked past. 'Hey, how are you doing? Thanks for coming out to see my girl. I think you'll like the show,' I said, adopting the role of proud dad.

One of them smiled and replied, 'Oh, we've seen it many times, Jimmy. But it's nice to see you here tonight.'

When I got back to my table, the show was almost ready to begin. I sat like a nervous stage mother waiting for the show to commence. There was a buzz in the air. Everywhere I looked there were celebrities and musicians. Daniel Johns from Silverchair bounced through the room shirtless like the rock star he is, with a beautiful girl on his arm. Each of them had a large glass of something that looked deadly. Daniel had a slightly crazed expression on his face, like he was looking for trouble. He thumped my back on the way past. 'Hey, Jimmy. What are we singing with her tonight?'

I didn't think I was singing anything. 'Whatever you like, Daniel. You dream it and I'll scream it.'

On the stage were a few props: two chairs and a table with bottles of whisky spread across it. I started to worry. Was Elly taking after her dad a little too much? Later, during the break, I was relieved to hear that the bottles were filled with tea.

Elly started the show with a routine about being disorganised. She picked up a large book and said, 'I've written my stage patter in this book. I'm a bit nervous and I might forget things. Okay, let me see where we are up to.' She smiled and flicked through her book. 'Ah, yes, here we go. Now I know where I am.'

She closed the book. 'Good evening.'

The crowd laughed.

Elly then proceeded to introduce each song she sang with a series of great gags. My girl was funny!

The owner of the bar, Aref Jaroudy, had been given the job of operating the smoke machine and the lights. As the night wore on, he was the butt of many jokes.

'Not enough smoke, man,' Elly would say waving her hand and gesturing for him to smoke the room out. Then it would be, 'Stop. You're killing me with the smoke now. Get it together or I'll have to put you back on wardrobe duty.'

The songs began and as she introduced each number she broke out a few stories that gave everyone in the room an insight into her struggles. Even me, and I knew all her stories.

'I don't know if you're aware of it, but I've got cerebral palsy. And although I would love to go out walking, I can't. So I'm going to do the next best thing and sing a song about it for you.' And she broke into the Patsy Cline song 'Walking After Midnight'. I looked around the room and saw I wasn't the only one crying.

The show was moving, confronting, even outrageous at times. And all of Elly's friends did everything they could to make it a success. I was mesmerised by my darling little girl as she held the audience in the palm of her hand. Jane and I sat with our arms round each other, feeling so proud and laughing along with the rest of the crowd.

Elly invited one of the young guys from the bar up on stage for Dusty Springfield's 'You Don't Own Me' and pushed and prodded him as she leaned close and sang softly in his ear, only to shove him away again as she hit the chorus – to the cheers of every woman in the room.

Then we were all silenced as Elly began to sing Radiohead's 'Creep'. When she whispered the line 'I wish I was special', I nearly fell apart.

At one point both Elly and Clayton left the stage, only to return in silver space suits for the David Bowie song 'Space Oddity'. Sometimes it has seemed to me that Elly feels she is not from this world. But this night she was right at home.

One of her gags involved pouring a large glass of what the crowd assumed was whisky and drinking it down in one. 'Ah, that's better. I drink to forget, you know. Now I've forgotten what it was I wanted to forget, so it's working for me.'

The audience roared, but I felt a tinge of pain in my heart, even though I knew it was just tea. Had she inherited some of my darker traits, my more destructive inclinations?

Elly invited me on stage then made me sit at a table and sing a song while she made faces behind my back. She was very funny and everyone was laughing, including me. Thirsty again, I grabbed one of the whisky bottles on her table and discovered that not all of them contained tea.

Elly gave me an innocent look. 'Oops! Sorry, Dad. That's just in case I get a sore throat.' Then she smiled at me and said, 'Thanks for your help, Dadda. Kitty will show you to your seat now.' As I walked off stage, she called out, 'In fact, Dad, my throat is a bit sore right now.' And she laughed and poured herself a big one.

The crowd roared again. I smiled awkwardly.

Further jokes and stories of struggle and survival were capped off by a rendition of Dolly Parton's 'I Will Always Love You'. That brought the house down, and the crowd gave Elly a huge ovation. After that, it was time for us oldies to get out of there so the kids could party on – no one wants to get drunk in front of their parents.

As we walked out, I thought about why the performance had been such a revelation. None of our family had ever seen or treated Elly as someone with a disability. We'd always wanted her to have as normal a life as possible. But perhaps that had blinded us to some of her suffering. That night, in front of a crowd of strangers, my daughter had shown us just how much physical and emotional pain she'd really had to deal with. She'd never wanted us to see it before because she never wanted us to worry about her. Now she'd demonstrated that she could stand proud and handle that pain with incredible style and grace.

It was one of the best nights of my life. My baby had found her mojo.

Downhill
Fast

'Come on, baby,' I pleaded with Jane, 'let's ski over there. There's no one heading that way at all.' Jane stood her ground. 'That's because it's too dangerous.'

'But I really want to go,' I insisted. 'Come on, we'll take it easy. Jurgen is with us. Jurgen always finds the best snow. He knows what you like to ski on.'

It was a freezing cold, windy day in Perisher Valley. We turned and watched as our instructor came flying down the hill, yodelling at the same time: 'Yodelay-heehoo!' Jurgen always yodels when he skis.

Whoosh! He came to a stop, spraying snow down the hill. '*Guten Morgen*. It is a beautiful day out zer. *Sehr gut!*' He smiled as he took off his goggles.

We were on one of our annual ski trips with the kids, in the early 1990s. Jane had introduced me to skiing when we'd first met and, I must say, I'd taken to going downhill like a duck to water. I seemed to be really suited to it – at least that was what people had been telling me all my life. At school they said, 'That boy's really going downhill.' People in the music industry repeatedly declared, 'Jesus, his career is going downhill.' I'm still here, though, and feel like I'm still climbing a hill and haven't yet reached the peak. Anyway, back to the story.

I'd first skied in Lech, in Austria, on holiday with Jane. As I was a beginner, I needed an instructor and Jane hooked me up with a guy called Heinz, who was the crankiest person I'd ever met. Every morning he'd be in a really bad mood with the world. He would say things like, 'Get out of the way, you stupid fucking tourists.' One day, at the top of a very steep hill, I told Heinz that I didn't think I could make it down. 'Well, take your fucking skis off and walk,' he replied. Then he jumped off the cliff and left me. I tried to catch up with him, but he was too fast. I wanted to kill him, but I hadn't yet mastered punching people and skiing at the same time (I've got the hang of it now).

After a few days I tried a different tack. I thought I would start the day with a big joint. I fired it up on the ski lift and offered it to Heinz. Suddenly he was the nicest, happiest guy alive. He started saying things like, 'Isn't it the best day? Look at that mountain! Enjoy your skiing!' – to the very same tourists he'd been screaming at the day before. We finally got on well for a while.

The other thing I remember about that trip is that when I went to check out of the hotel, they told me they didn't take credit cards. So I sent a message to my manager at the time to send me cash. Meanwhile I kept skiing. By the time the money arrived, I needed more. This went on for about three weeks. When I finally had enough cash to pay the bill, I had run out of pot, but I could ski with the best of them.

That was forty years ago. In more recent times we've always skied in Australia with the same instructors. Jurgen is from Austria and besides being a yodeller and a great skier is also a blacksmith – yes, an old-fashioned blacksmith – who makes incredible ironwork. Gates and fire tools and anything else you'd like made out of iron. Jurgen also plays the didgeridoo and is the happiest person I know. Our other instructor is Pavo. He's from Finland and tough as nails but a gentle soul too. He usually skis slowly and carefully with Jane while Jurgen skis wildly with me. Don't get me wrong, though: either of these guys can ski fast and safe. The only one who's really out of control is me.

For some reason, on this day in Perisher, Pavo was off and Jane had to ski with Jurgen and me. She wasn't happy about it. And we didn't have the best conditions for skiing. Every report had said the weather would be perfect, but here we were with bad visibility and high winds, and to make matters worse, it had rained overnight. Which meant that there was a very good chance that the higher we went, the more ice we would find.

I didn't care. I was keen as mustard and ready to take on anything. As you've probably guessed by now, I ski like I do everything else: hard and fast, and without thinking about it too much. Jane is a much better skier than me, but cautious.

I wanted Jane to ski with us because I love doing everything with her. But she wasn't into it. So I was doing my best to talk her into it.

'If you ski with us, we'll go nice and slow. You can follow Jurgen's tracks, and if it's icy we'll come straight back to the front of the mountain where it's more sheltered.'

I was slowly winning her over.

'Oh, I don't know.'

I could see her thinking about it.

'Okay, but as long as you turn around and come back if it's bad. Do you promise?'

I looked at Jurgen.

'*Ja*, ve promise,' he said sincerely.

I joined in. 'I promise too.'

Jurgen, who is as honest as the day is long, looked at Jane again and said, '*Ja*, Jane, if it is bad, ve vill come straight back. But it vill be supa. Trust me.'

So off we headed to work our way across Mount Perisher towards the Eyre T-bar, site of some of the longest, hardest runs on the mountain.

I was happy. Jane was worried. Jurgen was yodelling. 'Yodelay-heehoo!'

As we hit the first ice, Jane yelled, 'I don't like this. I want to go back.'

We all stopped and pulled down our masks.

'Vell,' said Jurgen with a worried look on his face, 'if you vant to go back, ve need to go to ze top and ski back. You can't valk from here. It's too difficult.'

I was worried too, but happy. At least I'd get one run down the mountain.

Jurgen reassured Jane. 'Ja, just stick close to me and it vill be supa.'

So we headed up the lift to the top of Mount Perisher. By the time we got to the summit, it was hard to even stand in the wind, let alone ski.

Jane was furious. 'I told you this was a bad idea. I'm skiing at my own pace. You two can do what you like.' And off she went. Very carefully.

It's often when you try to ski slowly, though, that you fall and hurt yourself. Sure enough, to our horror, Jane crashed a short way down the first part of the run. We skied quickly down to her.

'You okay, baby?' I shouted over the wind.

'No, I'm not! I think I've done my knee in.' Jane was in tears, and not happy with me.

'Okay,' said Jurgen, 'you guys stay here and I vill get ze ski patrol.' And he skied off, yodelling, to get help. He seemed to be yodelling even more than normal. I wondered if it was a nervous thing.

It felt like only a few minutes before the ski patrol arrived with the banana boat. A banana boat is a sort of sliding stretcher that the patrollers strap injured skiers into to get them down the mountain. One of the patrollers skis at the front and one at the back, while the injured skier travels down the hill head-first, I guess so you can't see where you are going and you worry less.

Soon Jane was strapped in and unable to move.

'We'll come down with you,' I said to Jane and the patrollers.

'No, we've got this,' one of them replied. 'This is what we do every day. It's probably better if you ski down with your instructor and we follow behind you more slowly.'

Jane wholeheartedly agreed. 'Yes, just go and I'll see you at the bottom.'

Jurgen led the way. 'Yodelay-heehoo!'

The snow was rock hard. Actually, it wasn't really snow, it was ice, so we flew down the hill. At the halfway mark, we decided to stop and see how Jane was travelling. Just as I looked up, I saw one of the patrollers fall, closely followed by the other. Soon Jane was on her own, flying head–first down the hill at breakneck speed. Strapped into the boat.

There was nothing we could do. She shot past us before we could move. Jurgen went into racing mode, but even he couldn't catch her.

Luckily, she made it to the bottom and ploughed into a big hill of fresh snow that stopped her as quickly as she had taken off. And very gently.

Jurgen reached Jane in seconds and quickly undid the straps on the banana boat. As I got to her, she was wiping the snow from her face. She was a lot paler than when I'd last seen her, but at least she was in one piece.

'Are you all right, my darling?' I asked hopefully.

'What do you think, Jimmy?' she snapped.

There followed one of the coldest nights of my life. And it had nothing to do with the weather.

Good to Be *Chieftain*

'Aye, laddie,' says the voice
on the phone, 'We'd like ye
tae be oor Chieftain at the
Brigadoon Highland Gathering
in Bundanoon next year.'

I've been asked before, but I've always been too busy. 'What do you think, Jane? Shall I do it this time? It's the fortieth anniversary.' I always look to Jane for guidance.

'I think it will be a good thing for you to do,' she replies enthusiastically. 'And I love seeing Scottish men in kilts. You know that.'

Jane is in and so am I. I've been looking for a good excuse to wear one of my many kilts and impress her.

Brigadoon is a Highland gathering that happens once a year in Bundanoon, in the Southern Highlands of New South Wales. Highland gatherings pop up all over Australia, indeed all over the world, but this one is right in my backyard. I've gone to it for a quick look a few times, and certain things about it appeal to me. The obvious one of course is that I am Scottish and love all things Scottish. But it's more than just that. It's partly to do with this lifelong search I seem to be on to find my place in the world. The need to belong burns in my heart. Being uprooted from Scotland at an early age and then moving from one place I didn't fit in to another place I didn't fit in for most of my life has left a hole in me that needs to be filled. Family and real friends have helped with that, but there is still a gap that only Scotland can fill. And a little piece of Scotland is carried in the hearts of the many people who are drawn to Bundanoon every year, looking for the same thing as me.

So I agree. The timing is good. I have the time off. And I really want to be a part of it.

I try not to be, but as the date gets closer, I'm increasingly excited. Shit. I hope it's good. I've been invited to the odd Scottish get-together before and they always sound like nightmares, but this should be great.

And I will be the Chieftain. But I don't know what's expected of me, so I ring one of the organisers.

'Yeah. Hi, it's Jimmy Barnes here. You know, the new Chieftain?'

The guy cuts me off. 'Och aye, Jimmy Barnes. Aye, aye,' he says in a broad Scottish brogue.

I cut him off. 'Just call me Chief!'

He's not sure whether to take me seriously or not.

I press on. 'I was just wondering, if you wouldn't mind telling me, what the hell does the Chieftain actually do? Can you send me a program or a timetable or something?'

He laughs. 'Aye, aw right, Chief, ah will, ah will.' And he hangs up.

It's nine o'clock at night. Maybe it's after his bedtime. He'll probably wake up the next day thinking it was a dream and ring one of his mates. 'Hey, Peter, ah had the weirdest dream last night. Jimmy Barnes rang me and told me tae call him Chief. He wanted me tae send him a program. Aye, it was weird, but ah think I'll send him one anyway. Just in case. He is the Chief.'

Two days later I receive the running order of the events. Pipe bands start playing at eight in the morning. That will wake the neighbours. At 9.45, I get started, leading the massed pipe bands through town then into the car park and onto the oval. Every pipe band that will be playing that day will be involved and I'll march at the front of them all. That sounds good. I'll need to be there early.

Then I have to judge the Tartan Warriors, a group of competitive strongmen, as they race each other to lift huge balls of granite known as the Bundanoon Stones onto barrels in the shortest time possible. That might be fun, getting sand

kicked in my face. Next I decide who wins the Tug o' War –
that'll be fun too, kind of – and I adjudicate the Tossing the
Caber, Hammer Throwing, Stone Putt, Weights for Distance
and Weights for Height competitions as well. I'll need a good
lie-down after that.

Then, believe it or not, I have to judge the Bonnie Bairns.
A fucking kids' beauty competition. Fuck me, really? They
need me to do that? Finally, we all go to a good old Scottish
knees-up for haggis, drinks and dancing. Well, I'll need a
drink by then and I guess if the haggis is good I could have a
wee bite or two, but I'm not dancing at all and the only time
my knees are going up is when I get home and put my feet
up to watch television.

I start to wonder what I've let myself in for. Too late to
back down now.

Meanwhile Jane is worried. 'Maybe you can go and do
this on your own. I'll just get in the way,' she says, trying to
weasel out of it.

'But Jane, every Chieftain needs a Mrs Chieftain by his
side. You know that.'

Margo Callaghan, a dear friend of ours, happens to be
there at the time. Margo is a beautiful, tall, Celtic-looking
woman with flowing red hair and pale white skin with
freckles. She is Australian and married to my friend Mark.

'I'll be Mrs Chieftain,' she says. 'I've always wanted to be
the chief's wife at the gathering—'

I butt in. 'Sorry, Margo. You can come along with us, but
I need my real Mrs Chieftain with me.'

Jane looks at me bewildered. 'How am I supposed to
look like a Scottish Mrs Chieftain?' It's true that, being from
Thailand, Jane doesn't look Scottish at all.

'They have highlands in Thailand, don't they?' I argue. 'We'll just say you are from the Highlands and not tell them which part.'

It is settled. A bunch of us will all go together. Jane and myself, Margo and Mark Callaghan, my youngest daughter, Elly-May, and her husband, Liam. Liam by the way is not only a real Highlander, but is also tall, red-headed and has a wild red beard. He comes from up near Aberdeen. A little town called Glenbuchat. Population four humans and forty cows. That's pronounced *coos*. Elly and Liam have a beautiful boy called Dylan and he, despite the fact that he is quarter Thai, has red hair and freckles too. In fact, he looks more like one of Margo's kids than any of ours.

One of Elly-May's best friends, Kitty, who is also Margo's daughter, will come along too. Kitty is another beauty, about six foot tall with red hair way down her back. We will all dress to kill, in kilts, sashes and sporrans. Two other friends, Paul Field and his wife, Pauline, will join the group later. Like us, those two welcome any excuse to wear a kilt. We decide then and there that our party will win the Best Dressed prize. I think I know the judge.

The day arrives. After many attempts to get out of it, Jane comes along with me, and she looks beautiful in her Scottish apparel. We get there before the others because we have chiefly duties to take care of. In my sporran I make sure I have everything I need: money and two hip flasks of whisky. It's going to be a long day.

At 9.45, the bands fire up. I use that term deliberately, because that's what the sound of a pipe band does to me. It starts a fire in my heart. And to be standing in the middle of

'Where did I leave those four hundred pipers?'
(Ted O'Donnell)

four hundred pipers sounds better than anything I have ever experienced before and I nearly break down in tears.

A soft-spoken, polite Scotsman called Alaistair Saunders is given the job of guiding me around the events. As the day goes on I realise that I don't have to worry about judging the events, I'm really just there to encourage the contestants. Thank goodness, as I'm no expert when it comes to something like tossing the caber. There is obviously a technique – the aim seems to be to send the log tumbling end over end as opposed to just flinging it up in the air to land flat on the ground. But beyond that, who knows?

'Would you like tae have a wee try, Jimmy?' one of the competitors asks me with a look in his eye that says, 'I dare you to try.'

I briefly ponder his suggestion, but I don't think anyone really wants to see a grown man fall backwards then have a large tree land on top of him. That's not entertainment.

'No, thanks,' I say. 'I threw a few gum trees this morning and I think I pulled a hamstring. But very kind of you to offer.'

I quickly limp away, feigning injury, but only make it as far as the Tartan Warriors. Each of these guys is the size of three of me, and as wide as he is tall. And they're pretty tall. They're picking up the big round Bundanoon Stones, each one weighing more than the last, and placing them on the barrels. I couldn't get my arms around one of the stones, never mind carry it anywhere. I quickly say hello then move on.

I'm stopped by another enthusiast. 'So, have ye seen much hammer tossing, Jimmy? Oh, it's a great sport.'

I agree to look on as the Tartan Warriors spin in circles and throw hammers across the oval.

'Would ye like a wee throw, Jimmy?'

I shake my head. 'I tell you what, though. If you find me a much smaller hammer and a pair of gloves, I'll get Jane to have a go.'

Alistair laughs, but I know he can smell the fear coming from me. 'Let's go over there, Jimmy. I think you'll like this event.' He walks me over to what is obviously the Bonnie Bairns competition. This should be much easier, I think.

'Hey, mister,' a voice calls out, 'choose carefully. The wean over there is ma baby and I love her more than life. Especially your life.'

I look up. The woman in front of me looks a lot like the guy I saw lifting stones a few minutes ago, only now he's wearing a dress.

'Sorry, sir, what did you say?' I ask with a smile.

'It's "Mrs", ya cheeky bastard.' She half-smiles back at me. I say 'half-smiles' because when she opens her mouth I see she only has half her teeth.

My official duties are done for a while, so I go for a walk to see the stalls and take photos with the punters. There are Clydesdale horses walking around and Scottish terriers for sale. If I had a bigger sporran, I'd buy myself a pup. But I have to say no and keep moving. There are HLTs for sale – haggis, lettuce and tomato sandwiches. No, there aren't really. I made that up. But I bet you once the organisers read this, there will be.

Everyone is friendly and happy to be a part of the event, and although I feel unworthy, they seem happy to have me as Chieftain. I'm happy to be here too. It's good to be Chieftain.

Later that day the four hundred pipers and scores of drummers line up and march across the oval towards me, the Chieftain. A wall of sound and human flesh marching as

It was a long, enjoyable day, but Dylan had had enough.

one and seemingly unstoppable. This is what it must have felt like to go into battle against the Scots. My heart swells with pride. I am Scottish and I do belong. This is the connection I need. These are my people, and they are not all living in Scotland. But they have Scotland living inside each and every one of them.

The rest of the day flies by. I am happy to be surrounded by the sounds of my home. All I have to deal with now is the knees-up. We go to the party, even though we are exhausted after being on our feet all day. In fact, Jane and I are both well and truly fried. It's been an emotional day.

Anyway, we make an entrance to the shindig and take our seats at the front of the stage. A band is playing folk songs and a few couples are dancing. Most people are waiting for the big moment when the haggis will be piped in by a lone bagpiper. It has to be said that haggis is an acquired taste, and some people never acquire a taste for it in this lifetime. Jane is one of those people. I like haggis if it is made well, but I'm sure I noticed this particular haggis sitting in the sun all day. It has certainly seen better days – like when it was a whole sheep, for instance. Now the stomach of that sheep is stuffed with its own insides and is being brought into a dance hall while a man plays music on another sheep's stomach. Next the poor haggis is cut open – life is tough for Scottish sheep – and that's our cue to leave.

It's been a long day, but I'd do it again in a heartbeat. Next time I hope to be playing in one of the pipe bands. I am taking lessons and so is Mrs Chieftain. Don't tell her I said this, but she's better at it than me.

The Covid
Chronicle

Suddenly it looks like we'll be travelling in the modern equivalent of the time of the Black Death. That is, if you believe everything you read online.

Friday, 21 February 2020

According to the cable news channels, the whole world could be infected with the coronavirus, or Covid-19, in the next twenty-four hours. Western countries already sold out of antiseptic wipes and waterless handwash days ago, which has led some conspiracy theorists to the conclusion that this was all planned, that some kind of germ warfare is happening, and that if you haven't already stocked up in advance, there's a good chance you won't make it through the next few days alive.

To me, it seems that the world has simply caught a cold. A new cold, right enough, but still just a cold. It appeared to have started in China, in a market where they can't afford refrigeration and keep cages of live wild animals stacked and ready for slaughter – badgers, beavers and hedgehogs and other delicacies I would never think of having as pets never mind eating. These in turn are piled above open tanks containing live shellfish, prawns and fish. A virus passed from the wild animals to the shellfish, they say, and then to humans. It's just a theory, but some people are already using it as an excuse to attack the Chinese. Can someone please create a vaccine for racism?

Anyway, a new superbug has emerged and although it seems to be less deadly than the last flu or SARS epidemic that did the rounds, there's no vaccine for it and people are dying. A lot of them are men in their mid-sixties. I think about my approaching birthday and all the smoke I've inhaled over the years and resolve that it will never take me alive.

All of this is happening just as Jane and I are about to start our first holiday in ages. I've been working for two years non-stop and desperately need a break. If I stay home, work will present itself and I won't be able to say no. I can already hear the call from my agent, Frank: 'This is a really special show. They need you to be a part of it.' And see the look on my publicist Rina's face as she pleads, 'We just need four or five interviews, that's all.'

The only way I'll get a break is if we go away, far away, somewhere I won't be called, recognised or photographed. So we decide to go ahead and book our trip.

'It's only in China at the moment,' I say to Jane. 'It's bound to be safe in Italy and Scotland, surely.'

Our plan is to fly to Singapore then catch a train to Thailand. After a few weeks on the beach charging our batteries, we'll continue to Istanbul – a place I've always wanted to see – then spend a few weeks in Italy and the south of France before hopping over to Scotland, where we'll tour stately homes and whisky distilleries. Then we'll head down to London before flying home to Sydney. What could possibly go wrong?

Monday, 24 February

A couple of days ago, we heard the virus had broken through the Chinese quarantine and had hit Korea. Japan is already in lockdown. Yesterday, on the eve of our departure, the first cases were discovered in Hong Kong and Singapore, and there are cases in Thailand too.

'It's only in Bangkok, though,' I reassured Jane, 'not at the beach we're going to.'

But now, at the airport in Sydney, reports of multiple cases in Italy are plastered over the newspapers.

'Fuck. It's not good. Maybe we should stay home?' I blurt out. But we're by now in the lounge, waiting to board a plane. Too late to turn back.

Time for a Singapore Sling at Raffles Hotel

Everyone is wearing masks. Jane and I had ours in our backpacks just in case, and when the first group of travellers walked past us coughing, we quickly pulled them out and put them on.

On the plane we wipe down every surface and clean our hands with sanitiser so many times our skin begins to peel. Then we sit back and try to relax.

'It'll be fine,' I say. 'Have a drink, my love, and enjoy the flight.' I don't sound convincing.

Tuesday, 25 February
On arrival in Singapore we head straight to Raffles Hotel. This is where we start the holiday. Tomorrow we'll be picked up and taken to the railway station to join the Eastern & Oriental Express train for a two-day journey to Thailand. Although we'll be in confined spaces with strangers, the train still seems like a good option. The less flying, breathing recycled air and passing through airports the better.

Wednesday, 26 February
The sparkling train is already at the platform when we arrive. A staff member greets us warmly and informs us that we've been upgraded from a 'State Room' to the 'Presidential Suite'. The day just got a whole lot better.

The suite is perfect. Jane and I have been married a long time and we each need our own space. The cabin is just big enough. We unpack our luggage then order afternoon tea. By the time we finish, the train is moving.

Time to explore. The bar and the dining cars are beautiful. Beyond them lies the open-air observation car. The first thing we notice is that this is where the smokers congregate.

We won't be spending much time there. After a single malt in the bar car, we head back to our suite to read and watch the countryside roll past.

Dinner on the Oriental Express is a big deal, so we dress appropriately. On our way to the dining car, we stop to catch a little of the entertainment: a magician and a piano player. Dinner is silver service and the whole event is great, especially as I'm dining with the best-looking girl in the world.

Thursday, 27 February
In the middle of the night I wake suddenly with a panic attack. It feels like someone is sitting on my chest. I haven't had one of these for a long time – it used to be every second night. Jane is sleeping soundly next to me, so I try to panic quietly. I get out of bed and stand near the air conditioner. That doesn't help, so I open the cabin door, hoping to breathe some cool fresh air in the hallway. But it's still about one hundred degrees out there and I have to come back in quickly. The only way I can control the panic is to distract myself, so I grab a book, read for a while under low light, and eventually pass out.

This morning I'm weary, but we have to prepare for an outing. The train has come to a stop and we have the choice of climbing up a mountain to a rubber plantation or taking a minibus to a farm to do some cooking. We choose the easy option and head to the bar car, where we are all to meet.

As we take a seat we hear a dreadful hacking sound. Directly across from us are an American couple, and the woman sounds like she's dying of something. It's the worst cough I've heard in years.

'Some cough you have there,' I offer.

Dinner for two: our first night on the Eastern & Oriental Express

She must see the panic in my eyes. 'Oh, don't worry, I only have a really bad cold.'

Jane and I start backing out of the carriage as quickly as we can, whip out our masks and put them straight on.

'Fuck, this is the last place I expected to catch the virus,' I say, probably just loudly enough for the woman to hear. 'Let's get out of here.'

Outside, one bus is going to the farm, the other to the mountain. The woman with the cough heads for the farm bus. That seals it: we're climbing. Jane's in platform boots, but she still prefers to do the trek. It's only a two-kilometre hike, though it's quite steep and it's very hot, but it turns out to be a great walk. The Malaysian farmland spreading out before us is beautiful, straight lines of rubber trees running as far as the eye can see.

We return to the train, which continues north then stops at the Malaysia–Thailand border for a quick passport check. We join the queue as late as possible to minimise our contact with other people, but as the line zigzags we keep coming within coughing distance of the sickly American. She's not happy to see us and we certainly aren't happy to see her.

Border guards take our temperature and look for symptoms of the virus, then we have to press our fingers onto a panel that reads our fingerprints – surely the perfect way to catch any bug. We pull out the hand sanitiser and scrub repeatedly. Luckily we've bought shares in Aesop and still have enough bottles of their Resurrection Rinse-Free Hand Wash to see us through the trip.

Come dinner time, we dress up again and take our seat at a table for two, but a friendly, smiling American couple opposite ask if we would like to join them. Were we in Australia we might politely decline, just in case they were mad Cold Chisel fans and we'd be in for a night of 'I love the band, I'm your biggest fan. Would it be okay if you signed my wife's arm and would you mind if I just ring my best friend in Toowoomba and get you to speak to him?' But these people didn't know us, so it would obviously just be normal conversation.

'So, you guys are Aussies then, are you?' the man asks as we sit down. He's soft-spoken and polite.

We both nod.

'I spent a bit of time there in the eighties, actually. I just love Australian music.'

I shoot a quick look at Jane. 'Really?' I say. 'What music do you like?'

'Oh. I loved Midnight Oil and Jimmy Barnes and Cold Chisel.'

For once in my life I don't know what to say. Is he kidding me or just making conversation?

'Sorry, what are your names?' I ask politely.

'Oh, pardon me, we should have introduced ourselves first. I'm Phil Tonbough and this is my wife, Jennifer. You guys are ...?'

I'm silent for a minute, wondering if I should lie. Fuck it. 'I'm Jimmy and this is my wife, Jane Barnes.'

Jane extends her hand.

The guy looks stunned. 'Er, you don't sing, do you?' he asks sheepishly.

'I do, actually.'

We all laugh. I'm pretty sure he didn't recognise me. It's just one of those strange things that happen now and again.

Phil turns out to be a very nice, quiet fellow and Jennifer is equally sweet. I don't even have to sign her arm or ring any of their friends. On parting, we exchange numbers and I tell them if they are ever in Australia to call us and we'll take them to a show.

Tomorrow the train will drop us off at Hua Hin, our favourite place in the world, where we'll spend a couple of weeks relaxing. Then all that remains is for Jane and me to get home without having to spend an extra few weeks in quarantine on Christmas Island. I wonder if you can book a suite with an ocean view. And do they have a spa? I doubt it.

Friday, 28 February

This place we stay at in Hua Hin is called Baan Kai Muk. *Baan* means house and *Kai Muk* means pearl. Jane has been coming here her whole life. It was originally the site of a wonderful old traditional teak house nestled among huge trees. The house was understated, practical and beautiful at the same time, and could sleep about twenty or more people. It was still here when I first visited more than forty years ago.

I had never stayed anywhere so beautiful. The rooms had big windows and ceiling fans, as well as air conditioning for people like me who couldn't cope with the heat, and the wide balconies could be closed in with wooden shutters. One room was filled with mattresses covered by one big mosquito net, and this was where the children slept. If you opened up the shutters, it was like camping outside, but they were inside the house and safe. Jane and I loved this idea so much that we have created a similar set-up for our grandkids on the veranda at our home in the Southern Highlands.

The house was built on stilts to stop it flooding in the wet season. In a Thai kitchen at ground level, Nom, the cook, conjured up a delicious feast for every meal. Outside the

The old teak house at Hua Hin, as it was when I first visited in early 1980s

house, on a platform near the gate that led to the beach, was a small wooden structure that looked like a doll's house. When it was built, Buddhist monks came to bless it and invite spirits to live in it or in nearby trees. Every day the maids would leave food and flowers there for the spirits to enjoy. That way, it was said, the spirits would never venture near the main house. After my time with my stepdad, Reg Barnes, and his family of spiritualists, I thought this was a great idea.

The old house was a magical place, but Jane's extended family grew so big that it was hard for everyone to book time there, so the difficult decision was made to tear it down and build apartments for all of the family to share. During construction, strange things started happening. Hammers would fly across the site for no reason. Wheelbarrows would tip over by themselves. After someone was injured, the family decided to call in the Buddhist monks to investigate. The monks reported that the spirits were unhappy about the changes. Removing the old trees meant they had nowhere to stay and the spirit house was not big enough for them all. So new trees were planted and a bigger spirit house was built and, after the monks returned to bless the house again and officially invite the spirits back, things settled down. A smaller version of the old teak house was rebuilt behind the apartments so that Nom, the cook, would have somewhere to live out her life. She has since passed away, and I imagine her now living in the spirit house with all her old friends.

Tuesday, 3 March
After a few days, we've settled into our usual routine in Hua Hin. Sleep until the sun shines through the window. A quick coffee then a walk on the beach. No need to nod or wave,

Daily offerings being laid out at the new, improved spirit house

talk to or shake hands with anyone, just walk. Head back to the pool as the sun starts to burn and swim for half an hour, then change and head to the market for breakfast.

You need shoes for the market, not thongs, as the ground is covered with pools of water from the washing of fish and chillies. The smell of shrimp paste, or guppy, hangs heavy in the air. It's not a place for the faint-hearted, and I've watched foreigners gagging as they walked through the market. We love it though.

Jane's favourite breakfast here is noodles with hot curry. I'm not quite so adventurous first thing in the morning but will often have a peanut-based curry with noodles and a large Thai iced coffee – sweet and strong, the way I like everything. After breakfast, we return to the sanctuary of our apartment and stay there for the rest of the morning, reading, writing and generally taking it easy. Come lunchtime we have to make a tough decision, though. Usually it's a toss-up between hot noodle soup or chicken and rice.

Around three, we are joined by Tina and Nikki. These two girls are stronger than bodybuilders and give Jane and me a two-hour massage every day. Thai massage is like a combination of torture and yoga, with a bit of stretching thrown in for good measure. It's so good, and after two hours I am ready to take on the world.

Hua Hin is where I feel most at home and most relaxed. If you haven't worked out why I love it so much, go back a couple of pages and read this again, please.

Sunday, 8 March
We've spent nine days following our routine and I've hardly thought about the coronavirus – except once when

I inadvertently flicked the television to cable news and saw it was panic stations all over the world. There was even a video of three women fighting over toilet paper in a Sydney supermarket. That was fucked. Imagine if things get tough and we run out of food. Then we might see the very worst kind of human behaviour.

In this little Thai beach town, the rest of the world and all its troubles still seem far away. But today we have to break the spell and drive up to Bangkok to attend the birthday party of Khun Pairat, a close friend of Jane's parents. He's turning ninety, so it's a big party. We sit with uncles and aunts who have looked after us for as long as I can remember. Many of these people are heavy hitters: ex–prime ministers and heads of banks and huge Thai companies. But today they are just family, and they treat us the way they treat their own children. We eat, drink a little and laugh as they talk about days gone by.

One great thing about Thailand, given the current situation, is that other people don't touch you. Instead of shaking hands, they *wai* – place their palms together and give a little bow. Originally the handshake was meant to show the other person that you were not carrying a weapon. The *wai* means 'I greet you in the place within me that is equal to the place within you.' Much more civilised, don't you think? Fuck it, I'm not shaking hands anymore. I want to greet people as equals. So if you meet me on the street, don't be offended if I don't shake hands. It's not just the virus, it's also about equality.

After the party finishes, we head to our hotel, the Mandarin Oriental, and I sit on the balcony of our room and watch Bangkok's river, the Chao Phraya, roll past. It reminds me of my childhood. It's like the Clyde in Glasgow or the Port River that runs through Port Adelaide, only this is a river on steroids – much bigger and the traffic that runs up and down it day and night is incredible. Huge rice barges, sometimes four of them tied together, are shunted along by tugs. Dozens of small boats dart around and ferry passengers across the river.

This city is full-on and the river is the heart of it all. I've watched breathtaking royal convoys of hundreds of boats all covered in jewels and gold glinting in the sunshine as they moved along the river, celebrating the King's birthday. I've travelled to the floating markets on long-tail boats powered by deafening diesel engines that pump out smoke as they speed through the river traffic and along the smaller canals that crisscross the city, passing kids screaming and laughing as they jump off platforms into the murky water, not caring at all about how busy the waterway is or even what's floating just below the surface. In fact, now, as I look closer at the colour of the water, I wonder if the new virus could even survive in there. Perhaps this water could be the cure.

It's something to think about. But it's late and I have to go to bed. Tomorrow we travel north to Chiang Mai.

Monday, 9 March

I wake up and turn on the news. The world is in meltdown. Story after story tells of more countries being shut down, more deaths, more people being quarantined. Fuck, I hope I can get home, and soon. This trip north is to visit some friends who came out to Australia last year. They want to show us their favourite places to eat and stay at in Thailand. But I am starting to worry a little about the bug. Not so much about catching it, but about passing it on to people who are

Rice barges on the Chao Phraya, reminders of days gone by

not as strong as me. So today we head to the airport wearing masks, sunglasses and gloves. I look like a cross between Michael Jackson and a Japanese taxi driver. Pretty funny, but as soon as I hear the first person in the airport cough, I'm happy to look weird.

Chiang Mai is beautiful, but there is a problem with the air quality, due to bushfires, it seems. So, as we face up to a virus that attacks anyone with a lung condition, I'm breathing air that might give me a lung condition. Holy fuck. I can't win.

We rush up to the hills where the air is better and, even more importantly, the food is superb. For the next two nights, we hole up in an amazing resort, the Four Seasons, and enjoy fabulous meals. No one here seems too worried about the virus just yet. Is that good or bad? I'm not sure.

Tuesday, 10 March

For our last night in Chiang Mai we go out to a beautiful hotel that has just opened, to celebrate with the owner, a friend of a friend. He's been partying since eleven in the morning and by the time we get there at seven in the evening he's having a really good time. He's sitting at a table, forcing glasses of wine down the throat of a young guy I assume is his boyfriend. If he is not his boyfriend, he will be by the end of the night. His party are being entertained by the hotel staff, who have been coerced into singing karaoke very badly. It's not long before the owner is looking for new talent and he turns to me. I fucking hate karaoke and try to dodge his gaze, but soon a microphone is being forced into my hand. Then I realise I'm happy to perform for Jane and our friends because the staff, as good as they are at hotel management, absolutely suck at singing.

Wednesday, 11 March

We wake to the news that the WHO is about to declare a full-blown pandemic. Oh shit. It's getting real. All that stuff I said about this being just a cold might have been off the mark. The world is shutting down and we still have at least a week before we are due to go home. I am starting to panic. Not because I feel threatened by all of this but simply because we are receiving calls and messages from all over the world, telling us to get home now before one of us dies. We hear that someone was punched in Sydney for coughing. I am afraid to sneeze in public now. I don't want anyone bleeding on me after I hit them back.

We head straight back to the safety of Hua Hin and start working out a plan of action. It has become obvious that we cannot go travelling around the world at this point, and it might be quite some time before we can continue our holiday. In Turkey people are beginning to panic about the threat from the virus. Italy is completely closed already, France is in lockdown and Scotland is just starting to feel the impact. So we will either have to bunker down in Hua Hin or make a break for home before they stop all flights to Australia. As nice as it is sitting by the sea in Thailand, we don't know how long this whole pandemic will last, and at some point we need to get home to our family. So we immediately cancel our onward flights to Europe and book the next available trip back to Sydney.

Friday, 13 March

I'm sitting at my computer as the sun is rising. The black sky slowly turns to bright orange and then to blue as the sun comes up. I can feel it on my face. It's shaping up to be a perfect day.

But then I make the mistake of listening to the news and checking my emails. Why do I do it?

'A total ban on all sporting events in America has been announced. The coronavirus is spreading faster than we can act,' an American newsreader says.

I quickly flick to the next channel. 'No football matches will be played in public until this threat is contained,' a BBC reporter with a serious face reports, standing in front of Big Ben.

Yet later in the day on ABC Radio the Australian prime minister says cheerfully that despite banning gatherings of more than five hundred people from next Monday, he'll be going to the rugby league on the weekend to see his 'beloved Sharks'.

What is wrong with him? Is he living in a different world from the rest of us? Seemingly, every world leader is asking their people to stay indoors and self-isolate. But not ours. 'Yeah, come on down and watch the footy with twenty thousand really smart blokes like me. Oh, and try not to cough.' Okay, he didn't actually say that, but ...

I turn off the radio and look at my computer. There are more messages from our children warning us to stay away from everyone. Emails from friends telling us to get home soon.

Yet, from where I sit, the world still looks pretty good. A fishing boat drifts past. I sip my coffee, eat another mango. When will the contagion hit this idyllic spot and snap me back to reality? Not today by the looks of it, unless it's coming by boat. I do know it's coming, though. It's slowly swallowing the world, spreading to somewhere new every day. It will hit Hua Hin sooner or later. Hopefully later. I need to start thinking about packing my bags and returning to the real world. But that's still a few days away.

I slip back into holiday mode. 'Jane, do you want to go for a swim?'

The water is cool and clear and when I dive below the surface the rest of the world disappears.

Saturday, 14 March

We wake to an unusual sound: kids swimming and playing in the pool. We stare at each other in disbelief.

'What are they doing in our pool?' I joke.

We realise it's the weekend, as that's the only time there seems to be anyone else at the apartment complex. For the rest of the week, we usually have the place to ourselves.

Even now, it's only a dad and his three kids in one of the other apartments. Maybe they too are fleeing the pandemic. We make jokes about it, with the virus in mind. And we try to avoid the other family. Just in case. Knowing the Thais as we do, we are sure they are just as germ-conscious as we are. And probably trying to miss us too. In fact, they are probably wondering who the foreigner is in *their* pool. After all, I am the stranger in this country.

It's a game of cat and mouse. We wake up early, run downstairs to the pool, swim and are gone before they wake. Then in the afternoon we wait until the wind picks up – Thais don't like swimming in the wind.

Sunday, 15 March

This morning I cross paths with the family and accidentally catch the eye of the father. He smiles at me and says, 'Sawasdee Krup,' the traditional Thai greeting. Then they all place their hands together and bow ever so slightly.

I return their greeting and ask them how they are. 'Sawasdee krup. Sabai dee maak krup?' I also place my palms together and bow, just to let them know that I'm not one of those handshaking heathens from across the sea. That seems to break the ice.

In the afternoon, the other family all arrive at the pool at the same time as Jane and me. It's like a Mexican stand-off. We look at them. They look at us. There's an awkward pause. Only for a second, but it's noticeable. Times like these, you wish you were wearing a poncho and a side gun. I'm sure I can hear someone whistling the theme from *The Good, the Bad and the Ugly*. We decide to keep walking and pretend we weren't going for a swim. I think they know what's going on. But as I'm the stranger in this land, I feel we should give way.

Tonight as we look out across the beach as the sun sets behind us, there seems to be more people here than I have ever seen before. Thai teenagers are swimming and taking banana boat rides and kite surfing. Some of them are riding those poor horses that are ridden in the burning sun all day by fat Western tourists who have seen Bo Derek riding a horse on the beach in the movie *Ten* and decided it's a cool thing to do. At least the Thai kids weigh a lot less.

When we head back to the apartment complex, there are more people swimming in our pool. Looks like it's a good time to be leaving. In any case, the news from home is that if we don't get back soon there might not be any flights or they might not let us in.

We start packing our bags. I hate to leave here. I haven't felt this relaxed in a long time.

Tomorrow we'll head up to Bangkok and go back to wearing gloves and masks at all times. But even if I'm wearing

Noodles and curry for breakfast at the market, Hua Hin

gloves, I refuse to shake hands ever again. The traditional Thai greeting is a reminder that equality is something we have to think about every day. The virus is having the same effect. It doesn't matter who you are, whether male or female, or what colour your skin is. We are all the same in the eyes of the virus. It has even moved into Peter Dutton. Poor virus.

Monday, 16 March

'I have a fever.'

'No you don't. It's just hot. In case you haven't noticed, it is about one hundred and ten degrees in the shade.'

'I have a cough.'

'No, you don't. You just choked on a glass of water.'

'And I have a headache.'

'Yes, you have, but I have been yelling at you to get it together and get out of bed for an hour.'

'Do you think I'll live?'

'Not if you keep this up. I might kill you.'

'Am I a hypochondriac?'

'Yes, Jimmy, you always have been a hypochondriac, but it's time to get up and start packing. Now!'

I'm okay, I tell myself. I'm tough. No fucking virus is getting me. I'm okay. I'm tough. No fucking virus is getting me. I'm okay. I'm tough …

I keep up this internal chant as I think about travelling through three airports to get home to isolate myself. Oh shit.

I'm okay. I'm tough …

Fuck it. I have to man up. Come on, pull yourself together, not apart. You are absolutely fine.

I'm okay. I'm t—

Shut the fuck up, you idiot. If anybody hears your internal voice, you'll get a one-way ticket to Christmas Island. And a free blood test. Oh God, it's starting to sound like a game show now: '… and All the Oxygen You Can Take In! And A New Car!'

Stop it. Control yourself. Jane told me watching all that afternoon television wasn't good for me.

Suddenly I'm aware of Jane in bed next to me and I realise that I've been dreaming. Thank fuck for that. It was only a nightmare. Even I didn't like me. I know I don't like me at the best of times, but that was a whole new level of dislike.

I shake it off and get up. We go for a walk on the beach, swim for the last time, then go to Nai Bier, our favourite noodle place, for breakfast – one last bowl of thick noodles with pork balls. Now all I have to do is shut my suitcases.

We are heading back to Bangkok, from where we'll fly home via Singapore. A lockdown has been announced in Australia, so we'll have to self-isolate when we get back, but that's fine. I love it when it's just Jane and me locked away. If I had my way, I'd isolate with her more often.

When we reach Bangkok, everything still looks almost normal: bad air pollution, heavy traffic and people everywhere. I'd half-expected to see packs of zombie-like figures walking the streets with their hands held out in front of them and blood dripping from their mouths – I told you I've been watching too much TV. There are some differences, though. Almost all the people on the streets are Thais rather than the hordes of Western tourists you usually see walking through these streets, wiping the sweat from their brows and pointing their cameras. Plus they are all wearing masks. And moving fast and with clear intention. Not stopping to talk, unless they have to, and then quickly moving on to wherever they are going.

On arrival at the Mandarin Oriental, I notice the hotel is strangely quiet. Before we walk into the foyer we are stopped by someone wanting to take our temperature. Both of us are normal and we're allowed in. I'm not sure what they would do if we had a fever. There are pump bottles of hand sanitiser everywhere we look – at the front doors, in reception, by the elevators. And there is an air of tension that was never here before. It seems that Thailand, the land of smiles, is on guard.

I watch the river again from our balcony. The sky is hazy, the sun red, half blocked out by the fumes from the millions of cars that move people across this massive city. Boats are still rushing by, but the river traffic doesn't seem quite as heavy as last week. The *Grand Pearl*, a huge ferry boat, drifts slowly past. Normally it would be showing the sights to huge groups of foreigners. Now it's empty. I can't see one single person on board. Most of the other tourist boats appear to be empty too. The long-tail boats that are used like taxis zigzag along the river, hoping to find a fare. And in the restaurants on the riverbank there are only a few people, most of them looking lost and concerned, just like me.

There's a knock at our door. The porters carry in our bags and I let out a sigh of relief. At least they are still the same as always, smiling and bowing, pressing their palms together and asking if there is anything they can do to make our stay more enjoyable. The virus is here, but the Thai people's spirit is not broken.

A friend in Australia has recommended a restaurant that she thinks we should try. It's our last night, and I've rarely had a bad meal in Bangkok, so what do we have to lose? But it turns out to be the worst meal I've ever eaten in Thailand. They don't even know how to cook rice. I refuse to eat it.

Jane is even more disappointed than me and is getting quite worked up about it. 'I don't want this to be my last meal of our trip,' she complains.

'Let's go to Uncle Chai's favourite fish-ball noodle place,' I suggest. This could be a mistake, as we haven't eaten there in twenty-five years. But the old place in the alley down by the wharfs is exactly the same. Nothing has changed. I even recognise the rats. And the food is still amazing. We leave satisfied that our last meal was memorable.

Back at the hotel, we wash the alleyway dirt off our skins, then sit and discuss the state of the world. In Australia people are snapping up everything they can get their hands on in supermarkets. In the Netherlands there are queues a kilometre long to buy pot – that's right, they're panic-buying marijuana. Imagine the come-down. They must be buying all the chocolate on the supermarket shelves too. That's what they do every night in Amsterdam, so I guess they were ready for it.

In America – only in America – the news reports are of people panic-buying guns. The lines go along streets and around corners. They are grabbing any firearms they can get their hands on. This will not end well. The virus will either bring out the best in humankind or it will bring out the worst. Time will tell.

Another half-empty party boat with lights flashing slips past our window with its music pumping and no one dancing. The party is over. I'm off to bed.

Tuesday, 17 March

Breakfast is quiet at first. It's like we have the place to ourselves. Twenty bowing, smiling staff and the two of us.

'Would you like coffee, sir?'

'Yes, please.'

I smile and nod. Or did I just bow back at him? It's funny when we Westerners bow, always a bit awkward and uncoordinated; we're never sure what to do with our hands. But I've been practising my new style of greeting.

'And what about a fresh juice for you, madam?' Jane is polite and cool as always.

'These people are so sweet and soft-spoken,' I say, straightening up my cutlery nervously.

Then a middle-aged American couple arrive. I hear their accents as soon as they walk in. It's nice to see someone else in the hotel.

As I walk over to the buffet to grab some food, they do the same. There is not a lot of room at the tables and everywhere I turn the husband seems to be in the way. He's one of those people with no spatial awareness and no matter which way I move he blocks the way, standing there with his hands on his hips, twisting around as he examines the food. I try to stand back, give him space. Then he turns quickly and nearly spills his food on me. He doesn't look up or say sorry, just pushes past like he owns the place. Someone might have to politely point out to him what he is doing wrong. I hope it is a sweet Thai person and not a nice 'gentle' Scotsman. If he gets home and does the same thing, he might become a statistic.

Bangkok airport is much busier than I expected. It's full of people. There are young couples, some obviously just off the islands down south, still wearing tie-dyed beach pants and with their hair braided with beads. Hordes of Australians in shorts and singlets smelling of beer. Russians and Eastern Europeans who don't look happy to be going back to the cold. Thousands of Chinese tourists desperate to get home. All are lined up in never-ending queues. Every single person at the airport is wearing a mask. Some travellers look pale and worn out, like they've been travelling all night to get here – only to find that their flights have been changed or cancelled. The joys of travelling in these challenging times.

We check in seven pieces of luggage – remember, we originally thought we were going away for nine weeks and travelling all over Asia and Europe. At least we don't have to see all those bags again until Sydney. Gloves on and masks pulled up, we navigate our way through the airport to the sanctuary of the lounge. If anyone coughs in the plane, there will be trouble. I was so relaxed for a while back there in Hua Hin, but now I'm back to my old aggressive self. If the virus doesn't kill you, the singer will. I'd better meditate or medicate, one of the two, before I board the plane.

The flight to Singapore is peaceful and uneventful, just the way I like my flights. Once again, we don our gloves and masks as we make our way to the train that runs between terminals. As we approach the platform, I see a familiar face, a former sportsman, now a TV pundit. Astonishingly, despite the mask, he recognises me from fifty metres away and walks straight over.

'Hey, Barnesy, how are you, mate?' He shoves out his hand. I'm so taken aback by the fact he's seen through my disguise that I instinctively shove my hand out and shake his. Fuck, I wasn't going to do that anymore.

Jane scowls at me.

There is a bit of small talk that naturally leads to the virus.

'I'm so upset about that,' he says. 'Can you believe that people are sucked into all that at home?'

I'm a bit stunned. Does he not see the mask and gloves and work out that I am freaked out by all of that shit too?

'People are *dying*. You do know that?' I say.

'Yeah, but it's only *old* people.'

'But they are people and they're dying. It's not bullshit.'

Jane can't hold her tongue a second longer. She leans in and hisses, 'In Italy, thirty- and forty-year-old men are dying.'

He's not impressed. 'Yeah, but surely they had some preexisting condition?'

Has he read the papers? No, these are perfectly healthy young men and they are dead, I think to myself. And if I don't get away from here soon, you might be too, mate.

'Yeah, okay then, travel safe,' I say as the train pulls up. He follows us on board and stands next to us.

Jane faces the other way. There follows an uncomfortable, silent three-minute train ride to Terminal Three.

'Yeah, we should catch up,' he says as we arrive.

I try to smile. 'Sure, all the best.'

Jane is already on her way out the door.

'Let's get to the lounge, shall we baby?' I call to her nervously.

She turns on me. 'Straightaway, you shook his hand. After all you have said.'

She's right. 'Yeah, I know. I just didn't have time to think. I'll be ready for the next person.'

I have to make a more conscious effort to stick to my new Thai-style greeting. But it's hard to shake off old habits. I come from a family where, if you don't shake a man's hand firmly and look straight into his eyes, you are in trouble. He might belt you for a start. I'll get it right next time, I tell myself. Thank God I was wearing gloves or Jane wouldn't be talking to me now. Next time I have to say it out loud: 'Nothing personal, mate, it's just the deadly fucking virus and all that. You know what I mean?'

On the television in the lounge, reporters are of course talking about the virus. Even Trump is admitting the US is in trouble and his government might have misread the situation. This is not a situation you want to misread. Especially if you are the leader of a country. But it seems a lot of our leaders are doing just that. More and more people are being infected every day and many of them are dying. It is getting worse by the second. I can't wait to get to my own house and take a long hot bath with some nice bath salts and a bottle or two of disinfectant.

Then we're on the plane and fortunately there is no one near me apart from my Jane. This is the only way to travel. I'm in heaven. Tonight I will sleep and be ready for whatever Sydney airport wants to throw at me. Outside the window the world below looks so small and all the people look like ants. Then I realise we haven't taken off yet, and they are ants. Shouldn't have had that drink.

Wednesday, 18 March
There is nothing like being in your own home, with all your own things. The air is clear and the sky is blue. After the pollution in Bangkok, it feels like I can finally breathe again. I was a bit bleary-eyed driving down the highway but I knew that the safety of my home was not too far away.

Our daughter Elly-May has been staying at the house and she has filled every cupboard with supplies, cleaned every surface with potent alcohol-based cleaners. Elly is like a doomsday prepper. We have enough flour and bread and rice and just about every other thing you can think of to last until the radiation subsides. Hang on, we haven't had a nuclear war. But Elly has shopped and prepped like we have. My wine cellar has been turned into a bunker with holes cut in the walls so we can poke our rifles out through them and fire at the neighbours as they stagger down my driveway looking for help. That is if they make it past the guard dogs, barbed wire and landmines. No, just joking, she's not that bad. There's only one dog. But it is deadly. It's a killer miniature white schnauzer named after Dolly Parton. One lick and you won't survive. Anyway, we don't have guns. We would much rather kill with our bare hands. Kidding again.

Elly is so happy to have us home. She was worried we wouldn't get back into the country. Now we are officially in isolation, so we sit with our masks on, on opposite sides of the room from her and her son, Dylan, and talk to each other. Or, rather, we shout. It's a big room.

At least we are together, almost. And in two weeks we'll give them both the biggest hugs, as long as we haven't come down with anything in the meantime.

'I love you, Elly-May,' I shout from our side of the room.

'I love you too, Dadda,' she shouts back, the sound of her voice echoing off the walls.

Then off to our own ends of the house we go. That's modern living in the age of contagion.

Home

Routines have never been my strong suit, but these days it seems I've changed. I love waking up in my own bed now, and knowing exactly where I am.

After years of touring, travelling and, I have to admit, running away from my problems, these days I'm finally starting to feel at ease.

I open my eyes and pull the curtains back and there is the river. Flowing slowly past the house. I watch the water and I feel calm. I can't help but think that my life has been a lot like that river. There were times when it rushed by, bursting over its banks, out of control, smashing, destroying and flattening everything that got in its way. But those times would always pass. The wind would die down and the sun would find a way through the clouds. The raging torrent would subside and there would be peace. Until the next storm. Now the storms in my life don't happen quite as often. In fact, they hardly happen at all. And when they do, I'm prepared for them and can ride them out.

I get out of bed, drink my coffee then sit at my desk and start to write. The act of writing used to be a painful process for me. Trawling through the wreckage that was my childhood caused me immense pain, but I had to do it. I needed to look at it all in the cold, clear light of day, so that I could let it all go. The longer it was hidden from the world, the longer it was killing me. It was as if I was permanently caught up in that storm that made the river so wild. My past was dragging me along, and dragging me down. It's still there of course, but it no longer pulls me under.

I can hear the voice of my five-year-old grandson, Dylan. His voice is loud and echoes from the kitchen down the hallway to my study. Dylan is excited. Every day he is excited. The world is a beautiful place for Dylan. Every morning he wakes up with a sense of wonder that is infectious. I look at him and try to see the world through his eyes. Untainted by my own broken childhood.

He runs to the study. 'Hey, Da. I saw a huge fish jump out of the water just out there. It might have been a shark. My dad and I are going to see if we can chase him up the river in the canoe.' He looks at me wide-eyed and full of life. 'Do you want to come with us?'

I'm busy writing, but it's an offer I can't refuse. How many times do you get asked to chase giant fish down a river?

'Sure, I'll come. Is it going to be dangerous?'

'Oh yes. There are crocodiles and hippopotamuses in that river. With huge teeth and tails that can smash the boat.'

'Well, I'd better come and look after you,' I say.

'My dad is with us. He's going to look after us. We will be safe.'

I get a lump in my throat.

'Of course we will.'

I'm so happy for Dylan. Every day he goes for rides on the river or long walks through the forest with his dad. Things he will remember for the rest of his life. And I get to share them with him. The only walks I remember my dad doing were the ones when he walked away.

'When are you going to go?' I ask.

'As soon as Dad finishes his work.'

He runs out of the room. I look down at my computer and type.

It's hard to write about anything bad when the whole world outside my window looks so beautiful. The leaves have turned a brilliant red and are starting to fall from the trees, leaving a crimson carpet that leads all the way down to the river.

The smells of chilli, spices and garlic drift from the kitchen. Jane is cooking Thai food. I close my eyes, and for a second I am carried away to our favourite beach in Thailand. But I'm not in another country, I am home. Everything I need and love is here.

I open my eyes and continue to write. This book has been a different experience compared to the last two. Partly it's because I've been reliving many happier, less fraught events from my life. But even when I've been writing about darker times or painful experiences, I find I am more removed from them now. As if I am watching them from a distance. I can revisit them, then move on, unhurt.

'Do you need anything, my love?' Jane is standing in the doorway, looking like an angel.

'I'm okay, baby,' I whisper.

'I'll bring you some tea and fresh shortbread I've just made,' she says, then turns and walks back to the kitchen.

I'm a lucky man. Lucky to have such a beautiful family. Lucky to be alive, really.

I sit and wait for my tea and think about what song I'll sing with my Jane. Every day, around sunset, we learn a new one. Jane has been practising the guitar, and guess what? She is really good at it. Jane can do anything. I have started taking piano lessons from my son, Jackie, and can almost find my way around the keyboard now, but it will be a long time before I can really play it. I've also started playing my bagpipes again. Not a lot, just enough to drive the family, the neighbours, the wildlife and anyone else within five kilometres completely mad.

My house is full of music and laughter and love, and even as I write these words my eyes begin to water just a little. I am

Dylan and me at our home on the river. Where I belong.

no longer consumed by pain and fear. These days I am living, not dying. The world has its challenges, but together Jane and I can deal with anything it throws at us.

The rain on the iron roof beats out a rhythm as Jane sits in my study playing me another song she has learned.

'I love you, my Jane,' I whisper to her as she finishes.

'And I just love playing this guitar,' she says proudly.

I stand and look at her for a second, pretending to be wounded. I can be so needy sometimes.

'Oh, and of course, I love you too, Jimmy. Even more than my guitar.' Then she walks over and throws her arms around me.

'That might be a bit of a stretch, baby,' I say, laughing.

Jane looks at me, and smiles.

Life is beautiful.

Acknowledgements

Some superstitious people think that life works according to the 'third time lucky' rule. I don't know if they are right, but it has seemed to be the case for me with this book, *Killing Time*. The process of creating my first two books was gruelling, but the road to this one has, thankfully, been much smoother. Of course, that is partly due to the subject matter but also because I have learned a bit about myself over the last six years and about publishing.

Just because I now know more about the writing process doesn't mean that I've needed the great team of people I had behind me last time any less. On the contrary, I think we worked together even harder to bring these stories to you. Everyone needs a great team behind them, and I would like to thank mine. I have definitely been lucky on this third book to have had their help.

Helen Littleton, my publisher at HarperCollins, has been my champion. She was the first person in the company to take a leap of faith and trust that I could actually write something worth reading, and I am so grateful for her unswerving belief. If you like any of my books, thank her; if you don't, blame me.

This time around Scott Forbes stepped into the editor's hot seat, having helped on the other two books, particularly with my Scottish dialogue. He'd been invaluable as we'd scrambled to get those books off to the presses several weeks after the absolutely final deadline. His calm and clever suggestions as the chapters of this book came together definitely kept me on track and helped me actually meet my deadline this time. Thanks, Scott.

Mark Campbell did the cover and internals. Fiona Luke did all the pre-press work on the pictures and cover, and Janelle Garside organised the printing, which must surely have been much less of a headache this time. Thanks to each of you. Pam Dunne and Nicola Young did the proofreading – I guess this is a good place to apologise for my spelling mistakes and typos!

Special mention to Graeme Jones, our gun typesetter, whom I neglected to credit on the two previous books. Maybe there is something to 'third time lucky' after all.

Alice Wood and Georgia Williams helped us spread the word about these words, so thanks to both of you, as well as Kathy Lipari, Justin Lees, the legendary Kathy McCabe and the rest of the HarperCollins team who've helped us draw extra attention to this book.

Closer to home, I would like to acknowledge and thank my great friend and manager John Watson for the countless phone calls he took to answer the millions of questions I needed answering as I wrote this book. I could not have done it without you, my friend. And, to his children, who have had to put up with me encouraging his endless dad jokes: sorry, kids.

Rina Ferris, my publicist of several years, deserves a special mention too. Actually she deserves more than that. Maybe a medal. Her faith and friendship are always appreciated by Jane and me. Thanks also to Warren Costello at my record company, Bloodlines, who helped with photos and other matters with his trademark combination of diligence and decency. Love you, Warren.

My nephew Jesse Lizotte took the cover photo. Despite my scowl in that picture, I'm actually always happy to see Jesse with a camera in his hand because it means he is about to come up with something great.

Most of all, I need to thank my family. The stories in this book would not have happened without them – the fact that so many of these chapters revolve around my Jane and the kids shows that they have always been the eye of my cyclone. When the world was spinning so fast that I thought I would slip and fall off forever, they were always there holding me down and keeping me safe. I love you, guys. Jane, you are my angel. My light. My love. My girl.

Some of the stories in *Killing Time* were written during the Covid-19 pandemic that continues to plague the planet as this book goes off to print. The necessary shutdowns have hurt a lot of people – many of whom were hurting already – so, understandably, most people won't look back fondly on this strange year. But the enforced time at home surrounded by my Jane, my kids and my grandkids has actually felt like a blessing to me.

With each book I've become more aware of how fortunate I am to have people who are actually willing to read my stuff. So, last but not least, a huge thanks to you, my readers, for making this possible. The process of writing these three books hasn't just helped me kill time during a pandemic but has also helped me make sense of both the world and myself.

Third time lucky.

Jimmy